The United States in the Pacific

THE UNITED STATES
IN THE PACIFIC————

Private Interests and
Public Policies, 1784–1899

Donald D. Johnson
[with Gary Dean Best]

PRAEGER

Westport, Connecticut
London

To Lenore Shirley Johnson, beloved wife of the late Donald Johnson, and to their three wonderful children, William Henry Johnson, Janice Ann Biles, and Andrea S. J. Wagner.

Library of Congress Cataloging-in-Publication Data

Johnson, Donald D. (Donald Dalton).
    The United States in the Pacific : private interests and public policies, 1784–1899 / Donald D. Johnson with Gary Dean Best.
        p.   cm.
    Includes bibliographical references and index.
    ISBN 0–275–95055–7 (alk. paper)
    1. Pacific Area—Foreign relations—United States.   2. United States—Foreign relations—Pacific Area.   I. Best, Gary Dean.
    II. Title.
    DU30.J84   1995
    382'.097309—dc20   94–41799

British Library Cataloguing in Publication Data is available.

Library of Congress Catalog Card Number: 94–41799
ISBN: 0–275–95055–7

First published in 1995

Praeger Publishers, 88 Post Road West, Westport, CT 06881
An imprint of Greenwood Publishing Group, Inc.

Printed in the United States of America

The paper used in this book complies with the Permanent Paper Standard issued by the National Information Standards Organization (Z39.48–1984).

10 9 8 7 6 5 4 3 2 1

CONTENTS

FOREWORD

Donald Dalton Johnson (1917–1993) began teaching in the History Department of the University of Hawai'i (UH) in 1949. His field was U.S. diplomatic history with special interests in American relations with Latin America and the Pacific. He originated the course "The United States in the Pacific" at UH, and taught it at many other institutions on the mainland and in the Pacific. It was my good fortune to take the course from him as an undergraduate at UH in the late 1960s.

Don Johnson was an inspiring teacher who rarely lectured from notes. More commonly he would bring to class a stack of books relating to the topic being covered that day, and he would then describe the contributions of each of the books to an understanding of that topic. Like most students in the class, I took copious notes.

The textbook for the class was an early mimeographed version of *The United States in the Pacific*. As the author noted in his preface, the manuscript was a labor of some four decades. The UH library has in its collection early versions from the 1950s, one of seventy-six and the other of 116 pages. Over the years the manuscript grew longer until by the time of his death, on Christmas Day 1993, it had reached 702 pages, including notes and bibliography. Even then, the manuscript was not ready for a publisher.

How, one might ask, could four decades of work produce an incomplete manuscript? An obvious explanation is that its author was distracted by other projects. In 1967, the Honolulu City Council commissioned Don to research and write a history of the government of the City and County of Honolulu. As he wrote in the preface to that work, "the subject and the materials available quickly overwhelmed the writer and mushroomed into a manuscript of more than 800 pages. Years passed in an effort to pare this into a shorter, manageable history and to arrange the details of publication."[1] The book was finally published in 1991 as *The City and County of Honolulu: A Governmental Chronicle.* Meanwhile, Don had also been commissioned to coauthor a history of the Hawai'i Government Employees Association, the principal public employees' union in the state, which was published in 1986.[2]

Such distractions aside, the principal reason why the manuscript was never completed—and might well never have been completed—can perhaps best be deduced from Don's attitude toward the subject. In his files are notes of opening remarks to dozens of ''The United States in the Pacific'' classes. The theme of them all is the same: ''This is an experimental course; it always has been, and I hope it always will be.'' Like the course it was designed to serve, the manuscript of ''The United States in the Pacific'' was ''experimental,'' constantly evolving as a result of the insights Don gained from his own research and from that of his students. Were he alive, it would doubtless be evolving still.

Both the course and the manuscript dealt with all aspects of the American presence in the Pacific, but the manuscript stopped with the attack on Pearl Harbor of December 7, 1941. Both included detailed consideration of the relations between the United States and the nations of East Asia—China, Japan, and Korea. After the death of Professor Charles Hunter, Don became responsible for the ''History of Hawai'i'' course as well, and the contents of his course and manuscript on ''The United States in the Pacific'' were thereafter enriched by his growing expertise on Hawai'i's history.

As was typical of most U.S. history specialists produced by graduate schools in the 1940s, Don's language training was in the languages of Europe. His facility in those languages made it possible for him to range widely in their literature concerning the Pacific and the international political and economic rivalries there that involved Americans and their government. His expertise in this area was probably unmatched in the United States.

During these four decades, however, increasing numbers of U.S. diplomatic historians with facility in East Asian languages were being produced by several graduate institutions, including the University of Hawai'i itself. The result was the publication of a number of books and articles on U.S. relations with East Asia that were based on research in the languages of Japan, China, and Korea, rather than only those in English and European languages. These offered better and more comprehensive surveys of U.S. relations with East Asian countries than Don's manuscript would have been able to include without extensive additions.

When I was asked, therefore, to prepare ''The United States in the Pacific'' for publication, I decided that the focus of the book should be on those areas in which Don Johnson's expertise was unmatched—the story of American activities on the ocean and in the islands that culminated in the acquisition of an American empire in the Pacific in the late 1890s. Space considerations would have dictated such a decision even if it had not otherwise been the natural one to make.

Don Johnson was for thirty years my mentor and one of my dearest friends.

I did my senior and M.A. theses under him in the area of U.S.–Japanese economic relations in the early twentieth century, abandoned the field briefly to do a Ph.D. dissertation on Herbert Hoover, and then returned to it with two years of research in Japan. After joining the faculty at UH at Hilo, my research and writing drifted in the direction of twentieth century U.S. political history even as I continued to teach "The United States in the Pacific" and, more recently, "The History of Hawai'i."

One criticism by a reader of the original manuscript had to do with its limited treatment of the effects on Pacific islanders, especially the Hawaiians, caused by the intrusion of Americans, as well as American influences on the islands. Aside from narrowing the focus of the book, as described above, and condensing parts of it slightly, my sole contribution has been to try to correct that deficiency by adding several pages, especially to what are now chapters 6 and 7 of the book. Lest Don be blamed for the viewpoint expressed in those additions, I must point out that my perspective on the missionary influence in Hawai'i is more negative than his was and that Don would probably not have agreed with my description of their effects on the Hawaiians.

I owe Don and Lenore Johnson an immense debt for all of their kindnesses to me over the years. Readying this manuscript for publication has been my attempt to repay some of those kindnesses. I hope that the finished product is worthy of its author.

Gary Dean Best
University of Hawai'i at Hilo

PREFACE

It all seemed so simple. Merchants trading to China began the American contact with the Pacific. Fur traders, sealers, whalers, and island and coastal merchants followed. They went there without government support or protection, for the weak Confederation of the 1780s was in no position to provide it. Later, as the federal government under the Constitution gained in strength, prestige, and wealth, Americans in the Pacific began to call on Washington first to protect and then to foster their interests. From China to California, from Alaska to Australia, it seemed clear that the interests of private business motivated and directed national policy.

All one needed to do, then, was to document the interests of Americans' businesses in the Pacific Basin to understand the roots of government policies. At the time the research for this study began it was very trendy to adopt an economic determinist approach to the history of American expansion.

Then the story became more complicated. While there were clear cases of private business initiative resulting in congressional advocacy or administrative action, there were other, disturbing, incidences of alleged economic arguments being used by those who were not businessmen to further causes of their own. At times those advocacies, using commercial rationalizations, even ran counter to the interests of businessmen actually involved in Pacific or Asian enterprises.

Further, groups such as missionaries, diplomats, military officers, and politicians had agendas of their own to serve. As the nineteenth century wore on, the motivation behind American public policies toward Pacific Basin countries and peoples became complex, confused, and at times even contradictory. Yet for more than a century commercial interests were so prominent that it was easy for politicians, publicists, and historians to base their evaluations of American national policies principally on economic grounds.

A more realistic view indicates that the motivations of U.S. policies toward this vast area have in fact been varied, complex, and often contradictory. Personal ambition, humanitarianism, missionary zeal, bureaucratic interest, and patriotic concern have played their part, whether in harmony or in opposition to the aims of merchants or investors. One major result of this has been frequent conflicts of view and action between Americans actually in the Pacific and those framing public policy at home.

This study surveys the activities of Americans who actually ventured into the Pacific before 1899 and the relation that existed between their special interests and the public policies designed to support or promote them. It does not pretend to end the controversies over the nature of the interests, both private and public, that created policy. The aim is to stimulate new thinking about the origins of national policies and their relations to the needs of Americans, and in some cases to those of the people of the Pacific base area they affected.

The literature on which a history of the United States in the Pacific may be based is simply enormous, and much of it is fascinating. It ranges from the soberest bureaucratic reports to the "gee whiz" writings of young seamen, and tourists, first exposed to exotic Pacific islands and their inhabitants. Statistical data on shipping, trade, and investments began early, but uncertainly, and increased gradually in consistency, reliability, and volume. Beyond this, of course, is an extensive literature of imagination, mixing fact and fantasy.

Upon this material a great pile of historical interpretation, political exhortation, and fiction has been built. Self-justifying memoirs have come from politicians, bureaucrats, and lobbyists. Businessmen have been noticeably more reticent about their conceptions or achievements. Scholars have created monuments of erudition and insight dealing with parts of the field, but very few have tried to deal with the whole.

There is still, then, need for a new look at the story of Americans in the Pacific and the ways in which their government became involved in protecting, furthering, or restraining their activities. There is still a need to inquire just what American interests really were, whose interests they were, and how the government policies supposedly designed for their well-being were suited to that end.

Over some four decades the author has consulted both primary and secondary materials in libraries and archives on both coasts of the mainland United States, in Hawai'i, and, for a brief time, in Australia. In Washington staff members of the National Archives and the Library of Congress were usually very helpful, as was the office of Hawai'i's former senator, Hiram L. Fong. Employees of the Departments of State and Commerce gave both advice and valuable data.

Most of the work has been put together in Honolulu at intervals during a teaching career at the University of Hawai'i at Manoa. Here, major support has come from the Sinclair and Hamilton libraries and their staffs, particularly Renee Heyum and the late Janet Bell. At the Archives of Hawai'i former archivist Agnes Conrad and at the Bishop Museum Library the late Margaret Titcomb became friends and valuable advisors. Rhoda E. A. Hackler kindly read much of the manuscript and offered valuable advice. Finally, my wife, Lenore Shirley Johnson, has been a constant support, with typing, proofreading, and tender, loving care.

INTRODUCTION

The Pacific was both a barrier and a highway for the first Americans who entered its basin. Its immense, watery distances made approach to the sought-for Asian coasts long and difficult. Yet its availability, its openness to ships of all nations, made it a road to possible riches through trade in the exotic products of the East.

This story begins in the first years of American independence, with ships and cargoes from the Atlantic ports of the United States seeking prize products of China and the "Indies." Pursuit of that trade also led Americans and their ships to ports in Africa, South Asia, Australia, the Pacific islands, and the Pacific coasts of the Americas. In each of those areas individual traders found profit, and the young nation found some of the markets needed to replace ports of trade closed or limited by America's new position outside the British Empire.

The first American policies in Asia and the Pacific, as Tyler Dennett once pointed out, were the policies of individual citizens who went there. Some of them also saw, or professed to see, advantages to their nation in the prospering of their trade. As the volume of that commerce and attendant investment grew, some of those concerned with it began to petition their government for assistance, and that involved the formulation of public policy. Tariff benefits at U.S. ports, diplomatic interposition with European governments, consular representation at Pacific Basin ports, naval patrols in the Pacific, and even a U.S. exploring expedition to reduce the dangers of uncharted seas followed special interest requests.

Whalers and missionaries expanded the list of American interest groups active in the Pacific. In response to appeals voiced in their names, though not always by the people involved, the United States government took a minor but increasingly active role in Pacific affairs during the early decades of the nineteenth century. In general, the official policy for years was the rather negative one of ensuring that Americans were treated no worse than the citizens of other nations by Pacific and Asian authorities.

In the mid-nineteenth century a combination of events profoundly altered the basis of American relations with the Pacific region that had prevailed since the *Empress of China* had sailed into that ocean in 1784. These events focused the attention of the American public and their government on the Pacific as never before, and began the steady and growing intrusion of public policy consider-ations into an area where heretofore the private interests of Americans had pre-dominated.

The first of these events was the outbreak of the Opium War between Great Britain and China, and the new basis for relations between China and the West that resulted from it. By the Treaty of Nanking, Great Britain obtained additional ports at which to trade and other concessions. For Americans to maintain equal-ity in the trade, the United States government, for the first time, had to exert itself to obtain the same treaty rights for its citizens through diplomacy that the British had obtained through force. The goal remained the same as in the days when private interests had predominated, and it was the British initiative—not an American governmental one—that transformed the methods by which the goal was now and would hereafter be pursued.

The acquisition of Oregon and California was the second event that altered America's relations with the Pacific. New considerations of military security were added to those of commerce and humanitarianism once the United States bordered the Pacific. Strategic interests ramified into the eastern Pacific and increased the concern of Navy and War Department bureaucracies. America's new ports on the Pacific coast breathed new life into old dreams of the wealth to be won through trade with "Asia's teeming millions" and captured the at-tention of publicists and some politicians, even if few legitimate businessmen. With the American frontier having reached its continental limits in the West, some clearly viewed the Pacific as a new "frontier" for American enterprise.

The growth of Pacific whaling and its expansion into the waters of the north-ern Pacific in the region of Japan likewise exerted an influence. It increased the American presence and investment in Hawai'i, and it focused attention on the hazards that might await shipwrecked crews washed up on the shores of "her-mit" Japan.

These three events, in combination, attracted the attention of some Americans to Japan, and even, to a lesser degree, beyond that hermit kingdom to the other— Korea. The new ports opened to trade by the Chinese moved some trade farther north along the coast, in closer proximity to Japan. The new American ports on the Pacific also meant more ships were now sailing to China by that more northerly route rather than the customary one from the south around Cape Horn or the Cape of Good Hope. Some merchants and publicists saw a logical exten-sion of that trade in the opening of Japan to commerce, at the same time that whaling interests sought a treaty that would provide humane treatment for ship-wrecked sailors there.

Thus, the mid-nineteenth century saw the signing of the first treaties with China, the enunciation of the first public policies toward the Kingdom of Ha-wai'i, and the "opening" of Japan, first to contact and then to trade. While this book does not describe the relations between the United States and the East Asian nations—which would require a book in itself for adequate treatment—the background of those events of the mid-nineteenth century must be kept in mind for their effect in drawing American public and governmental attention to the Pacific. Curiously enough, this projection of public policy into the Pacific increased as the second half of the century drew to an end, even as private interests were in many cases declining.

There has, however, always been an element of fantasy in U.S. policies to-ward the Pacific world, and it thrived particularly from the mid-nineteenth century onward. The appeals that were made to the government for action during this period more often arose from fanciful commercial, missionary, or naval hopes for the future than from present realities, and they commonly involved fundamental ignorance or misunderstanding of the societies with which they proposed to deal.

The confident expectations of those who urged an aggressive, even expansive, national policy in the Pacific failed in that nothing happened in the time frame they had imagined. The slow pace of social and economic change in Asia and the low purchasing power of its populace retarded the growth of market potential. Anti-imperial prejudice and sectional politics at home frustrated territorial expansionists. Missionary enthusiasm often wore itself out on the resistance of ethical and religious systems older than Christianity, on the inertia of traditional cultures, and on the opposition of suspicious European colonialists.

For most of the later nineteenth century the interests of Americans seemed to turn more inward, to the development of new national frontiers in industry and agriculture. Politically, this seemed to involve a decreased concern with foreign relations, made more possible by the absence of any immediate threat from Europe. Economically, it involved a relative decline in the importance of foreign trade as a part of the entire national economy. The merchant marine of the United States declined in size and importance, as did the major firms pursuing trade interests in the Pacific. The whaling fleet dwindled, and the number of Americans annually visiting Pacific ports decreased.

In keeping with this limited American private stake in the Pacific, Washington appeared willing to let other powers take the lead in charting the course of Western relations with the Pacific islands and nations. In the eastern Pacific, notably in Hawai'i and Samoa, a more forceful stand might occasionally be taken, but no general policy of vigorous assertion of U.S. power in the Pacific developed before the late 1890s.

This period of relative quiescence ended with what still appears to be dramatic suddenness. At a stroke, the United States reached across the Pacific and added

Hawai'i, part of Samoa, Wake, Guam, and the Philippines to its territorial holdings. The motives for this action remain controversial to this day. The results, with the possible exception of Hawai'i, are difficult to relate to previously established, tangible interests of Americans in those areas. Though theorists and vote-seekers continued to advance arguments based on trade and investment potentials in the Pacific, American businessmen continued to look mainly to Europe and the Pacific for opportunities.

The national government thus involved itself more in the international politics of the Pacific than it had to that date in those of the Atlantic, although the material stake of Americans in the East was not one-tenth as great. It soon became apparent that the commitment also exceeded the military or political power that the United States could, or would, exert in the western Pacific. By 1899 the imbalance between private interests, public policies, and national power had been established that would characterize American relations with the Pacific down to World War II and beyond.

1

THE BEGINNINGS

BARRIERS

What force could possibly drive the inhabitants of a raw, underdeveloped nation on the North Temperate coast of the Atlantic through the tropics, months and thousands of miles from home, to the distant, exotic coasts of the Pacific? It was a mixture of need and imagination that led these "Yankees" to risk their lives and fortunes in unfamiliar waters and among peoples alien, "heathen," and possibly hostile. The rich trade of Asia, especially China, was the goal. The Pacific was the highway to it.

The Pacific and East Asia were half a world away from the seventeenth-century settlers of British North America, the very symbol of remoteness. Yet, as transplanted Europeans at least some of the colonists knew that those distant regions existed. Europe's discovery of America, after all, had resulted from the search for a westward route to the Orient. The instructions to the first settlers of Virginia indicate that the quest for a new passage to Asia was a part of the promoters' concept. The search for a more direct route would continue throughout the colonial period.[1]

Even in Europe, however, relatively little was known about the Pacific at the time English settlements began to dot the Atlantic coast of what is now the United States. Spanish explorers from Magellan to Quiros had touched only a small part of the great ocean, and details of their discoveries, and those of the Portuguese and Dutch, were not publicized as a matter of policy at first. The Portuguese had concentrated their interests in the Southwest Pacific or, more properly, in South and Southeast Asia. The great age of Dutch and English explorers was only dawning in the early seventeenth century, and their maps and journals, though numerous in published form, still left much room for speculation and error.[2]

The best educated among the first English settlers probably knew something of the contacts with the East made by traders in classic times. Knowledge of the exploits of later travelers like Carpini or the Polos by land, or da Gama or Magellan by sea, was even more common. As Englishmen, the voyages of Drake and Cavendish would have informed them at least of the existence of the great ocean to the west and of strange peoples who inhabited its shores.[3]

For British colonists in North America to develop a tangible and direct interest in Asia and the Pacific, however, several obstacles first had to be overcome. The first was their preoccupation with the problems of planting settlements and then surviving under wilderness conditions. The frightful mortality rates among the first settlers of Jamestown and Plymouth testify to the magnitude of that problem. The struggle for bare subsistence left no opportunity for distant ventures or speculations overseas.

A second obstacle was general ignorance of the possibilities of commerce with the Orient. Because of the primitive living conditions, the first generation born in the colonies was less educated than the original settlers, particularly in such subjects as the geography and commerce of remote lands.[4] Although the British East India Company had begun its activities early in that century, neither the information nor the exotic products it brought from the East appeared significantly in the North American colonies until the late 1600s.

A third barrier between the first Anglo-Americans and the Orient was sheer distance. With the slow and uncertain means of transportation available to them, the journey to the Pacific represented a longer and more hazardous venture than colonial merchants or sailors were prepared to undertake. There was, however, a remarkable growth of maritime enterprise along the eastern seaboard before 1700, and hardy ships and seamen were being produced there. Yet, habit, limited knowledge, and shortages of capital combined to limit their activity almost entirely to the North Atlantic.[5]

Finally, the legal monopoly granted by the Crown to the East India Company over all British trade between the Cape of Good Hope and Cape Horn barred colonial as well as home subjects from trade there except with the Company's consent. Breaches in that monopoly were relatively few and brief down to the early nineteenth century, though evidence of the wealth being brought to Europe by Company agents produced jealous protests and occasional challenges from rival merchants.[6]

In the face of this imposing array of discouragements, colonial ventures beyond the capes and into the Pacific Basin were long deferred. Yet, the seafaring tradition brought with them from Britain, the difficulty of wresting a living from the soil of the American wilderness, the abundance of cheap timber, and the proximity of the North Atlantic fisheries all combined to encourage maritime enterprise. By 1700 Anglo-American seamen and colony-built vessels were competing with Europeans, including those from the mother country, on the fishing grounds, and they were trading the products of the sea and of their own soil along American coasts and in Europe itself. Then, events in both Europe and America pushed some of them further a-sea.

OPPORTUNITIES AND TEMPTATIONS

From the late seventeenth to the early nineteenth century Great Britain was involved in a series of imperial wars that included hostilities in America and South Asia as well as within Europe. In the first of these wars (1689–1697) seamen from American ports were enlisted in the crews of privateers, privately owned ships commissioned to prey on enemy commerce. Privateering thus augmented a nation's seapower, and to encourage it the captains and crews shared in the value of the prizes they were able to seize.

Men from Britain's West Indian colonies, as well as others from the Carolinas, Maryland, Pennsylvania, New York, Rhode Island, and Massachusetts, engaged in privateering ventures that went beyond Atlantic waters. Some of these wartime sailors crossed the hazy boundary between privateering and piracy, reluctant to pass up a rich prize just because it belonged to a neutral or friendly nation, or because the war for which their letters of marque had been issued had inconveniently ended.[7]

The first Anglo-American colonists to actually see the shore of the Pacific may have been among the buccaneers who reached the coast of Panama and the Isthmus of Darien in the 1680s.[8] More significant were those who sailed east of the Cape of Good Hope with commissions to harass enemy, chiefly French, shipping. Some of these took prizes, including cargoes of Eastern products, and brought them back to colonial harbors. Choosing ports with the most friendly or least vigilant authorities, these sailors displayed Arabian gold, pearls, precious stones, and exotic oriental fabrics to those unfamiliar with such riches.

Sir Thomas Lawrence reported from Maryland Colony that some of the privateer-pirates claimed returns of 1,000 to 1,500 pounds sterling per man as a result of their voyages, tempting other sailors and colonials to go along with them and disrupting normal maritime activity in several colonies.[9] One sheriff of New York was reported to have 2,500 pounds worth of East India products hidden in his own home, and William B. Weeden described that port as ''flushed with Arabian gold and East Indian wares.''[10]

The wealth brought back by privateers and pirates was comparatively limited, but it was spectacular and it attracted both public and private attention. Toward the end of the seventeenth century, piratical activity became so notorious and so damaging to trade and authority that the Crown took strong measures to end it. When some of the freebooters went so far as to attack ships of the East India Company, it proved their undoing. A series of spectacular trials in English and colonial courts, the passage of new laws against piracy, the infliction of harsh punishments and executions, and more effective naval patrols combined to extinguish most of this illicit enterprise.

For three-quarters of a century thereafter the few Anglo-Americans who traveled east of Africa were those employed by the East India Company.[11] It does not appear that wartime privateers from American ports reached the Pacific Ocean during those years, their furthest voyages having been confined to the Red Sea, the Persian Gulf, and the western Indian Ocean.

Meanwhile, a few Eastern products, particularly East Indian cottons, had already reached colonial ports through legitimate trade, and late in the seventeenth century Chinese tea began to arrive. These goods came through the East India Company and Great Britain, but some also were smuggled in from Europe, especially by the Dutch. At first expensive luxuries, in time some became items of common importation and use. Tea, certain spices, and Eastern cottons were among these.[12]

A series of letters exchanged between John Higginson, of Salem, and his brother Nathaniel, then in India working for the Company, shows how early the East India trade had reached Massachusetts. Writing in October 1699, John responded to his brother's inquiry:

What you propose of living in Boston and managing a wholesale trade of East India goods, I approve of, as best for you. That is a place of great trade, and all the neighboring colonies are mostly supplied from thence. All sorts of calicoes, algiers, remwalls, muslin, silks for clothing and linings; all sorts of spice are vendible with us. . . . In the late war time, all East India goods were extremely dear. . . . but now are abated about a quarter part in value. Some of the China war toys, and lacquer ware will sell well, but no great quantity.[13]

Noticeably missing from Higginson's list of "East India goods" is tea, a product that later would be very important in Americans' search for direct trade with China. The tea trade was then held in strict monopoly by the East India Company. It had, in fact, only been introduced into the English home market in the latter part of the seventeenth century. It was scarce and expensive enough then to make it a luxury item and something of a status symbol down to the end of that century, and it showed no indication that it would soon become the national drink of the English.[14]

Tea was introduced into the American colonies late in that century, again as a rare, exotic, and expensive item. Two merchants were licensed to sell tea "in publique" in Boston in 1690, and for years thereafter it was sold by apothecaries rather than by grocers. But fashion had its followers, even in staid New England. Alice Morse Erle reports, "Many queer mistakes were made through ignorance of its proper use. Many colonists put the tea into water, boiled it for a time, threw the liquid away, and ate the tea leaves. In Salem they did not find the leaves were attractive, so they put butter and salt on them."[15]

Tea seems to have come fairly rapidly into common use in colonial port towns in the eighteenth century. Alert to tides of fashion in the mother country, some upper-crust citizens first bought the imported leaves as rarities, others for their reported medicinal properties. As the East India Company's China trade grew, the supply of tea increased and the price fell. Dutch smuggling of tea, spices, and other products of their Eastern trade contributed to the price reduction until at least some of these goods were within the reach of others than just the colonial aristocracy.

By the time of the American Revolution colonial consumption of tea was common enough to make the East India Company's monopoly a very unpopular restriction. Among the economic sanctions adopted against increased British regulation of colonial commerce after 1763, one of those most frequently noted by historians was a boycott of tea imports. Colonials tried to find local substitutes to replace this commodity. Infusions of ribwort, sage, throughwort, loosestrife, raspberry, and strawberry leaves were brewed in the effort. During the Revolution the drinking of some of these must have been reckoned among the hardships of war.[16]

The colonies also shared, to some extent, in the vogue for things oriental that swept Europe's upper classes in the eighteenth century. Chinese lacquerware, willowware, and porcelain appeared in residences and public buildings. George Washington had Chinaware pieces in his residence at Mount Vernon. The colonial governor's palace in Williamsburg boasted Chinese wallpaper, and Eastern pagodas and other motifs appeared in items of interior and exterior design in Philadelphia and New England.[17]

In short, by the time of the American Revolution many inhabitants of the colonies were aware of East Asia and of reasons why a direct contact with it might be profitable. At the same time the colonial maritime industries had developed a technology that made voyages to the other side of the world possible. American ships had already sailed into the South Atlantic and the Mediterranean, and colonial shipbuilders were supplying a variety of craft, including East Indiamen, for purchasers in the British Isles. Now it appeared that only Britain's restrictive navigation acts and monopolies stood in the way of riches such as those the East India Company was reputed to be reaping.[18]

The eighteenth-century voyages of English mariners like Anson, Byron, Wallis, and Cook attracted more attention to the Pacific, and the published accounts of these and other expeditions became known in America to at least an influential few. As fellow Englishmen they could take pride in these achievements in distant parts. As seamen or merchants it must have occurred to some that they, too, might venture there if only legal barriers could be removed. There were merchants in Britain who shared this desire to end chartered monopolies, but no redress seemed likely through parliamentary action.[19]

COMES THE REVOLUTION

The American Revolution and the new conditions of political independence that followed it changed the picture for Anglo-American merchants, virtually compelling them to enter every possible branch of oceanic commerce. A vital part of the economy of the liberated colonies was dependent upon foreign trade, which had been disrupted and curtailed by British naval action during the long war. Peace found seamen and shipbuilders ready for action and merchants, at least those who had capital, eager to resume business in order to supply long-deprived American consumers. Supplies of timber and naval stores, some of which had formerly been reserved for British naval or mercantile use, were now available for American ships or for sale to the highest bidder.

Scarcely had the peace been signed in 1783 when American ships were on the seas once more, some of them sharpened by wartime privateering experiences. Outside the British mercantile system now, they were literally forced to find new overseas markets for the produce of American fields, forests, and fisheries and to seek the manufacturers that their basically extractive economy did not provide. Cash poor, they had to win from export and carrying trades the specie or credit with which to buy what they lacked.[20]

In this search merchants and mariners of the young United States turned first to the familiar Atlantic. Then a few of them ventured into the Pacific Basin in the hope of securing directly those products of the Orient with which American consumers were already familiar. If this also meant new markets for American produce, well and good, but it was to buy ''East India goods'' that they first headed toward Asia and the Pacific. American merchants hoped to replace British middlemen, and especially the East India Company, in their own domestic market. Sharing with many Englishmen an often exaggerated view of the Company's profits, Americans were merely the latest victim of an old European dream of the vast riches of the East and the certain wealth that awaited those who might trade there.

Tyler Dennett, in his classic *Americans in Eastern Asia,* says, ''Americans went to the Far East because they had to. They had to go everywhere.''[21] Imports, largely from Great Britain, rose sharply in 1784–1785, amounting to some $30 million for the two years and involving a large extension of credit by the English. Exports, however, were down, and an unusually large percentage of them were being carried in foreign ships, again mostly British. Indeed, it appeared that the British, rather than the Americans, were reaping most of the economic benefits of U.S. independence. American agriculture and manufacturing, together with the maritime industries, were seriously dislocated and depressed. Furthermore, for several years after the war it appeared likely that in Europe's remaining colonies fewer ports than before the Revolution would be open to American ships and goods.[22]

The British government, adopting the mercantilist views of Lord Sheffield, an influential writer on trade policy, for a time declined to negotiate a commercial treaty with its loosely federated former colonies and tried to close most of its remaining American possessions to U.S. goods.[23] The French, allied to the Americans by treaty, nevertheless proved unable or unwilling to replace the British as their major customer and supplier and for a time, at least, even resorted to restrictions on their home and colonial trade similar to those of the British.

Spain, too, resumed restrictive commercial policies once peace had been restored, and in the Jay-Gardoqui negotiations of 1785–1786 refused to agree to a commercial treaty except on terms that the American Congress could not accept.

Elsewhere in Europe the development of markets and credit arrangements moved slowly and uncertainly. To fill the Americans' cup of woe, the young Confederation was saddled with a public debt estimated to exceed $40 million. Congress, under the Articles of Confederation, lacked the taxing or commerce-regulating powers needed to meet even the interest on these obligations, and some of them were owed to the very governments from whom commercial favors were now being sought.

It would be easy to exaggerate the desperate plight of American commerce in the 1780s and, thus, to overestimate the importance of the new trade with Asia for the nation's survival. Merrill Jensen has suggested that by the end of that decade a new and broader basis of American economic life had already appeared for at least a significant part of the country.[24] Nevertheless, it must be remembered that the direct American trade with the "East Indies" was born in the darkest period of postwar economic depression and uncertainty. The trade then seemed to offer the very important dual advantage of commercial profit and elimination of European middlemen, a step toward economic independence.

A further point needs to be emphasized. Though there was more drama in the long voyages to exotic, distant ports, the great bulk of U.S. trade continued to be carried on the North Atlantic. After the Revolution, as before, the largest single supplier of manufactures, and purchaser of American products, continued to be Great Britain. After Britain ranked France and other nations on the European continent. In the late 1780s and after, moreover, even the trade with the British, Spanish, and French colonies in the Americas played a larger role in the economy of the young republic than did that with all the shores and islands of the Pacific.

Finally, in the first years after the Revolution, no one could be sure that the ports of Europe and of Europe's colonies would be opened to American ships as widely as they subsequently were. The European wars that followed the French Revolution and raged on through the era of Napoleon swept many European merchant ships from the seas, compelling Continental powers for a time to open home and colonial ports to neutral American traders, thus creating opportunities that could not have been foreseen by those who first proposed American ventures to the East in 1783 and 1784.

VENTURES TO ASIA BEGIN

Kenneth Scott Latourette has described a number of proposals for voyages to the East that appeared in maritime communities of the northeastern United States in 1783 and 1784.[25] If action did not result at first, it was usually for lack of resources, as was the case with a proposal before the Connecticut legislature in

1784. The uncertainty of gain in the East by comparison with more familiar trades was another deterrent.

Among those seeking to arouse American interest in the commercial possibilities of the Pacific at that time was John Ledyard, a native of Connecticut. Something of a rolling stone in his youth, Ledyard had sailed as a corporal of marines with Captain James Cook on the great explorer's third and last voyage to the Pacific. While on that expedition Ledyard had been impressed, as were other members of the ships' company, with the possibility of trading furs, obtained for trinkets on the northwestern coast of North America, for valuable tea, textiles, and other products of the Chinese. In Ledyard's words, "we purchased while here about fifteen hundred beaver, besides other skins, but took none but the best, having no thoughts at that time of using them to any other advantage, than converting them to the purposes of clothing. But it afterwards happened that skins, which did not cost the purchaser sixpence sterling, sold in China for one hundred dollars."[26] Ever the entrepreneur, Ledyard was so intrigued by the nature of the fur trade that when his ship touched at the island of Unalaska he learned all he could about the business from Russians engaged in the business there.

Ledyard returned to Connecticut at the end of 1782 and spent the winter rewriting from memory his narrative of the Cook expedition, his original diary having been sequestered with all others by the British Admiralty to prevent their publication prior to that of the official account. In the spring of 1783 he began an intensive effort to persuade American shipowners to undertake a voyage to the Northwest Coast for furs to trade in China.

Some American shipowners and merchants were already considering ventures to the East Indies at the time Ledyard first voiced his proposals. Their plans, however, involved entering into competition with Europeans on the already established trade route via the Cape of Good Hope and the Indian Ocean. Ledyard, on the other hand, was suggesting the possibility of going west around Cape Horn.

In direct competition with the Europeans, the Americans' only possible advantages rested on the cheapness of their vessels, the energy and shrewdness of their masters and crews, and their freedom from the hampering restrictions of governmental charters, monopolies, or regulations. At the same time, however, venturers from the United States suffered from the lack of a diversified industrial system that could produce domestic manufactures for export, from the absence of a large reservoir of liquid capital, and from the fact that they did not have the naval protection or government subsidies that others enjoyed. Ledyard's proposal seemed to offer, however, a new type of East Indies trade in which Americans, if they could beat the Europeans to it, might overcome those disadvantages.

From what can be gathered of his first proposals to New England, New York, and Philadelphia merchants, Ledyard contemplated establishing permanent trading posts on the Northwest Coast to which cheap trinkets, textiles, and bits of metal would be sent to exchange for furs with the native inhabitants of the area. Jared Sparks, Ledyard's early biographer, connected this plan with a potential extension of American territorial claims to the northwest. Sparks claimed that Thomas Jefferson, whom Ledyard later met in Paris, saw this expansive possibility and supported his efforts for that reason. Sparks even suggested that Ledyard's subsequent proposal to cross North America by land from the Oregon coast to the Atlantic gave Jefferson the idea that later resulted in the Lewis and Clark expedition.[27] There is, however, no conclusive evidence to support any of these claims in either Ledyard's or Jefferson's papers.

Ledyard constantly altered and embroidered his proposals, but his main goal was simply a commercial venture that might enrich him and his countrymen. It should be noted that Ledyard was not himself a merchant by profession, and those who were tended to be much more cautious than he in advocating such a far-flung enterprise. No suggestion of government action or policy appears in records of his thinking.

Whatever may have been the ultimate national significance of Ledyard's advocacy of the Northwest fur trade, his first efforts brought him only disappointments. At least three times he appeared on the verge of securing the necessary backing from American merchants, the most notable of whom was Revolutionary War financier Robert Morris. Each time, however, untoward events appeared to frustrate the plan before it could be carried into execution. Jefferson hinted that perhaps Ledyard was his own worst enemy.[28] Although he possessed the ability to talk his way into the confidence of shipping men of at least three nations, and of public figures like Jefferson, John Paul Jones, and the English scientist Sir Joseph Banks, Ledyard also suffered from an excess of enthusiasm and an impatience that frightened off one potential backer after another before his death in 1788.

Despite his own failure to find patronage, Ledyard's proposals had not fallen on deaf ears. By the time of his death the first citizens of the United States were, in fact, already in the Pacific Basin and engaged in the fur trade. Publication of the official journals of Cook's expedition in 1784 confirmed what the Yankee traveler had said, and others took up his plan. In September of 1787 a group of men, mostly from Boston, sent off two ships to try the Cape Horn route to the Pacific and the fur trade.[29]

Even before this, however, other American ships had entered the trade via the Cape of Good Hope route. The first such venture on record was that of the sloop *Harriet,* which sailed from Boston in December 1783. That particular ship did not reach the Orient, for it was able to load at the Cape a cargo of tea being brought on an East Indiaman. The master of the Company's ship apparently felt that it would be less dangerous to ensure the American's profit in this way than to encourage his entry into the Company's jealously guarded preserve at Canton. By July 1784 the *Harriet*'s cargo was being offered for retail sale in Boston.[30]

The first U.S. vessel known to have actually reached China was the *Empress of China,* which sailed from New York on February 22, 1784. The plan for this venture had been some time in preparation, and the presence of Robert Morris as one of the principals involved in it is one piece of evidence of the possible influence of Ledyard's advocacy upon this enterprise. Morris had mentioned his plan to enter the business in a letter to John Jay, then secretary for foreign affairs, on November 27, 1783.[31]

In this enterprise the noted Philadelphia financier joined with Daniel Parker and Company of New York to fit out the *Empress of China.* It was not an altogether happy or successful partnership, and it was limited to this one venture.

An important part of the preparation for the expedition was the selection of Major Samuel Shaw, a veteran of the Revolution, as supercargo. The function of that position was to handle the disposition of the cargo and purchase of China goods for import to the United States. Shaw left both an extensive account of the voyage and one of the clearest illustrations of the relationship between private interests and public policy that has come down from that early period.[32]

Various aspects of this pioneer voyage will be discussed in connection with the Old China Trade. Here it is significant to note that the ship carried documents from both the state of New York and the Congress of the United States attesting to its good character and to those of the owners. How much faith could be placed in a letter from a government so lacking in power and prestige as the Congress then was is difficult to say. At any rate, the letter itself was impressive enough. As it emerged from a special committee composed of James Monroe, George Partridge, and Hugh Williamson, the letter read as follows:

Most serene, serene, most puissant, puissant, high, illustrious, noble, honorable, venerable, wise, and prudent Emperors, Kings, Republics, Princes, Dukes, Earls, Barons, Lords, Burgomasters, Councillors, as also judges, officers, justiciaries and regents of all the good cities and places, whether ecclesiastical or secular, who shall see these Patents or hear them read:

We the United States in Congress assembled make known, that John Green, captain of the ship called the Empress of China, is a citizen of the United States of America, and that the ship which he commands belongs to citizens of the said United States, and as we wish to see the said John Green prosper in his lawful affairs, our prayer is to all the beforementioned, and to each of them separately, that they may please to receive him with goodness, and treat him in a becoming manner, permitting him upon the usual tolls and expenses in passing and repassing, to pass, navigate and frequent the ports, passes and territories, to the end, to transact his business where and in what manner he shall judge proper, whereof we shall be willingly indebted.[33]

This letter seems to have been approved by Congress at the request of Daniel Parker, the New York merchant, supported by a note from Gouverneur Morris to his friend Charles Thomson, the secretary of Congress. Morris wrote: "You will oblige me and others of your friends" to comply with this request. In the absence of a sizeable, entrenched federal bureaucracy the matter was quickly settled between friends.[34]

The *Empress*'s letter was modeled on one issued shortly before to Philip

Moore of Philadelphia for the ship *United States.* In a memorial to Congress Moore had gone so far as to suggest the desirability of stationing a U.S. consul at Canton, a unique proposal for government aid for that time.[35] Beset by problems at home, Congress showed little interest in this sort of expansive step in support of a trade not yet established with a nation not in diplomatic contact with the West.

The *United States,* incidentally, seems not to have reached China, completing its import cargo in India or Southeast Asia. It may be the vessel referred to by a London newspaper in March 1785 in these possibly wishful terms: "The Americans have given up all thought of a China trade, which never can be carried on to advantage without some settlement in the East Indies. The ship they fitted out for China, soon after the peace, has been offered to sale in France for a sum less than the outfit.''[36]

Armed with the letter from Congress (and guns still retained from Revolutionary War privateering days), the *Empress of China* set sail for China via the Cape Verde Islands, Cape of Good Hope, Indian Ocean, and Sunda Strait. During the five-month voyage the ship made two significant contacts. One was with inhabitants of Java, with whom they traded amicably and about whom Shaw recorded rather hopeful observations concerning future commerce. The second was with the officers of two French ships, who welcomed the Americans as allies in the recent war and who offered to lead the *Empress* to China by a new passage between the islands of Billiton and Banca. Upon their arrival at Macao, on China's south coast, the French continued to assist the Americans by introducing them to the French consul there and acquainting them with the methods by which trade was then conducted with the Chinese.[37]

Having reached Macao on August 23, 1784, the *Empress of China* was the first U.S. vessel to show the flag in an East Asian port. Under the circumstances, the ship was as much a curiosity to the Chinese and Europeans there as the former, at least, were to the Americans. Shaw reports that their reception was polite and, with the possible exception of the British, even friendly. The Americans were permitted to trade, even though they had not brought the usual "presents" for Chinese officials.

Major Shaw wrote a detailed account of the whole experience for presentation to the members of Congress in Philadelphia, and hoped that Congress would publish the letter in order that other Americans might be informed of the China trade possibilities. Congress, however, declined to publish the letter, apparently after first agreeing to do so. Instead, it passed a resolution: "That Mr. Shaw be informed that Congress feel a peculiar satisfaction in the successful issue of the first effort of the Citizens of America to establish a direct trade with China.''[38]

On its voyage home the *Empress* sailed from Whampoa, the anchorage for foreign ships at Canton, on December 28, 1784, and returned via Sunda Strait. Arriving in New York on May 11, 1785, the ship and her company were the objects of much attention, and the expedition was hailed as a great achievement for the young nation. As a commercial venture, however, it fell short of the high hopes of the entrepreneurs. Though it showed a profit of $30,727 on a total investment of about $120,000, including the value of the ship, it was not enough to save Daniel Parker & Company from bankruptcy or to provide Major Shaw with the fortune he had hoped to make. It was, nevertheless, enough to encourage others to pursue the same trade.[39]

Even before this first voyage was completed, Congress had issued several more sea-letters for projected voyages to China, using that prepared for the *Empress of China* as a model. By 1790 twenty-eight American ships are known to have cleared Canton, and by 1800 more than one hundred did so.[40] Though the annual figures fluctuated considerably, it is clear that the years following Shaw's first voyage saw the establishment of a continuing American interest in the East Indies trade. By the beginning of the nineteenth century the American stake in the West's maritime trade with China was second in volume, though a rather distant second, to that of Great Britain.[41]

The term "East Indies trade," as noted previously, was used to cover all the commerce with China, Southeast Asia, the shores and islands of the Indian Ocean, and even the Persian Gulf. These latter parts of the trade, some of them developed at first as way stations on the long voyage to Canton, provided refreshment for the crews, shelter from storms or foes, and varieties of trade goods more saleable to the Chinese than American native products. In the 1790s certain of these auxiliary trades, as in Indian textiles or Sumatran pepper, occasionally reached a volume that even exceeded that with China.[42]

The volume of all this Asian commerce still, however, represented only a minor part of the total foreign trade of the United States. This needs to be emphasized because some writers have viewed the new trade with the East as *the* major factor in the post-Revolutionary economy. One writer went so far as to make it the key to the whole period down to the Civil War.[43] The immense profits returned by some of the voyages are certainly impressive, but against these must be counted disastrous losses of investments, cargoes, and ships. It is impossible to strike an accurate balance by which to measure the overall profitability of the first American voyages to China or to compare their value with those sent to Europe or to Europe's American colonies.

Despite the sanguine expectations of Shaw and others, the markets for American goods in Asia or Asian goods in America proved limited, and both markets soon suffered from periodic conditions of oversupply.[44] Enormous profits were reaped by fortunate voyages at the high season, however, and they were enough to whet the appetites of merchants in Salem, Boston, Providence, New York, Philadelphia, and Baltimore, to name only the most prominent ports. Each had sent vessels to the Orient before 1795, and a few merchant houses, usually one involved in other trades as well, founded fortunes on the Eastern commerce.[45]

MEANWHILE, BACK IN CONGRESS . . .

Beyond its congratulatory resolution on the completion of the first voyage, Congress did not, indeed could not, provide notable support of this new commercial interest. Until after 1789 that body lacked the power and perhaps the inclination to take an aggressive position in fostering or protecting American trade in such a remote part of the globe. Until the 1790s the various states jealously guarded their power to regulate commerce. Neither Shaw nor other advocates of Pacific ventures at first expected government intervention in their behalf.

In November 1785 John Adams, then U.S. minister to Great Britain, suggested to Secretary John Jay that Congress might at least help publicize the opportunities of the East Indies trade so that others might be encouraged to follow. Showing a shrewd appreciation of the forces at work, Adams wrote:

> There is no better advice to be given to the merchants of the United States than to push their commerce to the East Indies as fast and as far as it will go.
>
> If information from persons who ought to know may be depended upon the tobacco and peltries, as well as the ginseng of the United States, are proper articles for the China market, and have been found to answer very well; and many other of our commodities may be found in demand there. But there is another resource which may prove of equal value at present. There are many persons in the European factories in India, particularly the English, who have accumulated large property, which they wish to transmit to Europe, but have not been able to do it, on account of the distance and the scarcity of freight. These would be glad to sell us their commodities, and take our bills of exchange upon Europe or America, payable in twelve or eighteen months, possibly in longer periods.
>
> These facts are known to individuals in America, but will probably be concealed from the public at large, lest the speculators and adventurers be too numerous for the profit of a few.[46]

Here is an early and classic expression of the conflict between private interest and what Adams and others conceived to be the interest of the whole nation. It may also give a clue to at least one reason why members of Congress were reluctant to spread Shaw's communication, or Adams's, on the public record.

Continuing, Adams indicated his understanding of where power really lay under the Articles of Confederation:

> The States may greatly encourage these enterprises by laying on duties upon the importation of all East India goods from Europe, and, indeed, by proceeding in time to prohibitions. This [latter], however, may never be necessary. Duties, judiciously calculated, and made high enough to give a clear advantage to the direct importation [by Americans] from India, will answer the end as effectually as prohibitions, and are less odious, and less liable to exceptions.

Finally, relating the private commercial interest to that of the nation as he saw it, Adams wrote:

> We should attend to this intercourse with the east with the more ardor, because the stronger footing we obtain in those countries, of more importance will our friendship be to the powers of Europe who have large connections there. The East Indies will probably be the object and the theatre of the next war; and the more familiar we are with every

thing relating to that country, the more will the contending parties desire to win us to their side, or, at least, what we ought to wish foremost, to keep us neutral.

This letter clearly illustrates the foresight and the frustration of at least one American leader of that troubled time. The Continental Congress, grappling with problems of unity among the states and lacking the power to levy tariff duties, could do little to urge American merchants to seek trade in Asia or to assist them in doing so. The individual states, on the other hand, enacted widely differing commercial regulations, some discriminating against others. Goods imported into Connecticut or Rhode Island, which did not at first pass strict protective or retaliatory duties, could then be shipped into Massachusetts, which did. The Carolinas had similar problems in the South. The futility of thirteen separate commercial systems was clear even before a British diplomat cited it to Adams as a reason for refusing to negotiate a commercial treaty with the United States.

Between 1785 and 1788, New York, Pennsylvania, and Massachusetts, to name but the principals, enacted duties that favored local over foreign shipping in the importation of tea, porcelain, and certain other oriental products. These were simply part of a general effort to encourage their states' maritime commerce and shipping and to discriminate against those nations, chiefly Great Britain, that were refusing to open some or all of their ports to American ships and cargoes.

It soon became apparent to the commercial interests of the nation that some congressional control over commerce was essential, or the country might dissolve in bankruptcy and disunion. In the movement toward stronger central authority, which many merchants supported, those involved in the China trade played a part. It is impossible to measure the precise importance of the role played by China or East Indies traders in the movement, however, for no sharp line distinguished the merchant dealing with Asia from the transatlantic or Caribbean trader. The same companies engaged in both. If they eventually won preferential duties for Asian goods imported in American ships, it was simply part of a general effort to win for the United States control over its own foreign trade. Strengthening the federal government was a major step in that direction.[47]

THE LURE OF THE CHINA TRADE

CONDITIONS AT CANTON

When the first Americans arrived to take part in the trade at Canton, they were entering a commerce that had long been established and maintained under conditions peculiar to itself. The discontinuous history of exchange of goods and ideas between China and the West goes back at least to Greek and Roman times, and one particular characteristic of that trade seems to have remained with it in virtually all periods—the one-sidedness of it.

The West, from the very beginning, had no large body of goods to export to the Orient that incorporated equal value for equal bulk or that the Chinese prized as highly as the West did the fabrics, spices, and other products of the East. The Romans had found it necessary to supplement their exports of merchandise to the East with specie, while striving to find some product that would tend to balance the trade. Those who followed them found a similarly unequal balance, and the drain of precious metals from the West that accompanied this luxury trade lent credence to belief in the fabulous riches that must characterize lands that produced such goods and needed so little that the West could offer.[1]

In practice, trade with China had come by the 1780s to be channeled through the single port of Canton, with Macao as an auxiliary base. Down to 1842 Canton remained the one official port through which maritime trade with China might legally be carried on.

THE BUSINESS SIDE

Pioneers of the early American trade with China were optimistic that they possessed a product that could be traded with the Chinese. The herb ginseng

(*Panax quinquefolia*) was much prized in the Orient for its real and supposed medicinal qualities, and the plant grew wild in the forests of eastern North America. Unfortunately for American hopes it was soon clear that the Chinese market for the herb was too limited to support an extensive trade. To make matters worse, the American herb was less highly valued than that produced in Korea and Manchuria. Though ginseng continued as an American export commodity to China, U.S. merchants were faced from the outset with the traditional Western problem of seeking other commodities saleable in China or making up the difference in specie.[2]

That hard cash would be an essential element for Americans in the China trade was very soon apparent. The export products available in the United States were generally ones that involved relatively small value for their bulk, in contrast to the oriental goods desired. A full cargo of American grain, cheese, rum, iron, and simple manufactures, even if saleable, would not exchange for half a cargo of Chinese teas, silks, cottons, lacquerware, porcelain, and the like. Before 1800 boxes and kegs of coins, chiefly Spanish, were being sent out in addition to every conceivable item that might find a market at Canton. Quite commonly, especially in the early years of the trade, a single cargo might carry goods and/or coins representing the separate ventures of many different persons or groups in the home port of the vessel.[3]

With the chronic shortage of hard money that characterized the economy of the young United States, the drain of specie to ports so distant to be exchanged for what were mostly luxury items was bound to occasional protest. As early as 1793, the *United States Chronicle* of Providence, Rhode Island, commented on a prejudice against the East Indies trade on that ground, and there were many more complaints in the years that followed.[4]

Timothy Pitkin printed figures for the years 1805 to 1825 that showed a total of more than $62 million in specie exported to Canton from the United States over that period, more than double the value of merchandise exported or reexported in the same trade during that period.[5] William C. Hunter wrote that the cargo of the *Citizen* (New York), on which he first sailed to Canton in 1824, was composed of 350,000 Spanish silver dollars in kegs, plus furs, lead, bar and scrap iron, and quicksilver.[6] This specie drain to the Orient continued at least into the late 1820s, when changes in China and in the West altered both the nature and the function of the trade.

Even without pressure from critics of the specie drain, the merchants of the Atlantic seaboard were certain to make every effort to find a more satisfactory basis for their trade with the Orient. One of the first important experiments to this end was the Northwest fur trade, suggested by John Ledyard and initiated by Kendrick and Gray in the *Columbia* and *Lady Washington* in 1787–1788. The fur trade, however, like that in ginseng, proved to have limitations both as to the market in China and the supply on the Northwest Coast of America. More will be said about this later, as well as something concerning the trades in sandalwood, *bêche-de-mer,* tortoise shell, and other products of the Pacific islands, all of which were sought as products for the China market.[7]

None of these commodities, nor all of them together, sufficed to equalize the balance of payment with China. For a time, from after the War of 1812 to the late 1830s, some American merchants managed to avoid carrying very large shipments of specie by first trading to Britain for cargoes of British manufactured goods and then disposing of these in China or along the way there. This trade became particularly irritating to English merchants who saw Americans reap the benefits of a trade from which they were barred by the East India Company's monopoly. Their complaint became one of the major ones brought against the Company in 1813 and 1833 by those who sought, successfully in 1834, to end that monopoly as it applied to the trade with China.[8]

AUXILIARY TRADES

Another way to avoid the shipment of specie to China was through what has been called a "chain trade" along the way. An example of this would be a vessel that set sail from Philadelphia with a cargo of American and West Indian goods, stopped at Spain or Portugal, touched at Gibraltar or picked up some opium at Smyrna, and then sailed along the coasts of Africa. Further stops might be made at Capetown, Mauritius, Bombay, Madras, Calcutta, Malacca, or Batavia before the ship reached Macao and Whampoa. By that time the character of the cargo might have changed completely, parts of it two or three times, enhancing its Canton value at each exchange. Even Baltic Sea ports were touched on occasion by American vessels ultimately destined for India or China, and, at the other end, Manila might come into the picture as a source of sugar and rice.[9]

Traffic with way stations of the Indian Ocean and Indonesia, as has been seen, began early and gave the name of "East Indies Trade" to all of the trade east of the Cape of Good Hope. Mauritius did not prove to be a major market for American produce, but it came to be valued as an excellent listening post for commercial information regarding the ports of South and Southeast Asia, and as a place where American or European cargoes could be exchanged for specie or bills of exchange that could be used at Canton.[10]

After the French opened the island to trade with American ships, the produce of India also became available to them there, which, in turn, forced the British to begin opening the ports of India to American ships for fear that the French and others would reap the advantages of being middlemen. Here was a clear demonstration of the way in which commercial forces, unsupported by any policy or action of the United States government, achieved international objectives.[11]

GROWTH OF THE TRADE

The American trade with China, begun in 1784, experienced a marked increase by the season of 1789–1790. In that year, however, with more than three million pounds of tea registered with the customs offices of the United States, the limitations of the American market were clearly demonstrated. Prices for oriental goods fell markedly, and a group of East Indies traders, forced to store much of the produce brought by their vessels, sought relief from Congress in postponing the payment of duties and allowing a major drawback on such goods as might be re-exported. Congress complied with the request, but the China traders had learned a lesson, and it would be several years before the trade would regain the level of that one season.[12]

The next session of Congress raised the duties on China goods imported in American ships, apparently in response to protests against favoritism to one group of merchants. This injured the tea traders so much that they responded with memorials and protests, and the favorable duties were promptly restored and remained fairly steady for the next thirty or forty years. Since a number of the principal men among the traders were also involved in other branches of trade and were prominent in local industrial, real estate, and public projects as well, their pleas were difficult to ignore.[13]

After 1789 the trade with China fluctuated very considerably over the years, so that average figures become of little value as a measure of its importance in the total American foreign trade. Moreover, the statistical data for a precise measurement of foreign trade in the early nineteenth century simply are not available. From the time of Pitkin to the present, those who have tried to deal with the period have offered explanations and apologies for possible inaccuracy in their estimates. Smuggling and other forms of illicit commerce, sloppy record keeping in consular offices, and the ravages of time in destruction of records all put the modern scholar at risk in trying to measure the China trade, East Indies trade, and the total foreign commerce of the United States in the early national period.

The outbreak of general war in Europe after 1792 offered special opportunities to neutral carriers, with American vessels soon taking a leading place. This is clear from the available trade figures for those years, especially for 1804–1808 and the single trading season of 1809–1810.[14] A heavy volume of re-exports from the United States in those years, exceeding at times the exports of domestic produce, reveals the importance of the carrying trade that had been opened to Americans by Europe's wars. Shifting efforts by the British and French to limit even trade of neutrals with their opponents brought high risks and losses, but unusually high profits as well. The attempts of the Jefferson and Madison administrations to protect neutral rights, as they saw them, by embargo and then by war, caused the only major interruptions in this commercial bonanza. During this period Asian products, especially from French and Dutch colonial ports, figured prominently among the re-exports.[15]

The War of 1812 brought a marked slump in virtually all branches of American maritime commerce, including the China trade. British seizures of American shipping extended to the Pacific and the coasts of China. Once the war was over, however, there was a brief upsurge of trade to take advantage of the higher prices resulting from war-created shortages of Asian products. This produced over-investment and glutted markets and coincided with a domestic business panic in 1819. Thereafter, though the general level of American trade with China rose above prewar levels, it was still subject to considerable annual variations in volume. Changing conditions in the trade, moreover, caused the business to become increasingly concentrated in the hands of a few firms, with a decline of small or one-shot ventures.[16]

Several factors combined to alter conditions of the trade in the late 1820s and early 1830s. There were technological advances on the Western side that made the production of cotton and other fabrics, as well as porcelain, cheap enough to reduce the demand for Asian products. Even Chinese designs and patterns could be duplicated. The result was that the East began increasingly to be viewed as a market, instead of a source of supply, except for tea, spices, and other specialty items. Moreover, the wars for independence in Spanish America reduced the supply of monetary silver on which the Canton market had heretofore relied, but increased international contacts by more stable American firms made possible the use of bills of exchange and other credit instruments in its place.[17]

On the Chinese side, there was increasing governmental concern over the growing trade in opium, at the reversal of the flow of cash created by that trade, and over the declining Western demand for China's cotton and ceramic products. Inevitably there would be administrative efforts to combat these threats to the fiscal and moral health of the empire that would alter the whole picture. The wonder is that it took so long.

In the peak years of 1805–1808, when Americans were handling their largest share of the colonial carrying trade, or grand cabotage, for Europeans, commerce in Asian products may have reached as high as 15 percent of total U.S. foreign trade. This almost certainly was the largest part that Eastern commerce ever played in the national economy of the United States, in part because in those early years foreign trade played a larger role in the economy that it would later when domestic manufacturing, agriculture, and internal commerce became more fully developed. By the 1820s and 1830s the conditions of the Canton trade had settled down, with a few large firms handling most of the American trade there. The value of the Asian commerce of the United States fell once again to a level of about 5 percent of its foreign trade, sometimes even less.

In the last two decades of the Old China Trade an average of thirty to forty American ships reached Canton per year, representing an aggregate import-export value of between $10 and $15 million annually. During this same period the total foreign trade of the United States multiplied several times in value, causing Asia and the Pacific to become even less important to American foreign trade than they had been in the first years of the nineteenth century.[18] Despite peaks in 1789–1790 and in 1805–1808, the trade that the *Empress of China* had begun in 1784 failed to live up to the expectations of its early enthusiasts.

PORTS AND MERCHANTS

The American merchants, shipowners, and mariners who entered the China trade came overwhelmingly from one section of the nation—the Northeast. The southern ports of Charleston and Norfolk apparently sent only one vessel each to the Orient over the entire period down to 1842. Even Baltimore, which had sent a ship to Canton as early as 1785, did not develop a major trade there. Philadelphia maintained its interest, though the peak of its activity had passed by the 1830s.[19] It was New York City, the pioneer port, which became the major center of the export trade to China, and after 1815, especially, the market for oriental goods came to center there.

Of the New England ports, Boston, Providence, and Salem were prominent in the early phases of the trade to China, but the role of Providence diminished sharply after 1826. Salem, after an early start at Canton, gave much greater attention to the pepper trade with Sumatra and maintained a rather extensive commerce with other ports of what is now Indonesia and ports of the Indian Ocean. After 1820 the importance of Salem as a major port declined, largely because of its unfavorable location in relation to the main marketing centers of the nation. Still, Salem has retained a special identification with the Old China Trade since, as Foster Dulles has written, ''no other port so carefully preserved the records of its commerce. We know more of its trade in Canton than we do of the trade of its rivals.''[20]

Boston merchants played a major role in the China trade from the beginning. As earlier noted, the *Harriet* was actually dispatched to the Orient from that port before the *Empress of China*. Other Boston vessels soon followed, and in 1787 Boston merchants pioneered the route to China via Cape Horn and the northwest fur coast. Even before the completion of *Columbia*'s voyage, Thomas H. Perkins, who would become a leading Boston merchant for years, had sailed with Captain James Magee aboard the *Astraea (Astrea)* to Canton by the old route with a stop at Batavia.[21]

Boston traders shared with those of New York and Philadelphia the principal role in bringing to the attention of the United States government the interests of those engaged in trade with the Orient. Surviving letters from them to John Jay, Alexander Hamilton, Thomas Jefferson, and James Madison during the early years of the trade indicate what must have been a wider correspondence than that of which we have record. Congressmen from the maritime districts of the northeastern states were certainly in touch with their prominent merchant constituents, though few of the latter actually ran for office themselves. One, Thomas Fitzsimons of Pennsylvania, did win election during the Articles of Confederation period, and he expressed the views of East Indies merchants while in office.[22]

Other merchants held office at the state or local level, or took part in political party affairs. Stephen Girard of Philadelphia played a prominent role in supporting the first two national banks and Madison's war efforts after 1812. John Jacob Astor corresponded with Madison and Monroe, and seems to have had access to Jefferson both during and after his presidency.[23]

The relative significance of petitions to Congress, private letters to members of the administration, or personal contacts in the interest of one commercial interest or another is impossible to recapture or to measure. Such prominent merchants as Robert Morris, Thomas H. Perkins, Joseph Peabody, members of the Derby and Crowninshield families of Salem, and the Wilcocks and Waln families of Philadelphia were active in political affairs at home at the same time that they were involved in various branches of Asian and Pacific commerce.

This means that insofar as there was any attempt to influence Washington in behalf of the interests of the trade with the Pacific, it was confined, geographically, to the northeastern states. Northeastern merchants could be found in both major politcal parties, but their major strength began among the Federalists and later moved to the Jeffersonian Republicans. And if the power they exercised over national policies was, as one writer has put it, enough to win "such favors as now seem incredible," considering the relatively minor national importance of their trade, that power was always limited, and it waned as the center of political strength in the nation shifted westward and southward.[24]

New tariff policies in 1816 were designed to expand trade rather than to protect American shippers. By the late 1820s the decline of political influence, or the shift of interest, among overseas merchants was further accelerated by the rise of manufacturing interests in the Northeast. This led many of the fortunes acquired in the Old China Trade to be invested in real estate, transportation, and manufacturing at home.[25]

The period between 1815 and 1835 was, then, one of readjustment for the China trade. Earlier favors, like preferential duties and drawbacks, which had been granted to the trade when it had been of limited volume and in goods largely defined as luxury items, were now criticized for the cost they added to the price of tea and other goods that had come into more common use. That the China trade survived this readjustment period was largely the result of more efficient management, at least for a time, in both shipping and merchandising.[26]

RELATIONS WITH EUROPEANS

One of the blessings of Chinese control at Canton was that no Europeans were in a position to interfere with American trade without risking Chinese sanctions. In the colonial ports that the British, Dutch, or French ruled, however, matters were different. Samuel Shaw encountered one of the earliest demonstrations of European jealousy at the hands of Dutch authorities at Batavia. Under the impression that he had received permission from the Dutch governor-general to trade there, Shaw sailed for Batavia on his third voyage to the East in 1790. Denied the necessary permits to do business there, Shaw registered formal protests to the Dutch authorities in Java about the discrimination practiced against him and his fellow countrymen, and he also dispatched a protest to the president of the United States.[27]

On July 14, 1791, Secretary of State Thomas Jefferson took up Shaw's complaint with the Dutch minister in Philadelphia. In the meantime, Thomas H. Perkins, then a young Boston merchant, had visited Batavia, found the Dutch ostensibly upset by the unethical behavior of some Americans there, and managed to smooth over the situation somewhat. The result was that a limited American trade continued there through the 1790s and into the period of the Napoleonic Wars, until the British seized control of Java. After the War of 1812 and the resumption of Dutch sovereignty at Batavia, there were repeated complaints by Americans of Dutch East India Company restrictions that limited their commerce.[28]

Americans enjoyed generally amicable relations with the French, not only at Canton but also in their colonies of Ile de France (Mauritius), Ile de Bourbon (Reunion), and their various stations in India. After a brief period of mercantilist restrictions by France, Americans found opportunities for favorable trade there, as well as for the gathering of commercial information.[29]

Commercial relations of a sort were established with the Spanish at Manila and a few minor Philippine ports. The trade there, connected mostly with that to China, reached such proportions in the 1830s that Russell and Company located an agent at Manila. Sugar, coffee, and rice were obtained from the Philippines, usually for trade at Canton, especially during the period when ships bringing rice were given reductions in port duties by the Chinese. Sales of American and European products at Manila were limited, however, as were formal political relations, by the exclusive Spanish policies that surrounded this distant colony.[30]

Both Spain and Portugal figured in America's early China trade, first as destinations for exports of fish, timber, and some re-exports. In both countries, U.S. ships picked up wines, oils, and citrus products that could be marketed along the way to China. The Canary, Madeira, and Cape Verde islands were frequently visited on outbound voyages for water, supplies, or refitting, and an occasional seaman was also taken on there. Portuguese ports in India and Southeast Asia also figured in many voyages, and, of course, Macao played an essential part in the approach to Canton.

Diplomatic relations with Spain grew increasingly troubled as the Spanish American wars for independence affected both trade and democratic sympathies in the United States. It does not appear, however, that those differences played any significant role in American activities in the western Pacific through the first half of the nineteenth century. Very few U.S. vessels touched at ports in Spanish America in the course of voyages to China, and it does not appear that their contacts there had any significant effects on the evolution of China trade policies.

As for the Portuguese in Macao, a number of American witnesses reported general hospitality, though some complained of high charges for lodging or other services there. And Samuel Shaw, Joseph Ingraham, and late comers noted that the Portuguese authorities at Macao, being dependent on the good will of the Chinese, were not willing to jeopardize their position by intervening on behalf of Americans. Portugal could not be relied on to help change a system of Sino-Western relations from which it had profited for so long a time.[31]

In addition to these relations with other Western nations that were connected to the China trade, there were also contacts with the Russians in northeastern Asia and in North America from Alaska to the California coast. The Russians, however, were not represented among the merchant community at Canton, though Ingraham reported in 1791 that trade in furs at that port was suspended by the Chinese over a dispute with the Russians. The imperial authorities apparently assumed that all furs arriving from the North Pacific must in some way derive from Russian sources.[32]

CONTACTS WITH JAPAN

The first American contacts with Japan likewise developed from the trade at Canton. In point of time, the first American contact with Japan was made not long after the first visit to China. In 1791 Captains John Kendrick and James Douglas, engaged in the fur trade voyages between China and the northwest coast of North America, touched on the southern Japanese coast, presumably at Wakayama. The first contact with Japan, then, sprang from a branch of the trade with China. From the outset, however, the experience of Americans in China and Japan differed notably, as did the kinds of interests they developed in the two countries. As a result, the ways in which American public policies toward Japan were formed often differed widely from the pattern set in China.

Kendrick and Douglas met with the refusal to enter into relations with foreigners that had been Japan's settled policy since the early seventeenth century. Moreover, the two Americans touched at a part of Japan that appears to have harbored particularly strong antiforeign views. Little is known of the impressions of Japan gleaned by these first two travelers to those coasts, and few Americans knew much about this first visit, and what little they knew was not likely to encourage others to attempt to open relations with the Japanese.

Strangely, it was the vagaries of European politics that created the next opportunity for American contact with Japan. In the wars that followed the French Revolution the Netherlands was overrun by French armies, and the Dutch government was forced into an uneasy alliance with the French. In these circumstances Dutch East India Company shipping in the Indian Ocean and China Sea was prey to the chief maritime opponents of the French—the British—and the annual Dutch vessel permitted by the Japanese to visit the island of Deshima in Nagasaki harbor was in imminent danger of being intercepted. Company agents in Java resorted to the subterfuge of hiring neutral American vessel to make the annual voyages for them. Between 1797 and 1808 about eight different American ships were hired to carry the cargoes between Batavia and Japan. Sailing under the U.S. flag on the open seas, the ships hoisted the Dutch flag upon reaching Japanese waters and were received in accordance with the old agreement.

The first of the American ships to make the voyage for the Dutch was the *Eliza,* from New York, commanded by William R. Stewart, an Englishman. The ship delivered her cargo and took on that for return without mishap in the summer of 1797. Rehired for a second voyage, Stewart appears to have conceived ulterior designs for his own profit. In a series of mysterious maneuvers he was in and out of Nagasaki without reporting back to his Dutch employers. He found the Japanese trade sufficiently attractive to return in 1803 on a trading venture of his own, this time sailing in a British ship from India. Dutch jealousy and Japanese suspicion were too much for the wily Stewart this time, however, and he sailed away empty-handed.

During the time of Stewart's adventures several other American vessels carried Dutch cargoes to and from Nagasaki, bearing with them a number of citizens of the United States who would later play prominent parts in the East Indies trade. Among these was the *Margaret,* owned chiefly by the Derby family of Salem, which reached Nagasaki in the summer of 1801 with a notable group of Yankee seamen and business figures aboard. George Cleveland, clerk to Captain Samuel Derby, wrote an entertaining, though highly unreliable, journal of the voyage and of the brief excursions ashore at the Japanese port.[33]

A few Americans were, thus, early acquainted with the trade that might be carried on with Japan, but they also knew well the jealousy with which that trade was guarded by both the Dutch and the Japanese. Nothing in the way of public policy was called for as a result of these encounters. What is more remarkable, no serious effort appears to have been made by American merchants to prospect on Japanese shores for commercial opportunities for nearly thirty years after their last voyage for the Dutch.

THE NORTHWEST FUR TRADE

While commerce along the established Indian Ocean route was developing, other Americans entered a new and different part of the China trade, one which in time would create Pacific interests quite distinct from those centering about Canton. This new interest began in 1787 when the ships *Columbia Rediviva* (commonly known simply as *Columbia*) and *Lady Washington* were sent out from Boston to at last follow the route proposed by John Ledyard. The entrepreneurs in this case were from Salem, New York, and Boston. The variety of individuals involved in financing the venture was designed at least partly to spread the risk of this unprecedented voyage.[34]

There is both significance and fascination in this venture. Sailing from Boston at the end of September 1787, the two vessels encountered the difficult weather conditions that would plague generations of American seamen traveling the Cape Horn route. Separated in a storm near the Horn in April 1788, the two ships were not reunited until months later when both anchored in Nootka Sound, on Vancouver Island, thousands of miles to the north. In the meantime, *Columbia,* commanded by John Kendrick, had been forced to put in at Mas a Tierra, one of the Juan Fernandez Islands, then under the authority of the Spanish viceroy of Chile. That brief contact caused one of the first exchanges of diplomatic correspondence with a European government concerning U.S. citizens in the Pacific.[35]

Plans for fur trading with the native inhabitants of the Northwest Coast had to be put off in 1788 because of the advanced season. Not until midsummer of 1789 could *Columbia,* now under Robert Gray, be sent to Canton with a cargo of pelts. On that Pacific crossing the ship visited Hawai'i, then called the Sandwich Islands.[36]

Gray found that several other vessels, mainly British, had preceded him with cargoes of furs to China that season, and that the market was favorable neither for what he had to sell nor for the oriental products, mainly tea, that he had come to buy. To make matters worse, his return to Boston came at the end of the largest season the direct American trade to China had yet enjoyed or would enjoy for some years thereafter. The limited market was already glutted.

Thus, this first American circumnavigation of the globe (*Columbia* returned via the Indian Ocean and the Cape of Good Hope) and venture into the Northwest fur trade was not a striking success. Nevertheless, it marked the beginning of a line of trade in which Americans, chiefly from Massachusetts, would play a leading role. British and other traders had preceded the Americans to the Northwest Coast, but by 1800 the American vessels trading there outnumbered all others combined, and the lucrative commerce based on furs flourished for at least a quarter-century.[37]

In the course of this trade incidental contacts occurred with Spanish American ports from Chile northward to Alta California. Fur-trading vessels made landfalls among the Pacific islands in eastern Polynesia, especially the Marquesas and Hawai'i. In time these contacts would develop interests of their own quite distinct from or only indirectly related to the trade with Asia, and would create new problems for the inhabitants of the islands and their rulers. And here, as in Asia, these relations would have to be handled by shipmasters, sailors, and traders, with little thought to aid or control from their government.[38]

WHALING

In addition to the commerce converging on Canton from both sides of the Pacific Ocean, another significant American interest appeared in the Pacific before 1800. This was whaling, which extended its frontier from the South Atlantic into the Southeast Pacific in the late 1780s. Increasing scarcity of whales had driven Europeans and Americans far afield from the familiar grounds of the

North Atlantic by the closing quarter of the eighteenth century. Then, when the South Atlantic proved to offer only limited whaling possibilities, whalers began to take heed of the reports of explorers and traders about an abundance of whales in the Pacific.[39]

The whaling interest supplemented the Northwest fur trade in the contacts it produced between citizens of the United States and the inhabitants of Spanish America and the Pacific islands. It differed from the fur trade, however, and from the China trade in general, in that its main concern had nothing to do with Asia, at least in the beginning. Few whalers ever entered the teeming ports at Macao or Whampoa, even in later days when the Japan fishery and those of the Southwest Pacific and Indian oceans developed. The whalers' field was the great ocean itself, and even when, eventually, they tried to influence public policy concerning the Pacific, their interest centered on matters of the sea, its islands, and its eastern shores, until the question of opening Japan arose in the 1840s and 1850s.

AT THE CENTURY'S END

By 1800, then, there were three distinct facets to the American economic interest in the Pacific Basin. The first and by far the most valuable was the commerce with China and other Asian contacts involved with it. Second, and dependent upon the first, was the fur trade with the Northwest Coast of North America and with the fur seal islands of the eastern and southern Pacific. Third was the whaling industry just developing in the southeastern Pacific.

All combined, these three interests probably did not amount to more than 10 percent of total U.S. maritime business down to 1800. Statistical data are lacking or unreliable, especially for the period of Europe's wars when it is particularly difficult to separate the Eastern trade from that of the North Atlantic. Some U.S. merchant vessels freighted East Indies cargoes directly to European ports, and even whale oil could be caught up in the bewildering variety of shifts in European trade policies that led to changes in ship registrations and midocean transshipments of oil. Even accepting the fact that foreign trade then played a larger part in the nation's money economy than it would a century later, these enterprises were still comparatively minor interests pursued in a remote part of the world.

It was not, therefore, reasonable to expect the administrations of George Washington or of New England's John Adams to devote much time or federal funding to the protection or promotion of Pacific commerce. Tariff preferences for oriental products carried in American ships appeared in the first federal tariff legislation after the enactment of the Constitution. Diplomatically, Thomas Jefferson tried to help the Spanish commander of the Juan Fernandez Islands who had been severely disciplined by his government for aiding the distressed *Columbia*. U.S. diplomats to European countries tried to secure the opening of their colonial ports in South and Southeast Asia to American trade.

The use of U.S. armed forces in the Pacific, or the establishment of diplomatic posts there, were governmental measures as yet out of the question. The dispatch of an American warship to the Dutch East Indies in 1800 to convoy merchant ships past unfriendly British or French patrols was an extreme case, and it was not soon repeated. The first consuls appointed to Canton, Manila, and Batavia were obliged to serve without formal recognition or authority.[40]

American merchants trading to the East were not always eager to have their government "meddling" in trade relations, even in the name of protection of their interests. Some of them felt quite able to handle their own affairs without government direction or regulation. John Adams, as noted above, was aware of the jealousy with which merchants guarded the secrets of their trade successes. Others were engaged in smuggling, at least by the rules of oriental officials or those of European colonies. Even sealers and whalers tried to protect hard-won knowledge of good hunting areas or avoid investigation of their treatment of crew members.

On the other hand, some did hope that their government might be helpful to their interests and asked for official recognition of them. John Kendrick, for example, sought State Department support for his land claims at Nootka Sound, claiming national as well as personal interest was involved. His heirs pursued the claim for years. And Joseph Ingraham, who followed Kendrick, claimed the northern Marquesas Islands for the United States.[41]

John Adams concluded his 1785 remarks on the opportunities for Americans and their nation in the East Indies trade with words fit for every generation: "Much will depend upon the behavior of our people who may go into those countries. If they endeavor, by an irreproachable integrity, humanity, and civility to conciliate the esteem of the natives, they may easily become the most favored nation; for the conduct of European nations in general, heretofore, has given us a great advantage."[42] However, control over the behavior of Americans anywhere outside the United States was, before 1800, largely beyond the reach of the government. Neither the federal nor the state governments were in a position to select or admonish those citizens who ventured abroad. Those who went were mostly ordinary seamen, drawn from the coastal areas of the northeastern states, possessed of the limited degree of learning or sophistication that might be expected.

Thousands of miles and months of rigorous sailing from their homes, they were often fearful of the strange people they encountered, or they were mistrustful or contemptuous. Many regarded the diverse peoples of the Pacific Basin simply as "heathen," or "Indians," their ethnocentric attitudes influenced by what little they knew of relations with the American Indians at home. These feelings appear in the journals and letters that have survived, mainly from the better educated among the ships' crews and officers.

The spokesmen for the first Americans in the Pacific were captains, supercargoes, other ships' officers, together with an occasional educated individual carried as a crewmember or passenger. A curious mixture of straightforward honesty and the same curiosity, fear, or contempt harbored by ordinary seamen can be found among them. As might be expected, the relations that developed were uneven, to say the least. Mutual benefactions and friendship were matched by cruelty, dishonest dealing, and dislike, whether in Asia, Spanish America, Europe's Asian colonies, or on the Pacific's many islands.

The first Americans who went to China and the Pacific were by no means a cross section of the people at home. They came, as noted, predominantly from the coastal maritime regions of the northeastern states. From common sailor to the most prominent merchant or shipowner, their interests were those of a minority of the American population. The great majority of that population were small farmers, farm workers, and artisans who were not directly involved in these distant ventures. As a consequence, there appeared from the outset at all levels of government a certain resistance to requests for special favors emanating from East Indies traders or whalers.

If John Adams felt that the American image (and resultant opportunities) in Asia would depend on the quality of those who went there, he could hardly have been gratified by what was happening in his own lifetime. A sprinkling of rascals accompanied the citizens of probity who dealt with Chinese, Malay, Polynesian, or Hispanic traders. Men of choler and violence manned and even commanded some of the vessels under the American flag.

In short, the kind of behavior that might have earned for citizens of the United States a reputation of being different from "bad" Europeans in their dealings with Asian and Pacific peoples was not the rule, though there were those at home who chose to believe that it was. This discrepancy between reality abroad and belief at home would characterize American relations in the Pacific for generations thereafter. It might, in fact, be the most enduring theme of the history.

3

FIRST AMERICANS IN OTHER PACIFIC AREAS

THE NORTHWEST FUR TRADE

The route to the Pacific around Cape Horn, pioneered for Americans by the *Columbia* and *Lady Washington* in 1787–1788, was soon followed by other vessels from New England ports. The principal interest that drew them there was the same fur trade from the Oregon-British Columbia coast to Canton that John Ledyard had first advertised to American shipowners. This enterprise also brought citizens of the young republic into contact with areas and peoples new and strange to them along the western coasts of Spanish America and among the islands of Polynesia. Still, the fur trade's ultimate objective, the market at Canton, tied it in with other commerce following the older route via the Atlantic and Indian oceans.[1]

From northeastern ports, among which Boston took an early and prominent lead, vessels bound for the Northwest Coast of North America took a southeasterly slant across the Atlantic toward the Cape Verde Islands. Thence, the track went southwestward toward the southern coast of Brazil and on south past Argentina to the Strait of Magellan or, more likely, Cape Horn. Landfalls along that part of the route most commonly took place at the Cape Verdes, often at some port in Brazil, and less frequently on the bleak Argentine or Falkland Island shores.

Fur trade captains normally tried to reach the stormy waters round the Horn during the Southern Hemisphere summer in order to minimize the difficulties of what, by general agreement, was apt to be a difficult passage. Joseph Ingraham, in the brig *Hope* in 1790, had a remarkably easy passage of the Horn, and in his log heaped scorn on other masters who spoke with dread of its hardships.

Still, the evidence on the other side was so abundant that passage of the Horn continued to be considered an achievement once it had been completed.[2]

The *Columbia,* it will be recalled, had such a difficult passage around the southern tip of South America that it had been compelled to put in at the Juan Fernandez island of Masatierra (Mas a Tierra), despite Spain's official hostility to foreign ships in those waters. Thereafter, many an American crew was happy, or fortunate, to put in at some Chilean port to recover from the rigors of the Cape Horn passage, and from these contacts the first U.S. intercourse with the inhabitants of Chile evolved. In time, a small commerce developed that linked Chile with the islands of eastern Polynesia and the American coasts to the north.[3]

A major early center of the Northwest fur trade was at Nootka Sound, on the western coast of Vancouver Island. Several vessels might simultaneously be found at anchor between trading visits up or down the coast. Here they refitted, refreshed, or sought information on the state of trade in one area or another. It was at Nootka Sound that John Meares, a pioneer English fur trader, claimed to have purchased land from the Indians in 1787 with the object of establishing a settled trading base. It was here also that an American, John Kendrick, secured deeds of a sort to lands around Friendly Cove.

Copies of Kendrick's deeds, bearing the names and marks of the principal chiefs of the area, were sent from China back to the United States in an effort to acquire governmental sanction for his claims. It is significant that both Meares and Kendrick, as well as Kendrick's heirs, appealed to their government on the grounds of national interest for support in pressing private land claims. Neither was successful, but both the British and American governments would later use the claims in arguing their respective national rights in the area.[4]

INTERNATIONAL COMPLICATIONS

Shortly after the first Americans reached Nootka Sound the Spanish government attempted to reassert an old, exclusive claim to the entire area on the grounds of prior discovery. This provoked an international crisis with the British, coinciding as it did with European differences between the two nations. During the controversy that followed, Spanish officers on the ground left the Americans on the coast undisturbed, apparently hoping to prevent them from forming common cause with the British. Captains Ingraham and Gray, masters of the *Hope* and *Columbia,* respectively, were entertained by both British and Spanish officers at Nootka. They signed a statement to Don Francisco de Bodega y Quadra, the Spanish commandant, which was generally supportive of the Spanish side. Ingraham, in fact, was highly critical of Meares's claims of what he had done there.[5]

Subsequent Anglo-Spanish negotiations at Nootka reached no definitive conclusion, and the matter of conflicting claims was taken up again in Europe. There the whole international balance was upset by the French Revolution and subsequent Continental wars, with neither Britain nor Spain able to make effective at that time a territorial claim to the Northwest Coast of North America. This result was of great importance to the American traders, even though their own government had not been involved in the negotiations, for it left the coast open to the free operation of American fur traders in the absence of any nation's exclusive territorial jurisdiction.[6]

Russian fur traders maintained a series of posts to the north of the main center of American activity. The Russian American Company aspired to a monopolist's position after 1799, but Americans were able to do business even with the company's settlers and officers. Russian or British furs were sometimes carried to China in American vessels in order to avoid Chinese restrictions on Russian trade by sea or the British East India Company's controls over British commerce on the Pacific.[7] American traders also carried foodstuffs and supplies to Russian American settlements and borrowed native fur hunters with their kayaks to assist in the search for furs as far south as the coast of Baja California. On at least one such expedition a sort of partnership arrangement was created between Russians and a Yankee captain.[8]

The activities of the Americans nevertheless presented more problems than promise to the agents of the Russian American Company, for some Yankee traders were not above selling firearms and firewater to natives for furs. These "blessings" of civilization complicated the task of maintaining Russian control in the area and formed the subject of Russian diplomatic protests to the United States beginning with the opening of formal relations between the two nations in 1810.

To have accepted the validity of their protests and other overtures would, however, have implied a recognition by the United States government of Russian sovereignty over an area of unknown extent in the Northwest, and this Washington was not prepared to offer. For its part, the Russian government was too concerned with retaining the friendship of the United States in a common stand against British expansion and interpretations of maritime law to make an issue of such a relatively minor matter. Thus, no formal agreements were reached then, nor does there appear to have been any demand for, or expectation of, government action by those engaged in the trade.[9]

After the War of 1812, however, the situation changed. Agreements between the United States and Great Britain in 1815 and 1818 called attention to a possible territorial claim by the United States in the Northwest. The claim would be based on discoveries by fur trade captains like Robert Gray and on later activity, including the attempted settlement at the mouth of the Columbia River by the Winship brothers.

In 1821 the House of Representatives established a committee to inquire into the status of American interests and claims in the Pacific Northwest. Under the chairmanship of Dr. John Floyd of Virginia, the committee produced an extensive report that reviewed both the history of the fur trade and the basis for U.S. claims to territory on the shores of the Pacific. Precisely what Floyd's motives were in pushing this question is not clear, though the influence of John Jacob

Astor and William Clark, of Lewis and Clark fame, has been suggested, particularly because of the part played by Senator Thomas Hart Benton in the subsequent debates.

In those debates, however, which continued into 1823, questions of broad (and speculative) national interest, the "threat" of occupation of Oregon by foreign powers, and the need to vindicate an American "right" to the territory seem to have figured more prominently than private interests.[10] Commercial interests entered the discussion only in arguments over the feasibility of transcontinental expansion for the nation and its economy, or in vague statements concerning the desirability of a port of commerce on the Pacific. Those in the House who advanced this last view did not, for the most part, represent the areas of the country whose citizens were actually engaged in Pacific trade, and the maritime fur commerce, which had first given rise to American interest in the area, was already in a state of decline.

THE MARITIME FUR TRADE AND ITS DECLINE

The Northwest Coast fur trade experienced its heyday in the first quarter of the nineteenth century, and from the late 1790s to about 1825 traders from the United States dominated the maritime traffic. One account gives the following figures for the period to 1814:

	Ships (counted separately; no ship twice)	
Years	British	American
1785–1794	25	15
1795–1804	9	50
1805–1814	3	40

The same source adds: "To the Americans the maritime fur trade was a means to an end; to the British, owing to monopolies, it was an end in itself. After 1793, the British vessels ceased to come from Europe. . . . After 1803 the British flag was not seen in the trade for more than a decade."[11]

Foster Dulles records that in one good year, 1801, fifteen American ships took to Canton some 18,000 sea otter skins, valued at more than $500,000. Between 1790 and 1812 he estimates that an average of 12,000 of these rich, glossy pelts were taken, plus an undetermined number of beaver, seal, and other skins.[12] After the War of 1812 the figures dropped dramatically as ruthless exploitation rendered the sea otter all but extinct, leading the Indians along the coasts to demand higher prices. Moreover, as the British and Russians based in "Oregon," Canada, and Alaska strengthened their holds upon fur-trading operations along the shore, profitable voyages by the sea-based Americans became more difficult.[13]

The Northwest fur trade was a risky and adventurous business at all times. While one voyage might bring tremendous profit, another might represent a total loss of trade goods, ship, and crew. Captain William Sturgis, one of the most active and successful (and vocal) of the Bostonians in the trade, reportedly grossed a return of $284,000 on an investment of $50,000 in one venture. Another trader reportedly received $8,000 worth of furs in exchange for one rusty iron chisel.[14] Still, from John Kendrick to John Jacob Astor there were those who lost heavily.

Much ingenuity had to be exerted in finding goods to catch the fancy of the Northwest Indian tribes, for their market was quickly saturated and needs or status symbols of one season could quickly become dregs on the market by the next. The experience of Joseph Ingraham is illustrative of the problems faced. When he found that the type of goods offered by the *Columbia* were no longer desired by the natives of the coast, Ingraham saved the day by having heavy iron collars and bracelets made by his smith out of rod iron from his ship's cargo. William Sturgis's *Journal* and its appendix provide a running account of shifting Indian tastes over the years 1799 to 1802. The master of the *Jefferson* sold worn-out sails, the crews' old clothing, trunks, boxes, seal oil, crockery, carpets, old ropes, rigging, and anchors for 300 skins. Even the ship's long boat went for the last thirty-five of these.[15]

The lawless conditions of trade on this wild coast led to frequent conflicts between native inhabitants and fur traders. Treachery and brutality were shown on both sides, and when trouble did arise there was no arbitrament but that of force. Captains learned to limit the number of Indians allowed on board their vessels at one time and to keep watch twenty-four hours a day. An armed man in the foretop, one captain observed, had a quieting effect on those on deck.

Those who failed to observe these precautions often suffered severe losses. In such notable cases as those of the *Boston* in 1802, and John Jacob Astor's *Tonquin* in 1811, cargo, ship, and virtually the entire ship's company were lost to Indian attacks. Despite the record of commercial uncertainty and violence, however, none of the powers whose citizens or subjects were involved acted to establish their rule over the land between the Spanish settlement at San Francisco Bay and the Russian establishments in Alaska for years.[16]

Tyler Dennett estimated the value of the fur trade of the United States with China between 1788 and the 1830s at between $15 and $20 million, based on the Canton value of all furs, including those shipped from the Atlantic coast and from the Pacific islands. He further estimated the value of exports from the United States to the Northwest Coast in the heyday of the trade, from 1789 to 1817, at around $163,000 annually.[17] This was never a major proportion of total U.S. foreign trade, and if the losses incurred in the business were subtracted from the estimated gains the figure would be even less impressive.

For a comparatively brief period the Northwest fur trade brought profit to a small group of American merchants and welcome relief from some of the drain of coinage involved in the China trade. It is curious that with the exception of

Astor almost none of the people active in this enterprise seem to have been identified with the fur trade in the eastern United States. A number of them, however, including Astor, were or would shortly become influential figures in the Northeast, and their interests were seconded in Washington by men like Benton, Floyd, and others with Western connections.[18]

In retrospect, it was not primarily the financial magnitude nor the political connections of the Northwest fur trade that marked its significance to the nation. Until the rise of Pacific whaling, the Northwest fur trade was the major motive bringing citizens of the United States into the eastern Pacific and acquainting them with the commercial potential of its waters, coasts, and islands. Through it the first bases for American territorial claims were made, even though the first such claims were ignored by Congress and the State Department.[19]

PACIFIC ISLAND PRODUCTS

As noted earlier, the search for items to sell to the Chinese began early in the American trade. Goods from Europe, Africa, and South and Southeast Asia were carried to Canton in American ships to supplement the meager offerings of the young republic's undeveloped economy. The quest for still more commodities soon spread to the islands of the Pacific as Yankee traders learned more about Chinese ways. The fur trade and its incidental contacts with Spanish America and the islands of Polynesia made some new products available. Then, when a few ships approached China by way of Australia and some of the islands of Melanesia, the quest was broadened still further. Sandalwood, *bêche-de-mer,* tortoise shell, pearls, and pearl shells were gathered among these islands, and edible birds' nests were sought in Indonesia and the western Carolines.

Sandalwood of presumed saleable quality was found in Hawai'i by Captains William Douglas and John Kendrick as early as 1790–1791.[20] Those who had been at Canton knew the price the fragrant wood brought there, and the first experiment in carrying the Hawaiian variety to China seems to have occurred very shortly after its discovery. The trade in Hawaiian sandalwood did not reach major proportions, however, until some twenty years after this first experiment, because the first traders did not understand the quality of wood desired by the Chinese. In the meantime, small quantities of low-grade wood were picked up occasionally on stops incidental to the refreshment of the ships' water and provisions or in minor trade with the island chiefs.

Before the Hawaiian sandalwood trade entered its major period of activity, roughly between 1810 and 1830, traffic in that product had already begun in Fiji, and American vessels were among those active in it. The peak of the Fijian sandalwood trade appears to have occurred in the 1808–1809 trading season.[21] An element of international rivalry entered into it, as British officials in New South Wales tried to encourage British trade in order to forestall the development of too strong an American influence. This was, however, a relatively small part of American enterprise in the Pacific, and though it involved contacts with

Australian ports that often conflicted with British law or policy, it did not occasion calls for policy decisions by the government of the United States.

Hawai'i was a different matter. About 1809–1810 the Hawaiian sandalwood trade began to assume greater importance than before, and King Kamehameha I imposed controls upon it. In 1811 he entered into a written agreement with Jonathan and Nathan Winship and William Heath Davis, Boston traders, granting them a monopoly on the sandalwood trade of Hawai'i for ten years. In return for this, the king was to receive 25 percent of the value of the product shipped. Cotton was also included in this arrangement, as experiments in growing cotton in Hawai'i were then under consideration.[22] Full development of the monopoly was, however, frustrated by the outbreak of the War of 1812.

After the death of Kamehameha I in 1819, the controls he had imposed upon exploitation of Hawai'i's limited supply of sandalwood were removed, and a period of virtually uncontrolled cutting began at the behest of the Hawaiian chiefs. Greed for Western goods encouraged upon them by American and other Western traders led to an orgy of exploitation of Hawaiian commoners by the chiefs in the pursuit and harvest of the trees. That exploitation and the resultant deaths of many of them were described by Western visitors of the time. The legacy of the trade was plundered forests, exhausted timber cutters, and a burden of debt upon the chiefs of the islands that could not be met with the depletion of the sandalwood. Those debts then served as a source of admonition and demands, first by the merchants to whom they were owed, and then by a series of American naval officers and commercial agents responding to their appeals for assistance as debt collectors.[23] The search for sandalwood, meanwhile, shifted southward once again, to places like the New Hebrides. There the American role was less prominent than it had been in Hawai'i.[24]

The sandalwood trade played a role in strengthening commercial ties between the United States and Hawai'i and in increasing American national interest there. The results of the trade by Americans in Fiji and the New Hebrides were not the same, largely because of the distance from major American trade routes and greater British activity and interest in the South and Southwest Pacific. Yet even there that branch of American commerce helped to acquaint Americans with the area and revealed the potentials and dangers of those islands for refreshment, for whaling, and for trade in other island commodities.

China traders soon discovered that the sea slug (*Holothuria*), more commonly referred to as *bêche-de-mer*, was prized as a delicacy by Chinese epicures when it was properly prepared. This product was obtained by the Chinese from the coasts and islands of South and Southeast Asia before the Spaniards, and later the English and Americans, found it among the islands of the Pacific. Thereafter its pursuit constituted another branch of that island commerce that grew up in the first half of the nineteenth century.

The principal sources of *bêche-de-mer* were Fiji, New Caledonia, the New Hebrides, and other islands groups in the Southern Hemisphere, and a few places, such as Palau, north of the equator. Into these waters Yankee captains sailed, establishing relations with island chiefs as a necessary preliminary before setting up the gathering and drying processes that had to be done ashore before the product was fit for shipping or sale. Several early accounts describe both the curing process and the resulting relationships between traders and islanders.[25]

Never a large enough item in itself to form an entire ship's cargo, *bêche-de-mer* served as a supplement to a variety of trading enterprises at Canton. Its pursuit helped to extend the acquaintance of Americans with islands that might not have gained their attention otherwise. Out of their successes and difficulties arose demands for naval patrols to redress grievances and to maintain some order among islanders and foreign seamen. The United States Navy began to do this on a sporadic and limited basis as early as the 1820s, though never on the scale achieved by the British, particularly in the South Pacific. The calls for an official U.S. exploring expedition to lessen the danger of navigation in ill-charted waters also gained support, directly or indirectly, from those engaged in this trade.[26]

Other Pacific island products that became objects of commerce included tortoise shell, pearl shell, arrowroot, and various fibers and woods and manufactures thereof. All were obtained at first in exchange for such things as beads, trinkets, lengths of cloth, and pieces of metal. The islanders eventually became more sophisticated and familiar with Western scales of values, however, and began to demand goods of more lasting value such as metal fishhooks, tools, ships, sails, and fabrics more durable than their own bark cloth. In many cases they also developed a taste for the foreigners' liquor and firearms, and in some cases overpledged their resources to purchase Western style clothing, furniture, and even precut houses, ill-suited though these items were to island climates and social settings. Here, as on the Northwest Coast of North America, the search for new status symbols vied with that for the useful products of the foreigners' material culture.

It should be noted that there was a great deal of imposition and exploitation in the commerce among the islands, especially where there was a disparity in need or desire between the two sides. Mariners months from home and desperately in need of water, firewood, or provisions at times resorted to chicanery or force, if either seemed feasible, in order to obtain them. Islanders might try to acquire by stealth or force the precious foreign products they coveted. And differing concepts of property and property rights provided additional grounds for misunderstandings and violence.

When these occurred it was impossible for Americans or other outsiders to appeal to recognized courts or governments or to use the consular channels customary among Western nations. The authority of Polynesian chiefs could be appealed to, but few of them possessed the power that the Kamehamehas came to exert in Hawai'i. Naval officers of several nations tried to draw up agreements or set rules of trade and contact with island leaders, but these were not backed by the force of law in the absence of stable, recognized governments. When "consuls" were sent to some of the island ports, there was no question of receiving the usual exequatur in return, nor could diplomatic officers be exchanged on a plane of equality. In any case, mutual interests in continued contact, backed by the threat of force, formed the basis on which island economies became linked with those of the United States and other Western nations.

CULTIVATED ISLAND PRODUCTS

American trade with the Pacific islands continued to include as one of its principal objects the securing of fresh water, wood, and provisions. This was particularly true when whaling ships predominated among those sailing the mid-ocean waters. The variety of commerce involved some dislocation of traditional island economies, but more distruptive were the efforts to achieve commercial levels of production of particular commodities such as sandalwood, shell, or *bêche-de-mer*. By the middle of the nineteenth century attention was turning to the production of at least two new crops, efficient traffic in which demanded regular cultivation over considerable areas and long periods of time. These products were copra and sugar.

Brief and small-scale experiments with the production of sugar from cane were made in Hawai'i before 1820, but not until the mid–1830s was a plantation of any size begun and maintained. This was on the island of Kaua'i. That experiment involved a combination of merchant, missionary, and Hawaiian energies.[27]

The attempt to improve and expand the plantation revealed three problems, each of which in time required the intervention of public policy in the search for a solution. One was the question of secure title to lands used in intensive agriculture. A second involved securing a reliable and continuous labor supply. Third was the problem of marketing the exportable product. Efforts to solve these problems would bring serious infringements upon the freedom of the Hawaiian and other island polities and disruptive influences on traditional patterns of economic and social life.

Efforts to market the oil pressed from the meat of the coconut were begun by British missionaries in Tahiti in the 1820s. Two decades later the son of John Williams, one of the most famous of the mission pioneers, acquired some small success with copra processing in Samoa. Also, increased use of soap in Europe and new methods of handling coconut oil combined to make its profitable export possible.[28]

It was the Germans, however, who were chiefly responsible for the subsequent development of the industry, with Americans playing but a small part in the copra business. The major center of settled activity for Americans, Hawai'i lay so close to the northern limit of the tropics that coconut growth was neither sufficiently abundant nor rapid to sustain an important commerce in competition with other islands. Elsewhere, an occasional planter or trader of U.S. citizenship appears in the scattered records, but neither their numbers nor their connections made them an interest group. The Central Polynesian Land and Commercial

Company, which staked extensive land claims in Samoa in the 1870s, was a speculative, not a copra-producing, venture. Late in the nineteenth century the United States did become a major consumer of copra and coconut oil, but the material was commonly purchased abroad.

Significantly, however, by the middle of the nineteenth century Western trade among the Pacific islands had developed an economic significance of its own, independent of the China market. A handful of American firms and individuals continued in this branch of commerce after 1840, but their share was not an important part of the nation's total foreign trade. It then declined in importance during the second half of the century, except in Hawai'i.[29] Even with the growth of plantation economies among the islands over the years, their limited populations lacked the purchasing power or the productivity to give reality to occasional newspaper or congressional outbursts about the "vast markets" they might someday represent.

As France, Britain, and Germany asserted power over one island group after another, they raised barriers of preference that helped curtail existing American trade. Land titles proved difficult for Americans to sustain or acquire under the European colonial regimes, partly because of the nebulous nature of the claims involved, but also because of Washington's disinclination to involve itself in international complications over such minor matters. A few Americans residing in the Pacific, and some naval officers, might chafe over European territorial expansion, but with the exception of Hawai'i, neither Congress nor the Executive Branch chose to involve itself in supporting national claims until well after 1850.[30]

MISSIONARY INFLUENCE

Missionaries from the United States, sent by the American Board of Commissioners for Foreign Missions (ABCFM), arrived in Hawai'i in 1820. They represented an interest different from the commercial concerns that hitherto had dominated the minds of Americans in the Pacific. The missionaries' original objective was to bring the light of Christian salvation and civilization to the heathen idolators of the islands (and to foreign sailors and traders among them), and they demanded neither the favor nor the aid of their government in beginning their work. In their relations with the Hawaiians, the ABCFM warned the early missionaries to avoid involvement in commercial or political matters and to limit their function to Christianizing and civilizing their island charges. As time would tell, however, the temptation to involve themselves in these matters proved irresistible in a society that knew no separation of church from state, religion from politics, or business from government.[31]

The missionaries arrived at a strategic moment in Hawaiian history. Kamehameha I had died the previous year, and his death was soon followed by the abolition of the traditional kapu system under his successor and of the Hawaiian religion, which had provided that system with its force and authority. It was into this vacuum that the missionaries flowed, with unique opportunities, it appeared to some, to create a Puritan commonwealth on these islands in the Pacific. Their advice was quickly sought by Hawaiian chiefs on matters of secular importance as well as on religious questions, and the Puritans did not hesitate to respond. Hiram Bingham and some of the others justified these secular actions: If they failed to help, then others with baser motives would surely step in. In that case, the opportunity to save, protect, and "civilize" the Hawaiians might be lost, threatened as they were by the immorality of foreign seamen and castaways and by the impositions of unscrupulous traders in a land far from the foreigners' accustomed legal restraints.[32]

Missionaries like Hiram Bingham, William Richards, and Gerrit P. Judd labored mightily to protect the Hawaiians from the temptations of the flesh and the avarice of the foreigners. The political power that they sought over the island people to isolate them from such influences was not, in their view, political at all. In typically Puritan fashion, however, they viewed the political authority that existed in Hawai'i as a suitable instrument for imposing and policing their narrow moralistic views on the people.[33]

The missionaries considered themselves agents of God, not agents of the United States or of the communities from which they came. Nevertheless, many of the ethical and social ideas they brought with them and tried to inculcate in the Hawaiians bore the stamp of the New England society from which most of the missionaries had come. Puritan doctrine and Yankee folkways were inextricably intermingled, sometimes producing contradictions. Although they did not seek consciously to extend the power of the United States over the Hawaiian group, some of the Puritans eventually concluded that if the islands were to fall under the control of any Western country they would prefer that it be the United States.

In the 1830s and 1840s it began to appear that European colonial expansion was threatening the independence of Hawai'i, even as it did the Marquesas, Tahiti, and New Zealand. British and French subjects, on the other hand, viewed the ABCFM mission in Hawai'i as an instrument of American expansion well before the Americans did.[34]

Except for one minor effort at missionary work in the Marquesas, the ABCFM did not attempt to expand its activities in the Pacific islands beyond Hawai'i before 1850. By agreement with the London Missionary Society, proselytizing south of the equator was left to the British.[35] Difficulties with the French, however, developed out of the support given by the French government to the extension of Catholic missions to Hawai'i. Even then, appeal for direct support by the United States government for help in maintaining their mission monopoly was not ABCFM policy. One United States Navy commander actually chided the Puritan missionaries in Hawai'i for their intolerance toward the Catholics in 1832.[36]

By the 1840s, however, as European encroachments on the Pacific islands spread, the missionary group in Hawai'i began to be considered by some in

Washington as an American interest of national significance. This is indicated by the reports of naval officers and commercial agents who represented Washington in the region over the years.[37] Mission partisans at home, moreover, were not without influence in Washington, and that influence was clear well before 1842 when the first statement of U.S. policy concerning Hawai'i was issued by President Tyler. Both the president and the House Foreign Affairs Committee referred to the importance of the missionaries' role on that occasion.[38] It is characteristic of much of American policy concerning the Pacific that such stress was placed upon a humanitarian interest as deserving of government support in the same breath that advanced recognition of a commercial interest as well.

THE EASTERN SHORE

Along the Pacific coast of South America such ports as Talcahuano, Valparaiso, Coquimbo, Mollendo, Paita, and even the closely guarded Callao saw the arrival of ships from the United States even before the end of Spanish rule. The ports of Central America seem to have been touched less frequently than those from Acapulco northward to San Francisco. Trading vessels heading for the sea otter coasts of the Northwest were soon followed by whalers and sealers. The latter vessels carried on their hunt in the waters off the coasts of Chile, Bolivia, Peru, and Ecuador, and on the islands adjoining them. For whalers active in the ''on-shore'' fishery, South American ports became bases of local operation and trade, despite restrictive Spanish regulations. Both whalers and itinerant traders, moreover, found markets there for North American and European manufactured goods in return for Chilean provisions, grain, and copper, or Peruvian silver.[39]

Some Spaniards in Chile complained that this illicit trade by Americans represented a subversive threat to Spanish authority, since the Yankees brought radical ideas as well as merchandise to that colony's secluded ports. At least two American traders, Richard Cleveland and William Shaler, set out on trading voyages just after 1800 with the idea of spreading democratic ideas. They and others testified to the eagerness of Chileans whom they met for news of the outside world that did not come through censored Spanish sources. By the second decade of the nineteenth century, the first of a small group of U.S. citizens were already resident in Chile, active in commerce and printing, and incidentally in the encouragement of views that were revolutionary in the atmosphere of that remote Spanish colony.[40]

As the wars for independence from Spanish rule drew near, the reception that American vessels might encounter in these Pacific coast ports became more uncertain. At times it was difficult to tell whether loyal Spanish forces would be more unfriendly to Americans than forces of the revolutionists. As the wars spread between 1810 and 1826, U.S. commerce there continued to grow, despite the confusion of Spanish warships, rebel cruisers, privateers, and outright pirates. Some American captains established cordial relations with Spanish officers and sympathizers, others with the rebel forces. One special agent from the United

States is said to have accepted a brevet commission in the Chilean revolutionary army.[41]

Arms and other military supplies were carried to the rebel forces by American ships, and Yankee vessels sometimes even served as troop carriers on the Chilean and Peruvian coasts, but services of that sort were apparently rendered for both sides depending on private initiative and the risk involved. Officially, the United States was neutral in the struggle between Spain and its colonies, especially while the question of Florida's possession was being negotiated between Spain and the United States. A U.S. commercial agent was sent to Chile before 1810, but he was not recognized as such by Spanish authorities there. Subsequent quasi-diplomatic and consular appointments to posts in Chile, Peru, Gran Colombia, Central America, and Mexico gave the United States a pioneer role in recognizing the independence of those new nations.[42]

In some areas of Latin America this created a legacy of good will, at least temporarily, though little was done by the United States government to follow up this auspicious beginning. In the half-century that followed the achievement of their independence no commercial or political ties developed between the Pacific coast nations of South America and the United States that were strong enough to require a major U.S. foreign policy orientation toward them. Rival British interests, both commercial and political, soon became more influential in those nations, with the possible exception of Mexico's northern provinces. North Americans, with few exceptions, seemed to turn their attention elsewhere.

THE UNITED STATES NAVY ON THE PACIFIC COAST

The United States Navy played a significant role in the development of American policy toward the Pacific coast nations of Latin America from the early nineteenth century. During the War of 1812, Captain David Porter sailed in the *Essex* to the Southeast Pacific to protect what was already a considerable volume of U.S. property engaged in whaling and commerce there. Porter had no specific instructions for his mission, and neither the Navy Department nor the Department of State accepted responsibility for claims he made to part of the Marquesas Islands in the name of the United States. He did not involve himself in the Chilean independence conflict, although his vessel was ultimately captured by a British squadron in Chilean waters.[43]

From 1817 U.S. Navy ships were regularly on the South American Pacific coast, largely, it appears, in response to complaints of seizures by Spanish or Spanish-American vessels. In 1821–1822 those units stationed in the eastern Pacific were officially grouped under the designation of the Pacific Station, or Pacific Squadron, although at times only a single ship was actually there. Valparaiso and Callao were the ports principally used as bases by American warships on that coast, even as they were by British and French ships employed on similar missions. The effect of the presence of the officers and men on social and political relations between North and South Americans is impossible to estimate. In the course of writing their routine reports to the Navy Department, however, the commanders of the Pacific Squadron were helping to form the atmosphere in which policy decisions would be made in Washington.[44]

Porter seems to have been one of the first navy officers to conceive of the Pacific as a zone of American national interest, and he lauded the value to the U.S. whaling industry of his destruction of British whaling in the eastern Pacific. He saw possible national benefit, or at least benefit to the whalers, in American possession of a base in Polynesia; hence his claim to Nukuhiva in the Marquesas. Finally, he seems to have suggested to the Madison administration that a naval expedition be sent to Japan to open contact with that nation, both for the glory of the nation and for the benefit of its commerce.[45] Few of his successors in that station seem to have had such broad-based views, but the navy's role as the protector of the nation's commerce in the Pacific was ever in their minds.

From the Pacific coasts naval patrols reached westward into Polynesia and eventually beyond, hunting mutineers, reproving wayward American residents, investigating claims by merchants and mariners, and seeking to draw up port regulations by agreements with island chiefs. In the early 1830s Commodore John Downes reached the Pacific Station after completing missions in Southeast Asia and Hawai'i, illustrating the global scope of the navy's responsibilities. Still, congressional unwillingness to devote large funds to naval expansion, coupled with bureaucratic conservatism within the Navy Department itself, severely limited U.S. naval activity in the Pacific until after the establishment of the East India (later Asiatic) Station in 1835 and the acquisition of the Pacific coastal portion of the United States over a decade later.[46]

The navy could not create trade, and it was trade, or rather the comparative lack of it, that did most to condition the attitudes of American policy makers toward the Pacific's southeastern shores. The volume of American shipping using the Cape Horn approach to the Pacific increased unsteadily through the first half of the nineteenth century, then reached a sudden peak in the years of the California gold rush.[47]

As the whale ships pushed westward and northward from the "off-shore" ground, the Pacific ports of South America became less important to them. The decline of the Northwest fur trade also brought fewer American ships to those same ports. Yet a more solid basis for trade existed in the direct exchange that developed between Latin American ports and those of the United States and Europe. Despite the suggestions, even entreaties, of consuls, ministers, and private entrepreneurs, however, North American business interests were slow to take advantage of the opportunities that existed there. For example, William Wheelwright, an American seeking to develop steamship and railroad enterprises in South America, discovered that he had to go to Great Britain to obtain financial backing.[48] By the middle of the nineteenth century, as a consequence, the British position in trade, investment, and often in political influence was greater than that of the United States in most of the Pacific coast republics south of Mexico.

AMERICANS AND AUSTRALASIA

American trade with Port Jackson (Sydney) began as early as 1792, when the *Philadelphia,* from the port of the same name, disposed of a mixed cargo of supplies at the raw penal colony recently established there by the British.[49] A chronic shortage of provisions and tools there paved the way for the continuance of a small trade. The peculiar conditions of the early New South Wales establishment, moreover, created an opportunity for an astonishingly large traffic in alcoholic beverages, which for a time virtually served as currency there.[50]

The British chartered companies' monopoly of Pacific commerce hindered the development of an adequate supply system or private trade with the mother country. For some years it also interfered with the development of British whaling and sealing in the South Pacific. As long as these artificial restraints on British enterprise remained, they provided ample opportunity in the region for traders from the United States. Early governors of New South Wales complained to London of the infiltration of Yankee traders, and they tried to reduce the "rum trade" and general dependence upon American suppliers. Another source of friction was the willingness of some American captains to provide passage for convicts escaping from the penal settlement.[51]

The British East India Company's monopolistic privileges were gradually limited or abrogated, however, and the development of British settlement in Australia permitted the growth of enterprise and commerce there. The War of 1812 virtually ended American trade with Australia, and it was not resumed until after 1833 when the British inaugurated more liberal trade laws.[52]

To some extent the earliest American trade with Australia was linked to that with the South Pacific islands and with China. As early as 1787 a route to China by way of the Tasman Sea had been discovered, and it was occasionally used later for commercial voyages. More common, however, was an indirect trade that involved Port Jackson and the sandalwood or *bêche-de-mer* sites in Melanesia and other island groups. On occasion American vessels were chartered by merchants of New South Wales to carry private ventures for them as a means of circumventing British restrictions or of merely getting shipping space at all. In such ventures as these escapees from Australia were sometimes taken away and settled on the islands and coasts of the Pacific, often to the new areas' detriment. Sealing and whaling ships were also occasionally involved in both trading and passenger violations of British colonial rules.[53]

A total of about seventy U.S. merchant vessels touched at Australian ports between 1792 and 1812, not including the increasing numbers of whalers that appeared there after 1800. Their trade with Port Jackson was a way of securing specie or British bills of credit that could be used later at Canton.[54]

It was not until the 1830s and 1840s that "middle ground" and Tasman Sea operations brought large numbers of American whalers into Australian and New Zealand waters, though a few had reached there earlier. By 1840 the volume of American activity around the North Island of New Zealand gave the Yankees a very important role in the commerce there before the British assumed sovereignty. Exclusive policies thereafter adopted by the British soon destroyed most of the commercial and property interests that Americans had established. One resident trader at Bay of Islands complained bitterly to the State Department, enclosing a map of lands he claimed to have purchased from the Maori, but Washington was not disposed to contest British control or policies.[55]

British officials and merchants continued to complain of American competition or unethical behavior in Australian ports, and various traders from the United States, in turn, protested against the discriminatory regulations or arbitrary interference by the British in their enterprises there. An air of injured self-righteousness pervades the complaints of both sides, but the small scale, or relative unimportance, of American interests there made their influence on either U.S. or British policy insignificant.[56]

Until the time of the California gold rush in the mid-nineteenth century, the combined volume of American trade with Australia and New Zealand was very minor. The competing nature of the economies of the two regions, coupled with the imperial ties of the two British colonies, offered little promise of close and extensive commercial ties. The one major hope for such a trade relationship lay in Australia's ability to export its great staple, wool, to the United States. But as early as the 1830s American wool-growers were able to secure protective tariff rates, which eliminated Australian competition. American exports to Australia and New Zealand were limited because ties of the people there to the British motherland served as barriers to extensive sales just as effectively as protective tariffs might. What Americans did export to Australia and New Zealand was more likely to travel in foreign, especially British, ships than in American ones, and the goods were often handled by British, Australian, or New Zealand agencies.[57]

4

WHALERS, SEALERS, AND EXPLORERS

BEGINNINGS

Whaling was one of the most colorful, adventuresome, and, at the same time, one of the most economically important of American interests in the Pacific for most of the nineteenth century. The literature dealing with it includes original logs and diaries, works of fiction, government documents, consular reports, and detailed documentary studies. Yet, in all of this, very little has been written about whaling as an influence upon national policy.[1]

In its heyday the whaling industry carried into the Pacific Basin each year a larger number of Americans than did any other branch of the nation's economy. Through the length and breadth of the great ocean, from American to Asian coasts, and from Arctic to Antarctic, the whalers pursued their quarry with equipment representing an investment of millions of dollars. In addition, businesses involved in supplying the whalers or in processing and disposing of their imported product employed thousands more, with corresponding investment of capital.[2]

The whalers' discoveries—their problems, successes, and failures—kept news of the Pacific before the people of the United States and their government from the start of the nineteenth century until its closing years. It would seem logical that during that period appeals must have been made to the government in the name of the whaling interests in an effort to influence public policy.

Several of the eighteenth-century explorers of the Pacific had reported an abundance of whales in various locations. When America's earliest China traders began their voyages, they made similar reports. These discoveries were most welcome at that time, since older Atlantic whaling grounds were being depleted. When even the newer South Atlantic fishery began to result in longer and less rewarding voyages, the reports made the Indian and Pacific oceans seem enticing.

There were serious obstacles to overcome, however, before whaling expeditions to the Pacific could be undertaken on a commercial basis. One of these was the danger of navigating in unfamiliar, only partly charted waters. Others were the problems of supplying vessels for even longer voyages and landing on strange, potentially hostile shores. For Europeans there were the additional problems created by the trading and navigating monopolies that had been granted to their East India Company and other chartered companies.[3]

Defying these difficulties, the *Emilia,* owned by the Enderby firm of Great Britain and commanded by transplanted Nantucketers, was the first to take whales in the southern Pacific in 1787–1788. But British whaling was handicapped in the late eighteenth and early nineteenth centuries by the monopolistic restrictions on enterprise between the capes then held by that nation's East India and South Seas companies.[4]

The first U.S. whaler known to have hunted in the Pacific was the Nantucket vessel *Beaver,* which sailed in August 1791, and returned home with a good cargo on February 3, 1793. That same season saw no fewer than six American whalers sail for the Pacific, including the *Rebecca,* which was the first New Bedford ship in that ocean. Alexander Starbuck's *History of the American Whale Fishery* lists forty-six American whaling voyages to the Pacific before 1800, most of them concentrated in the Southeast Pacific, near the west coast of South America, in what was referred to as the "on-shore" fishery.[5]

The growth of Pacific whaling, indeed of the whaling industry in general, was irregular in the 1790s. Through the 1780s and 1790s, European wars and discriminatory policies against the products of American fisheries hampered the industry. The outbreak of war between Britain and France in 1793 brought to American whalers the same kind of interference that was afflicting seagoing commerce in general. French, Spanish, and British warships, privateers, and "pirates" seized American ships in port and at sea until whale shipowners cried out to their government for protection. Then late in the decade the American "quasi-war" with France added still further to the uncertainties of whalers, causing many to abandon the business, others to find their ships seized by the French without compensation.[6]

THE SEALERS

Fur sealing was closely allied to whaling in its earliest days in the Pacific. As early as 1783 an American ship from Stonington, Connecticut, visited the Falkland Islands in the South Atlantic, and the industry appears to have spread to the Pacific within the next decade, although the exact date of the first voyage there is uncertain. Some ships occasionally combined whaling with seal hunting, but differences in the habitat of the animals sought, coupled with the different methods of treating and marketing the two products, tended to encourage specialization.[7]

In this early period fur seals were commonly found on islands in the high southern latitudes. Whaling and sealing could be combined most easily at places like the Juan Fernandez Islands, off the coast of Chile, and other islands near Australia and New Zealand. In both areas Americans were soon prominent in the ruthless pursuit of seals, which would eventually exhaust the supply. It is estimated that from the single island of Mas Afuera, in the Juan Fernandez group, between one and three million seals were taken by 1805. Once the herds of this and other groups were depleted, the search passed on to other parts of the Pacific, including the coast of California and its adjacent islands. In the Far North the search for seal skins was combined with that for the more valuable sea otter and land animal pelts.[8]

Sealers frequently spent weeks in the frigid Far South or Far North of the Pacific, sometimes leaving crew members on shore to pursue their prey while the ships cruised on to other hunting areas. They set up temporary lodgings on islands that were generally barren and uninhabited, and when the herds on the islands were destroyed or frightened off, all interest in them vanished. No American national claims to islands emerged from the sealers' activities, but sealers were the basis for the first U.S. claims to discoveries and rights in the Antarctic continent.[9]

Unlike whaling, the pursuit of the fur seal as a branch of commerce was closely related to the China trade. Though the sealers often returned to their home ports to dispose of cargo, the ultimate destination of the pelts was commonly Canton. There the price received for a sealskin is reported to have varied between forty-two cents and two dollars or more, depending on the market. James Kirker suggests that a reasonable average for the entire period of the trade in the southeastern Pacific was about ninety cents. Charles Scammon describes a later period, extending to the 1870s, during which American sealing was largely carried on in the northern Pacific by a much smaller number of vessels. He cites a value of nine dollars for a dressed pelt in the European market in 1873.[10]

No accurate estimate of the total number of ships and men involved in the sealing trade is available, but the total would certainly be but a small fraction of the figures for whaling. One source claims thirty American sealing vessels operated on the coast of Chile in 1801, but it would be dangerous to extrapolate from that figure to a general one for that year or later. The number of ships clearly declined after the early years of the nineteenth century, but the importance of the sealers as a national interest cannot be dismissed merely on the basis of their small numbers or narrowly sectional home base. Their discoveries, especially in the high south latitudes, and their numerous contacts and conflicts with Spanish and British rivals or officials were enough to draw national attention.[11]

GROWTH AND MOVEMENT OF PACIFIC WHALING

Down to 1820 the Pacific whale fishery found its main field south of the equator, and even after that date the South Pacific remained an important region of activity. As the years passed, overfishing of an area or the spirit of adventure led whalers to push on in search of new areas where their quarry might be more plentiful. In this they were sometimes assisted by reports from merchant captains, who sent word home or exchanged views at sea concerning whale sightings in new areas. This role of merchant pioneers should be recalled to counter exaggerated claims sometimes made for the whalers as discoverers.[12]

American whaling experienced a remarkable growth after the War of 1812, encouraged for much of the time by high prices and limited competition. Captain George Washington Gardner, a Nantucketer, took the *Globe* westward from the South American coast in 1818 and discovered a rich harvest in the area between 105° and 125° west longitude and 5° and 10° south latitude, which came to be known as the "off-shore" fishery. There was also a "middle ground" in the Tasman Sea, between Australia and New Zealand.[13]

Vessels on the off-shore ground began to visit many of the islands of Polynesia, where they found no colonial or governmental authorities that their government could, or would, recognize. Their contacts there, partly as a consequence of this lack of formal relations, were frequently disastrous to the native peoples—introducing new diseases, alcohol, and placing new demands on the limited resources of the islands.

In the absence of normal intergovernmental channels for the settlement of debts and grievances in the islands, whalers joined merchants in relying on the limited services of the United States Navy and a handful of commercial agents. The dispatches to the Departments of State and the Treasury from commercial agents in such posts as Honolulu, Papeete, Lauthala, and Apia provide a fascinating commentary on the behavior of American masters and seamen on the whaling grounds and their relations with island peoples and their chiefs. Their accounts, combined with the protests of returned sailors, led to agitation for federal laws to guarantee seamen's rights. Through the years, however, naval officers, commercial agents, and consuls were far more likely to side with the owners and masters of vessels than with the common seaman.[14]

In 1819 the port of Honolulu was visited by its first two American whale ships, and the following year an American and an English whaler opened the fishery off the eastern coast of Japan. By 1822 there were reported to be more than thirty whalers on the "Japan grounds," and thereafter new fisheries were also developed in the North Pacific toward Alaska and the Aleutians (around 1835), in the Sea of Okhotsk (1847), and in the Bering Sea and Arctic Ocean (before 1850). All of this increased the importance of the northern, rather than the southern, Pacific as a center of American whaling, and made Honolulu more and more important as a center for the industry. The movement north also brought increasing use of the Mexican and California coasts and contacts with the Spanish-Mexican authorities and populace there.[15]

In addition to these major Pacific grounds, American whalers also operated in the Indian Ocean during the first half of the nineteenth century and among the islands of Indonesia, the Philippines, and the Carolines, though these did not become major whaling grounds. Still, the activities of these vessels extended the geographic knowledge of American mariners and their contacts with Pacific peoples.[16]

WHALING AND HAWAI'I

The increasing importance of whaling in the North Pacific caused the American stake in Hawai'i to assume very significant proportions. The inhospitable climate of the far northern shores and the hostility of many Russian, Spanish, or Japanese authorities on their coasts made Honolulu the only good and readily accessible port in the entire area. Between 1820 and 1860 whaling became the mainstay of the money economy of Hawai'i, taking up the slack left by the decline of the Northwest fur trade and of that in sandalwood. Had it not been for whaling the economic interest of Americans in the islands might have dwindled, despite a small transpacific commerce that involved the islands with the California-Mexico coast and East Asia. Without this new economic interest, and the extensive shipping that accompanied it, missionary and commercial groups in Hawai'i would almost certainly have been insufficient to maintain the American position against French or British designs on the islands.

Coincidentally, missionaries of the ABCFM reached the Hawaiian Islands at almost precisely the same time as the first whalers. The attention of the New England churchmen had originally been drawn to the islands because of the activity of the early American traders, not the whalers. Their purpose was not only to convert the heathen but also to provide a more Christian influence upon the seamen who visited or resided among them. Once in Hawai'i the missionaries found the growing number of whalers an unexpected influence with which they had to contend, and much of their reporting home had to do with whalers and their impact on the island community.[17]

The presence and influence of American traders, however, predated both the whalers and missionaries, and after 1815 the first of them, probably James Hunnewell, actually took up temporary residence in Honolulu to sell off a cargo of goods. This trade stood on its own before the arrival of the whalers, but by the end of the 1820s the provision of supplies and ship chandlery for the North Pacific whale fleet had become a major part of the business. Through the 1830s and 1840s the whaling interest continued to grow, leading some in the Hawaiian government to deplore the reliance of the kingdom's economy on this one industry. So important did it become during this period that both the Hawaiian and American governments were compelled to develop public policies to deal with it and with each other. Whaling gave Americans a dominant position in the international affairs of the kingdom that neither missionary nor merchant influences alone were capable of at that time.

The growth of whaling's importance to Hawai'i was sudden and dramatic. After the appearance of the pioneers in the trade in 1819, at least sixty such arrivals were listed in 1822. From 1827 to 1830 the average was 140 per year. Since many of the whalers pursued their business to the north of the islands in the summer and to the south in the winter, they made two stops per year in Hawaiian ports. Thus the number of separate vessels reported was always less than the total number of recorded "arrivals."[18]

Honolulu was not alone in attracting whaling ships. The efforts of the missionaries to reduce the attractions of that port for whaling crews, combined with the rising port and market prices, drove some of the whalers to try other ports after 1825, and Lahaina, on the island of Maui, became known as a whalers' port. Even Hilo, on the island of Hawai'i, drew some patronage, though neither of these ports could offer a sheltered harbor such as Honolulu possessed.[19]

In 1823 a small shipyard was established in Honolulu to improve the usefulness of the port as a center for repairing and refitting whalers and other vessels engaged in general trade. A few unseaworthy hulks were moored in the harbor for use as floating warehouses or as storage places for whale oil awaiting transshipment to homeward bound carriers. By 1829 it was estimated that the value of U.S. commerce passing through Honolulu annually had reached $5,270,000, a figure that far exceeded the volume of trade or investment by any other nation at that time. As the dominance of the Americans in the whale fishery of the northern Pacific increased in succeeding years, the primacy of that nation's influence in Hawai'i grew correspondingly.[20]

Not all American whalers were in the North Pacific, however. After the British liberalized their trading regulations in 1833, American whaling ships found Australian ports more hospitable and whaling in that area increased. By the 1840s vessels from the United States were welcomed at Sydney, where their presence had previously been discouraged, and a minor fishery developed in the "middle ground" between Australia and New Zealand, where British and colonial whalers were already active. In 1836 forty-nine American ships were said to be active at New Zealand's North Island, and in the next two or three years Americans seem to have been the most frequent whaling visitors to the South Island as well.[21]

AMERICAN WHALING AT ITS PEAK

Through the 1830s and 1840s whaling voyages continued to become longer and more expensive as whales were killed in larger numbers on the more familiar grounds or were sought further north. Voyages that had once taken two years, or a bit more, lengthened now to three, four, or by the 1850s even to five years. This required additional emphasis on Pacific ports as supply and repair stations, bringing Americans into closer relations with the residents of many islands and accessible coasts, and linking the peoples of those shores in economic relations with the whalers.

On occasion efforts were made to base whaling operations in Pacific ports rather than in New England. American merchants in Honolulu and San Francisco tried outfitting whalers, but their share of the business was never large and some sort of tie-in with the East Coast masters of the trade was always desirable, if not essential.[22]

The growth of whaling brought more Westerners to ports like Honolulu to profit from the developing trade. Their more sophisticated trading practices drove up the price of supplies, threatening the whaling industry for a time with extinction from diminishing profits. The expanding demand for illuminants, and the special qualities of spermaceti oil, however, kept the price level generally high enough to make whaling profitable for the thrifty, the able, and the fortunate. Until the arrival of refined petroleum illuminants after the American Civil War, the whaling industry remained an important part of the nation's maritime economy.[23]

While it is impossible to measure exactly the importance of the whaling industry to the total economy of the United States, a few figures indicate its general significance. From almost nothing at the end of the War of 1812, whaling tonnage increased to some 35,391 gross tons by 1820; to 82,316 by 1831; and to 157,405 a decade later. From 1845 to 1860 it averaged above 185,000 tons, with a peak of nearly 200,000 tons in 1858. It has been estimated that between 1829 and 1845 whaling ships rose from 10 percent to 21 percent of the total American tonnage engaged in foreign commerce. Another source has concluded that Americans in 1847 owned at least 722 of the world's 900 whaling vessels, not counting foreign whalers owned or operated by Nantucketers.[24]

As for the income derived from whaling, one source has concluded: "In 1838 the value of the oil and bone brought into New Bedford alone was $2,490,051: and during the ensuing forty years, with six annual exceptions, it remained between $2,000,000 and $6,000,000. . . . In order to supply whaling products in such quantities it was necessary to kill some 10,000 whales each year." Another historian has estimated that the value of the whalers' product reached $6 million for the first time in 1835 and peaked in 1854 at $10,802,594.20. "The average catch," he writes, "was worth about half the estimated value of the fleet, or say near the actual value," making "a well-handled whaler . . . a most profitable ship until after the petroleum industry was developed."[25]

In addition to sperm oil for illumination, lubrication, or the manufacture of candles, "whale oil" produced by the right whale or others was used in quantity for cheaper illuminants or lubricants. Whalebone was a valuable auxiliary product of the industry, used in making "stays, corsets, riding and carriage whips, umbrellas and other objects, requiring both strength and flexibility." Ambergris was another incidental product of the whale fishery, rare but extremely valuable since it was prized as an ingredient in perfumery and, in some lands, as an aphrodisiac. The handling and processing of these products for domestic use or for export were important for their own contributions to the American economy.[26]

It has been estimated that 17,500 officers and men shipped aboard whaling vessels in 1844 and that they used or consumed annually some $3.8 million worth of commodities. In the early days of Pacific whaling the ships were primarily crewed by young men drawn from the seaports and nearby areas of New England, New York, and even from the mid-Atlantic states. By Melville's time, however, such young men found far better opportunities in commercial voyages or onshore, and crews increasingly consisted of foreigners, often the riffraff of Atlantic and Pacific ports.

In addition to those who actually took to the sea, many other Americans were involved in the manufacture of ships, boats, harpoons, and other specialized whaling paraphernalia. The raising of provisions for whalers, the manufacture of their clothing, and the production of the timber and cooperage needed in their trade all involved still others in the economy of the industry. One writer has suggested that with the inclusion of subsidiary crafts and trades about $70 million worth of property and some 70,000 persons were involved directly and indirectly in whaling as early as 1833, well before its period of maximum growth.[27] According to one source: "During the prosperous era of whaling there were more than 50 New England ports, as well as several ports in the States south of New England, at which whaling vessels were registered."[28]

Even at its peak, however, whaling represented only a small portion of American foreign trade or total maritime enterprise, and in its period of greatest volume the whaling ship, on average, was a less profitable venture for owners and seamen than a merchant ship engaged in the carrying trade. In 1854, for example, when whaling was grossing less than $11 million, the total value of American foreign commerce exceeded $583 million.[29] Furthermore, the business involved directly only a very small part of the nation, however widely dispersed its indirect influences might be. Only a small portion of the Atlantic seaboard, approximately a dozen ports, were engaged in whaling to any considerable extent. This fact constantly had to be borne in mind by those who approached the government for favors. Even inland districts of the maritime states at times showed indifference or hostility to the requests of the whaling interests.

WHALERS AND GOVERNMENT

There was no whalers' "lobby" in the nineteenth century. After the American Revolution Nantucketers made representations, occasionally supported by mainland merchant groups, in favor of tariffs or bounties that might assist their cause at home and urged diplomatic pressure to open European markets to their products. Outside of Nantucket, however, there is no conclusive evidence of any united whalers' campaign, let alone continuing organization, to support the interests of whalers before state and national governments, and the Nantucketers achieved scant success in their own efforts.[30]

The growth of the whaling industry took place without the assistance of government and mostly without naval protection. Edmund Fanning appealed to the Madison administration in 1810–1812 for an exploring expedition that would, among other things, provide benefits to American whalers and sealers, and the voyages of the whalers were often cited as a major training source for sailors and masters who might be needed by the navy in time of war. But Fanning's proposal failed to produce action, and after the War of 1812 there was no serious attempt at new legislation or executive action until the latter years of the John Quincy Adams administration, when the activities of Jeremiah Reynolds again raised the issue of an exploring expedition.[31]

American whaling expanded to the threshold of its "golden age" without a lobbying organization and with precious little in the way of governmental attention. While Captain David Porter's naval activity in the Pacific during the War of 1812 helped clear the way for American whalers by damaging their British rivals, there is no evidence that Porter's action followed any specific orders or calculated policy of the Navy Department.[32]

The whaling industry's supporters were not without imagination. Samuel Haynes Jenks, editor of the *Nantucket Inquirer,* recommended in November 1822 that a canal be built across the Isthmus of Darien to shorten the voyage to the Pacific, only to have the idea opposed by a New Bedford newspaper lest it lead to overexpansion of Pacific whaling and the depletion of the whale supply there.[33] In the ensuing years others advocated a government exploring expedition, naval patrols among the islands to ensure proper treatment of Americans trading and fishing there, improved consular or diplomatic representation in the region to the same end, and even, eventually, the opening of Japanese and possibly other ports to whalers and merchants.

When Jeremiah Reynolds began his agitation in behalf of a Pacific exploring expedition he did so on his own, without any encouragement from whaling interests. Reynolds became a one-man lobby, and he made the cause his own to the point of antagonizing Fanning and others who were more closely associated with the whaling district and who had favored such an expedition before Reynolds made it his cause.

Reynolds sought backing from whalers and any others who would support him, and he succeeded in getting a government subsidy for his effort. The Jackson administration, however, had no interest in Reynolds's proposal until it became necessary to court votes in the northeastern states in the mid and late 1830s. Reynolds then rose to prominence again and addressed a joint session of Congress for three hours. Eventually his efforts would lead to the dispatch of the expedition under Lieutenant Charles Wilkes, but before then Reynolds would overplay his hand and alienate those responsible for the voyage. When the expedition was actually prepared, Reynolds was excluded from participation, a fate publicized by his friend Edgar Allan Poe.[34]

Doubtless the whaling industry influenced the government's decision to organize the exploring expedition, both directly and indirectly, but the extent of its influence has probably been exaggerated by some. Certainly, New Bedford, which became the leading whaling port before 1840, joined with Nantucket and other communities in keeping whaling and the Pacific before the public. The *Whalemen's Shipping List and Merchants' Transcript,* published in New Bedford from 1843 to 1914, was one of several periodicals that gave continuing coverage to the subject. The *North American Review, Niles' Register, Hunt's Merchants' Magazine,* and other periodicals of wider circulation also published articles on whaling as an industry of national interest. Yet even at the height of its prosperity and far-flung activity, the whaling industry had its opponents, active or passive, whenever political action on a national scale was proposed, especially in the South and West. The spokesmen for whaling sought to portray their industry in terms of its importance to the economy and to the defense of the entire nation, but they found few who were convinced of this.[35]

THE WILKES EXPEDITION

Largely due to the continuing efforts of Reynolds and Fanning, petitions and memorials requesting an exploring expedition continued to reach Congress in the early 1830s. Fanning was now emphasizing the commercial gains that Americans could expect to reap as a result of a better knowledge of the Pacific islands, and he was more influential now as a result of a book he had published about a private expedition he had led to the Antarctic in 1829–1831. In 1835 the House of Representatives again passed a bill supporting such an expedition, but the Senate once more failed to act. In 1836, though, a bill supporting such an expedition passed both houses of Congress and was signed by President Andrew Jackson on May 14, 1836.[36]

Planning for the expedition was put under the command of its designated officer in charge, Captain Thomas ap Catesby Jones, a veteran of a previous Pacific trip and a longtime supporter of the expedition concept. A great deal of progress was made in the first three months, but this was followed by interminable delays. Congress, which had shown no hurry to approve the voyage, was now eager to get it underway. The congressional frustration is well illustrated by Congressman (and former President) John Quincy Adams's statement to one naval officer: "I told him that all I wanted to hear about the exploring expedition was that it had sailed."[37]

Finally, in November 1837 the expedition was assembled in New York City harbor and was awaiting its sailing orders when Jones suddenly resigned over a supposed slight in the sailing orders. His resignation caused new delays because it was impossible to find another senior naval officer who would take command of the expedition. Eventually, command of the expedition was offered to a lower-ranking officer, Lieutenant Charles E. Wilkes. Wilkes was really a naval scientist, formerly head of the Naval Department of Charts and Instruments, and his appointment to head an expedition in which the ships were actually commanded by officers senior to him caused a storm of protest not only among those senior officers but among junior ones as well. This led to new delays, with the dispute taken up in Congress.[38]

Part of the problem had to do with Reynolds, who wanted to accompany the expedition in some capacity. Certainly he had earned that right since he had been a prime mover in getting congressional support for it. But Reynolds had antagonized those responsible for organizing the expedition, and there was opposition to having him along. Reynolds lobbied energetically in his own behalf with Congress, but the question finally came to Wilkes for a decision, and Wilkes turned him down. Finally, on August 18, 1838, over two years and two months after Congress had authorized it, the United States Exploring Expedition set sail for the Pacific under Wilkes's command.[39]

The expedition sailed on a course charted from detailed instructions furnished by the Navy Department. The chief purpose of the expedition was to explore and survey the South Pacific in order to facilitate American commerce and whaling in that region. The officers and scientists of the expedition were also to, in the words of the instructions, "extend the bounds of science and promote the acquisition of knowledge." In addition to visiting the island groups of Samoa, the Societies, Fiji, and Hawai'i, Wilkes was instructed to travel to the Antarctic, the Northwest Coast of America, and even Japan, with his return tentatively scheduled for the summer of 1841. Wilkes was, however, allowed considerable discretion in deciding how much time was necessary.[40]

The expedition stopped over for a month at Rio de Janeiro to make repairs on one of its ships, then sailed on in July of 1839. While traveling around the tip of South America, Wilkes made his first south polar exploration and then sailed to Valparaiso, Chile, to await the arrival of one of his tenders, the *Sea Gull*. Unfortunately, the *Sea Gull* had disappeared off Cape Horn during a storm with all hands on board and she and her crew were never seen again. The remaining ships then set sail for the Tuamotus.[41]

After approximately a month exploring some fifteen islands of the Tuamotus group, during which many specimens were gathered and observations recorded, the expedition proceeded to Matavia Bay, Tahiti. During a stay of about a month Wilkes made meteorological observations from an observatory he had established there, and also surveyed the four principal harbors of Tahiti. He also filled his log with detailed observations on the native culture, some of them based on inaccurate information.[42]

After leaving Tahiti and the other Society islands, the expedition proceeded to Samoa where it spent five weeks surveying the entire group. Wilkes, himself, surveyed and explored the island of Tutuila, whose principal harbor at Pago Pago he praised highly. Besides surveying the group and gathering the specimens and scientific data that they found, the expedition also appointed a consul to represent American interests in Samoa, and especially to serve the interests of the whalers who occasionally put in at Samoan ports.[43]

Australia followed Samoa in the expedition's itinerary. It reminded them of home, with similar housing and "the identity of language." Late in December

1839, Wilkes returned to the south polar regions without the scientists, and this exploration of Antarctica consumed the next three months.[44]

After a week in Sydney, Wilkes sailed with the expedition to Bay of Islands, New Zealand, for a week and then to Tongatabu, largest of the Tonga Islands, where they arrived in late April 1840. Wilkes spent much of his time in Tonga observing the culture and people of the islands. Wilkes found the Tongans superior to the Tahitians both in their appearance and in their morals. After less than two weeks at Tongatabu, Wilkes sailed for the Fiji Islands, which were one of the major objectives of the voyage.[45]

The expedition spent three months in the Fijis, with an operational base at Ovalau where Wilkes erected a meteorological observatory. While the surveying of the islands went on, Wilkes negotiated sets of commercial agreements with the various chiefs—much as he had already done in Samoa. The expedition's visit to Fiji was, however, marred by a series of incidents that escalated in severity.

It began with the successful effort, through guile and the use of hostages, to capture a Fijian chief, Vendovi, who was held responsible for the massacre some six years earlier of ten crew members of a Salem merchant ship, the *Charles Dagget*. Word of this action spread through the islands like wildfire, and thereafter no Fijians would board the expedition's ships. Boats conducting surveys off the coasts of the islands began to observe demonstrations of hostile intent on the part of the Fijians, and in July one such boat was captured by the Fijians after it went aground. The contents of the boat were seized, but its crew was returned unharmed to the expedition's base of operations.

The headstrong Wilkes demanded the return of the boat and all its contents. The chiefs restored the boat but could not round up all its contents, which included clothes, instruments, and other small items that had been taken by members of the village. Wilkes thereupon decided that the entire village must be punished, and he landed with a force of marines and burned the village to the ground. This, however, only caused relations with the natives to deteriorate further, and a subsequent incident resulted in the deaths of two of Wilkes's officers, including his own nephew.

Once again Wilkes retaliated with force, determined, as he put it, "to inflict the punishment it merited . . . not by burning towns alone, but in the blood of the plotters and actors of the massacre." The two villages adjudged guilty of the crime were attacked with only one serious casualty on the American side. When the Fijians made overtures for peace, Wilkes required the natives of the two villages to return all belongings of the two slain officers and to load his ships with water and provisions—3,000 gallons of water, 12 pigs, 3,000 coconuts, and a supply of yams.[46]

In August Wilkes set sail for Hawai'i where he found the people a marked contrast with the Fijians. In his description of the Fijians, Wilkes had very little positive to say. They were, he wrote, "degraded beyond the conception of civilized people." By contrast, Wilkes had been in Honolulu for only a day or two when he wrote that the Hawaiians were so civilized that he could scarcely believe they were Polynesians. While his ships were in Honolulu, the enlistments of a number of his crew expired, and rather than sign on American drifters there Wilkes enlisted fifty Hawaiian volunteers to take their place.[47]

Wilkes set up an observatory in Honolulu, then sailed to the island of Hawai'i with the American commercial agent and a prominent missionary, Dr. Gerrit P. Judd. He climbed to the top of Mauna Loa and established a metereological observatory there, then he and his party explored and surveyed Kilauea volcano on their way to Hilo. Wilkes next spent a couple of weeks on the island of Maui before returning to Honolulu on March 19, 1841. Meanwhile, the members of the scientific group accompanying the expedition explored the flora and fauna of the Hawaiians Islands, gathering hundreds of specimens.[48]

Wilkes then spent about four months exploring the Pacific Northwest Coast of North America, laying a claim to that area for the United States by so doing. During a brief return to Honolulu in November 1841, Wilkes assembled statistics furnished him by the missionaries and several merchants on Hawaiian schools and trade.[49]

Although Japan originally had been one of the objectives of the expedition, so much time had been consumed in the Pacific by the end of 1841 that Wilkes decided to terminate his explorations and return to the United States. After stops at Manila and Singapore, the expedition sailed around the Cape of Good Hope and arrived back in New York City on June 9, 1842, after nearly four years of absence.[50]

AFTERMATH

What had this first and only official American voyage of exploration accomplished in those four years? For Americans interested in commerce and navigation in the Pacific, the Wilkes expedition had assembled a mass of information that ranged from detailed maps and charts based on accurate surveying and meteorological information, descriptions of headlands and entrances to the various ports, data on the availability of provisions and the temperament of the natives, statistics on populations, imports and exports, port regulations, rates of exchange, and other useful information for mercantile interests. Wilkes felt that ''no opportunity had been omitted to gain useful information, which, when published, must be of great use to our commercial operations.''[51]

The expedition had also plotted known whaling grounds, ocean currents, and gathered other meteorological data. A leading commercial magazine of the time agreed with Wilkes that the data on the various islands were alone worth the entire cost of the expedition. In addition, there was the vast addition to knowledge furnished by the scientific group that had accompanied the expedition, which included specimens as well as drawings of other specimens and of the natives and their costumes.[52]

In sum, however, the expedition achieved only limited success. In part this was because it had been launched under a Democratic administration and returned to find a Whig president in the White House, who showed little interest in the expedition. Not until nearly two years after its return did the administration even solicit bids for the printing of the material the expedition had assembled. The attitude of the Whig administration was also revealed in the dismissal by the secretary of the navy of the scientific members of the expedition even before they had filed their reports.

The American people, too, showed little enthusiasm for the expedition. Its progress had been reported by few national periodicals, and it was largely New England newspapers that occasionally published some of the stream of information that the expedition was sending back. The romantic appeal of Polynesia that had been evident in America in the 1830s had apparently ebbed by the early 1840s, replaced perhaps by a new preoccupation with events in the western part of North America.[53]

EFFECTS OF THE WHALERS ON PACIFIC ISLANDERS

The effects of the American whalers in the Pacific were obviously greatest in Hawai'i (this will be discussed in chapter 6). In the rest of the Pacific, however, American whalers inevitably exerted an influence as well. By their sheer numbers they eclipsed the previous contacts between merchants and Pacific islanders. Virtually all of the remaining islands and atolls that had not lost their innocence as a result of the contacts with China traders saw that innocence swept away by the intrusions of the whalers and, to a lesser extent, the sealers.

Many of the early traders had introduced diseases, alcoholic beverages, and firearms into the islands of the Pacific. The dissemination of these continued under the whalers, and contributed to a population decline in the islands and to the chronic warfare that raged in some of them. The whalers also popularized the practice of prostitution among island women. Where the sexual favors of Polynesian women had heretofore been given freely or in exchange for small gifts, those favors began to be commoditized in the 1820s in New Zealand and Hawai'i. Ships' officers even carried women with them when they sailed away, dropping these "whalers' trollops" off at whatever island was nearby when they tired of them.[54]

Those ports that became popular with the whalers quickly grew in population, examples being Kororareka (now Russell) at Bay of Islands, New Zealand, and Lahaina, Hawai'i, and developed businesses that furnished the ships with provisions and the crews with recreation. Agriculture geared to providing the needs of the ships flourished in the vicinities of these towns.[55] At the same time, the whaling fleets carried off from the Pacific islands many of their best young men as crew members, further contributing to the population decline. One estimate placed the number of Hawaiian men who shipped out on whaling ships in 1842 as approximately 1,000.[56] In all of these influences, the whalers contributed potently to the upheaval of the traditional lifestyles of the natives.

TOWARD A PACIFIC POLICY

By the middle of the nineteenth century some form of public policy making had been forced upon the United States, as it had been upon Britain and France, by the number of their citizens active in the central and eastern Pacific and the value of their property there. In the islands small groups of merchants, missionaries, or planters had begun to gather in ports such as Honolulu, Papeete, Apia, and Levuka. Isolated traders took up more or less lasting residences on atolls, high islands, or in towns along the Spanish American coasts. There they pursued their varied interests and also served as intermediaries between the local peoples and passing whaling, trading, and naval ships.

In time some of these expatriates called upon their home governments for protection from islanders, other foreigners, or each other. The sending of naval patrols to "show the flag" and awe the natives or other Westerners was one form of reaction, and in time it became a more or less regularized process, especially after the creation of the Pacific Squadron. Before about 1840 Pacific appointments were not as prestigious in the navy as those to the Atlantic, Caribbean, or Mediterranean stations, and only a handful of officers seem to have taken enough interest in the area to propose major naval expansion there.

Another form of governmental action was the appointment of consular agents to Pacific posts to help fix legal responsibilities for debts, damages, or property rights. Among Americans it was common in the early years for individual traders or the firms they represented to seek consular appointments as a means to enhance their local prestige and business fortunes. Later it became more common practice for political party followers at home to seek those appointments as patronage in the hope of making their fortunes or their mark. The consuls' major concerns seem to have been private ones, questions of national interest being raised only when they were threatened by native violence or upstaged by European rivals.[57]

Opinions about the desirability of intervention by their government seem to have varied widely among Americans resident in the Pacific islands. Those skirting the edges of the law or living outside it scarcely welcomed the introduction of authority. On occasion, even those who at first welcomed naval intervention turned against it when the results did not meet their expectations. In the single year 1826, for example, American missionaries or merchants in Honolulu were alternately cheered and embittered by the actions of two naval commanders, John "Mad Jack" Percival and Thomas ap Catesby Jones. Percival condemned missionary-inspired rules against Hawaiian women visiting ships in the harbor, while Jones supported the missionaries and angered the merchants in doing so.[58]

As for commercial agents, the careers of John Coffin Jones at Honolulu, Moerenhout at Papeete, and John Brown Williams in Fiji were full of turmoil and complaint, with very limited support or instruction from Washington. Not one of the three escaped the censure of their fellow citizens or the displeasure of the State or Treasury departments, or both. There were able men who served in satisfactory fashion at some Pacific ports, but considering the manner in which agents were selected and the comparative unimportance or financial unattractiveness of most of the posts, such men would seem to have been lucky choices for their country rather than the result of good management. In the making of national policy their role was of very little significance.[59]

As for claims to Pacific real estate in the name of the United States, Washington's policy, if one may call it that, was throughout this period one of disinterest except, of course, for the Pacific Northwest. The claims of Joseph Ingraham and David Porter in the Marquesas were ignored, as was John Kendrick's fanciful idea of a claim to Nootka Sound until copies of his "deeds" were used later in discussions of the northwest border with Great Britain. Occasionally strong expansionist rhetoric could be heard in Congress—as early as the fur trade investigations of the early 1820s—but John Astor appears to have been the only American with sufficient economic interest in the Pacific to raise the issue of territorial expansion there before the 1840s. When Britain and France first began to assert sovereignty in the Pacific, the United States was prepared neither to oppose nor emulate them.

So far as there was any official U.S. policy toward the Pacific islands at all down to the mid-nineteenth century, it was merely that of maintaining for its citizens freedom and equality of commercial opportunity. Only in Hawai'i, where American merchants and missionaries held a strong position, supported by influential connections at home, would a form of international caveat be enunciated in 1842 by President John Tyler.

5

TO THE PACIFIC COAST

THE LURE OF CONTINENTALISM

When the United States expanded to include the Pacific coast within its territory in the 1840s, it resulted from a variety of influences. Among these, the growth of American interests in the Pacific certainly played an important role, although the extent of that influence is subject to debate.

A combination of maritime enterprises, overland expansion of fur trade and agrarian frontiers, and perhaps the early influence of sea-to-sea colonial charters had prepared the minds of some Americans to think in terms of expansion to the western limits of the continent. Unquestionably, the maritime trade that linked the Northwest Coast with Canton originally familiarized Americans with the Oregon and California coasts, but that interest, by itself, was never strong enough to stimulate an extension of the nation's borders to the Pacific. It was the addition of several transcontinental movements by fur traders, farm settlers, and missionaries, and the development of routes of communication to serve them, that provided the necessary political clout to carry the acquisitions through.[1]

As noted in an earlier chapter, the fur trade to Canton began New England's maritime interest in the Pacific coast of North America from 1788 through the 1820s. Out of the ventures of men like John Kendrick, Robert Gray, Joseph Ingraham, the Winships, and John Jacob Astor, there developed the idea of a national stake in that remote area that was ever before the eyes of both private citizens and government officials. Nearly all the principal figures in that trade spoke at one time or another of the national as well as the private interests there. Several suggested the possibility of establishing a national claim to territory and the creation of an outpost under the U.S. flag. If the concept of a national interest there could be planted, it would lend further credence to the works of private enterprise.

Gray's exploration of the mouth of the Columbia River in 1792 laid the basis for a later American claim to the territory by right of prior discovery. Copies of John Kendrick's deeds to lands around Nootka Sound, marked by chiefs of various tribes in the region, are still retained in Department of State archives. If they were not more actively pressed into use as foundations for an American claim to the territory, it is probably because the Lewis and Clark expedition and Astoria offered a surer basis.[2]

THE OREGON QUESTION

The question of who should possess or control the Pacific's eastern shore to the north of California had a considerable history before citizens of the United States became concerned with it. The Spanish could claim priority of discovery because of their voyages of exploration, particularly in the sixteenth and eighteenth centuries. Spain's galleon trade to Manila had helped to create interest in the region, though actual contacts resulting from it were mostly south of Oregon.[3]

After Sir Francis Drake's voyage in the sixteenth century, British contact with the area lapsed until the explorations of Cook and Vancouver in the late eighteenth century. For France, the voyage of La Perouse also came in that latter period, about the same time that the first British and American fur traders were arriving there. Russians, meanwhile, had been active in the Aleutians and Alaska. Four European countries were, thus, at least potential claimants to interests on the Pacific coast of North America. The European powers did not trouble themselves with the territorial claims or rights of the many tribes of Native Americans already resident in the areas, except when it was necessary or expedient.

The significant point is that despite the early Spanish claim to the entire northern Pacific, including its American coast, no serious international controversy occurred until about 1790 because no Western nation had developed direct, tangible interests in the occupation of any part between San Francisco Bay and Alaska.

Despite their earlier contacts, the four European nations really had no established advantage over that of America. Once the maritime fur trade began, however, Spanish authorities became concerned over the frequency of foreign visits to Vancouver Island and the coasts north and south of it. Their weak and belated efforts to reassert a claim already two centuries old now threatened American as well as British and Russian interests there.

John Meares, one of the earliest British fur trade captains, conceived of the idea of establishing a permanent settlement on Vancouver Island at Nootka Sound to advance his own and his nation's interests. To win his government's support for the idea, he greatly exaggerated the extent of his claim and the work he had begun there. Yet out of Meares's claims, and Spanish efforts to frustrate any such British activity, there arose the Nootka Sound controversy of 1789–1790.[4]

Although that dispute came about more out of the vagaries of European diplomacy than from North American concerns, the United States was indirectly involved. If either Britain or Spain had won recognition of an exclusive claim to Oregon and attempted to enforce that claim, any hope for the maintenance of an American interest there—present or future, private or national—would have gone glimmering. More important to President Washington's administration, however, was the possible effect that Anglo-Spanish hostilities might have on U.S. neutrality, particularly if either demanded passage for its military forces through the western portion of the United States.[5]

By a convention agreed upon peaceably on October 28, 1790, Spain and Great Britain effectually postponed any exclusive claims to territory not actually occupied by their forces or subjects. The stalemate over the issue was of greatest benefit to the United States in the years that followed. In the absence of any exclusive foreign claim to the area, Americans could freely pursue their trade without need for governmental support. As noted in the opening chapter, Americans quickly began to dominate the Northwest coastal fur trade and did so for at least two or three decades. When the major British fur trade companies, Hudson's Bay and Northwest, eclipsed the Americans through their expansion overland, U.S. concern with the Northwest Coast declined until transcontinental fur traders, missionaries, and farm settlers revived it later.[6]

GROWING AMERICAN PRIVATE INTEREST

As late as 1810 four Western nations—Spain, Britain, Russia, and the United States—continued their interest in the Oregon region, but none had yet established a land base there. Employees of Britain's Northwest Company had crossed the main ranges of the Rockies and established posts on their western slopes. Agents of the Missouri Fur Company built a post on the upper Snake River in 1808. But not until 1810–1812 were the first real attempts at settlements made on the coast. First, the brothers Jonathan and Nathan Winship of Massachusetts tried to create a trading base and fort on the lower Columbia in 1810. The hostility of Native American tribes who resented this attempt to usurp their role as middlemen in the trade forced the Americans to abandon their effort.[7] The following year John Jacob Astor's Pacific Fur Company founded a base at Astoria, nearer to the mouth of the Columbia, barely beating out a party representing the British.

Both of these American efforts were privately planned and financed, but both Astor and the British Northwest Company received at least passive support from their respective governments. Former president Thomas Jefferson hailed Astor's achievement with enthusiasm, calling it "the germ of a great, free and independent empire on that side of our continent."[8]

That any effort to establish an American claim to sovereignty in Oregon was futile was made clear in 1812, when the Russian American Company established a new settlement near Bodega Bay, on the California coast not far north of San Francisco. Despite Spanish orders to evacuate land claimed by Spain, the Russians not only remained but also constructed a small fort (Fort Ross) and permanent buildings. Though the outpost was not conspicuously successful in its purpose, which was to provide provisions for the trading enterprises in Russian Alaska, it remained in Russian hands for nearly thirty years. Russian activity in the northern Pacific expanded, moreover, in the second decade of the century to include considerable interest in the Hawaiian Islands.[9]

PUBLIC POLICIES

The reports of increasing foreign activity on the Northwest Coast began to arouse concern in the United States after the War of 1812, especially in the northeastern maritime areas. Now the first public policies designed to protect the Pacific coast interests of Americans reached the diplomatic stage. Under the terms of the Treaty of Ghent, Astoria would be recognized as an American post "captured" by the British sloop of war *Raccoon,* thus validating this American national claim there, even though Astor's agents had sold the property to the Northwest Company before the *Raccoon* arrived.

Secretary of State James Monroe wrote to the American negotiators at Ghent on March 22, 1814:

On no pretext can the British government set up a claim to territory south of the north boundary of the United States. It is not believed that they have any claim whatever to territory on the Pacific Ocean. You will, however, be careful should a definition of boundary be attempted, not to countenance in any manner or in any quarter, a pretention in the British government to territory south of that line.[10]

It seems clear that Monroe was here regarding the existing forty-ninth parallel boundary between the United States and Canada as extending all the way to the Pacific, although no formal agreement to that effect was reached.

As early as July 1815, Monroe sought the restoration of Astoria to American hands by the British, and when negotiations brought no result, Captain James Biddle was ordered in September 1817 to sail secretly in the U.S.S. *Ontario* to take formal possession of the post under the terms of the treaty. A leak in U.S. Navy secrecy alerted the British minister in Washington and produced protests, but negotiations in London found a British government more concerned with restoring good relations with the United States than in preserving a minor claim to a distant post. A convention was signed between the two countries in October 1818 that resolved a number of border questions and provided for British recognition of existence of the American claim to Astoria, "without, however, admitting the right of that government to the possession in question."[11]

The two governments agreed that for the next ten years citizens of either nation could freely enter and pursue their interests in the northwestern country west of the Rocky Mountains without prejudice to the claims there of either nation. During that decade Britain's Northwest Company, which merged after 1821 with the Hudson's Bay Company, established its position even more strongly with posts and fur traders. At the same time, the American maritime trade declined in importance, and no fur-trading or farming settlers from the United States arrived to back up their nation's claims.[12]

The Adams-Onis Treaty of 1819 with Spain, aptly termed the "Transcontinental Treaty" by Samuel Flagg Bemis, clarified the Oregon question further. While that treaty dealt chiefly with the cession of Florida to the United States, it also contained a provision providing for Spanish recognition of the forty-second parallel as the northward limit of its possessions on the Pacific coast, thus abandoning Spain's claims to Oregon. Secretary of State John Quincy Adams, a son of Massachusetts, certainly was aware of the maritime interests involved and harbored a general concern for commerce there—commerce in which Bostonians had played such a major role.[13]

In the years after 1820 several different lines of interest joined to apply pressure on the United States government to adopt a more aggressive policy toward the whole Far West. Fur traders were one group, with Astor and a group of St. Louis merchants at first competing, then cooperating, to further the growth of their overland expansion. This was clearly a business interest group with specific and limited aims. Allied to this were the increasingly powerful voices of members of Congress, including Congressman Dr. John Floyd of Virginia and Senator Thomas Hart Benton of Missouri. Floyd was tied by family and friendship to men who had participated in westward exploration and trading, and in December 1820, as earlier noted, he persuaded the House of Representatives to appoint him chairman of a new committee "to inquire into the situation of the settlements upon the Pacific Ocean, and the expediency of occupying the Columbia River."[14]

Benton had just been elected to the Senate, but he had already advocated westward expansion in speeches and as editor of the *St. Louis Enquirer*. His arguments went far beyond the interests of the fur traders, to include the prospect of future commerce with the Pacific and Asia across a trans-American route for which St. Louis would likely serve as a valuable entrepôt. Both Floyd and Benton also advocated expansion as a matter of national pride and duty—to combat the activities of British interests in the northwest and the Spanish further south. (Floyd and Benton roomed in Brown's Hotel in Washington during the winter of 1820 and 1821, as did agents of John Jacob Astor.[15])

Just over a month after its creation, Floyd's committee presented such a lengthy and detailed report to the House of Representatives as to indicate that there must have been considerable prior preparation on his part, or by someone else, before the committee was set up. The report traced the history of the fur business and land claims in America in an effort to establish a basis for a U.S.

claim to the Oregon country. While the law and logic of the report appear a bit fanciful at times, the enthusiasm was strong. Rationalizing its proposal to push the American claim there and to support it by settlement, the report argued:

From every reflection which the committee have been able to bestow upon the facts connected with this subject, they are inclined to believe the Columbia, in a commercial point of view, a position of the utmost importance; the fisheries on that coast, its open sea, and its position in regard to China, which offers the best market for the vast quantities of furs taken in those regions, and our increasing trade throughout that ocean, seems to demand immediate attention.[16]

Later in the report a description of the Oregon country called attention to its supplies of wood for shipbuilding, fertile soil for farming, and grass for livestock. American occupation, moreover, would have the advantage of pacifying the Indians of the region. Then, after another reference to the growing American commerce on the Pacific, the report dragged in the potential advantages to the whaling industry of a port in Oregon. Later in the report the Columbia was referred to "as the only point on the globe where a naval power can reach the East India possessions of our eternal enemy, Great Britain." Clearly Floyd and his committee were amassing every justification possible for American expansion into the region.[17]

The Russians had expanded down the coast as far as Fort Ross, the report noted, and when combined with the British activity in the region, it pointed to the need for prompt action by the United States if Americans were not to be shut out. What action should the United States take? The Floyd committee urged the immediate establishment of a settlement at the mouth of the Columbia, which would include the wives and children of those moving there. At the conclusion of the report came a proposed bill authorizing and requiring the president to occupy "that portion of the territory of the United States on the waters of the Columbia River." Much of the bill dealt with the regulation of Indian affairs and control of trade (largely in furs) in Indian lands, thus revealing the influence of Astor and his St. Louis allies in the framing of its contents.[18]

Congressional debate on establishing a military post at the mouth of the Columbia and encouraging settlement there to forestall British or Russian occupation continued for at least three years. In the end, however, no action was taken to implement the proposal. Diplomatic negotiations with Britain and Russia resulted in agreements that seemed, for the time being, to remove any immediate threat to American claims to access to the Northwest Coast.

INTERNATIONAL RIVALRIES

For Americans actually visiting the Northwest Coast in the 1820s, however, the situation was made more difficult than before by the increased activity of their Russian and British rivals. A decree by the Russian czar in 1821 claimed

Russian control of the northern Pacific and its shores down to the fifty-first parallel, which seemed to pose a potential threat to American trade with the Russian settlements there and to the use of Aleuts or Alaskan natives in the pursuit of pelts farther south.[19]

The expansion of British activity represented an even greater problem, particularly their policy of trapping out the regions south and east of the Columbia where Americans were becoming active. In fact, the threat of American competition had been one of the arguments used in bringing about the merger of the Northwest and Hudson's Bay companies. There was even a suspicion that the British and Russians were cooperating in opposing the "Yankees" at both the operating and diplomatic levels.[20]

Protracted international negotiations followed during years of declining yields for the American fur trade along the coast. In the course of negotiations with Russia, Secretary of State John Quincy Adams stated clearly to both British and Russian ministers in Washington the opposition of the United States to any extension of European domains in North America, a view amplified by President Monroe in his famous message to Congress of December 2, 1823, later referred to as the Monroe Doctrine. That remarkable statement was more theory or wishful thinking than true government policy, since the United States clearly lacked the power to prevent Europe from establishing new bases in the Western Hemisphere. But the canny Adams had reason to believe that no such establishment was imminent. In proposing the statement to Monroe he hoped to touch the national pride and at the same time defend the tangible interests of the "Boston men" on the Pacific coast.[21]

Still, at the very moment that Adams was protesting Russian and British claims, and Benton was asserting in the Senate the indisputable right of the United States to Oregon, Congress continued to reject the proposals of Floyd and others to implement occupation of the mouth of the Columbia. Both Eastern property interests and Southern and Western farm groups found reasons to protest the diversion of national energies to such a remote area.

In April 1824 Russia signed a treaty with the United States that established the southern boundary of Russia's American domains at 54°40' north latitude. The following February an Anglo-Russian treaty was signed to the same effect. This left just Britain and the United States (and of course the aborigines) to claim the coastal area between 42° and 54°40'. There the matter might presumably have rested until at least the expiration of the ten-year "joint occupation" agreed to by the British and Americans in 1818.[22]

The prospect of that expiration, however, concerned both President Adams and Senator Benton. The only non-native settlements in the region were those of the British Hudson's Bay Company, and American dominance of the maritime fur trade seemed to be diminishing as the land-based activities of the British and Russians expanded, causing furs to become scarcer. Even Astor seemed to be losing interest in the Oregon country. It was feared that if this state of affairs continued to prevail in 1828, then nothing would prevent the British from allowing the "joint occupation" agreement to lapse and then to claim the whole for themselves. Curiously enough, the initiative to forestall such an outcome was taken by the United States government before there was any pressure from would-be settlers on the land and at a time when agitation by fur trade interests seemed to be fading. Though Senator Benton's talk of vast economic potential in the Northwest rose to greater and greater extremes, the government's initiative was derived more from political motivations than from actual knowledge of the area or pressure from interest groups.[23]

The Adams administration sent Albert Gallatin to London in 1826 to begin negotiations for a renewal of the Oregon convention of 1818 or to settle on a boundary with the British. Adams was at that time willing to agree to a continuation of the forty-ninth parallel line westward from the Rockies to the Pacific. He would even concede to the British the right of free navigation of the Columbia River, a magnanimous gesture considering that the only "civilized" residents of the area at that time were British subjects. In dealing with British Foreign Minister George Canning, however, Gallatin found himself confronting the British equivalent of a Benton. Like the Missouri senator, Canning saw great commercial potential in Oregon, including transpacific trade to Asia, but it was for the British to develop it and not the United States. Canning, therefore, viewed Britain's recognition of an American claim to the area in 1818 as a mistake, and he now set out to undo it and to claim the Columbia for Great Britain.

It is a tribute to the diplomatic skills of Gallatin and to the determination of President Adams that the result of the negotiations of 1826–1827 was a new convention so much to the advantage of the United States. Political pressures on both sides of the Atlantic made Canning no less willing than the Americans to adopt a delaying compromise. Since no mutually satisfactory boundary agreement could be reached, the "joint occupation" formula was renewed, this time without a definite term, but subject to renunciation by either party on twelve months' notice.

Any settlement of the issue made at that time on the basis of actual occupation would surely have been to Britain's advantage. In agreeing to delay a settlement through renewal of the "joint occupation" provision the British gave American fur traders and farmers, together with missionaries, an opportunity to establish themselves in Oregon. Gallatin felt in 1827 that the British at least partly recognized this possibility yet were prepared to see it come about rather than force an Anglo-American confrontation over the issue.[24]

THE AMERICANIZATION OF OREGON

Some of the first Americans to reach Oregon overland in the 1820s, like fur trader Jedediah Smith, were interested in extending the influence of the United States into the area even as they were pursuing their private concerns. Between 1830 and 1840 the American fur-trading pioneers were followed by a growing number of fellow countrymen, including missionaries, farmers, adventurers, and a few apparently attracted by the possibilities of maritime industry. They found that the British Hudson's Bay Company, centered then at Fort Vancouver on the Columbia, represented virtually the only "law west of the Rockies." These Americans were not reticent about stating the claims of their own nation to equal status in the region, and that status was recognized to a degree by the regional superintendent of the British company, Dr. John McLoughlin. At the same time, however, McLoughlin and other agents of the Hudson's Bay Company attempted to discourage American settlement in the Oregon country and warned their superiors of the need for more support if Britain's and their own claims were to be maintained.[25]

Among the Americans who moved into Oregon intending to found a permanent settlement was Benjamin Louis Eulalie de Bonneville, a graduate of the U.S. Military Academy at West Point. In 1832 he successfully led some twenty light wagons through South Pass in the Rockies, proving the feasibility of this overland route. The story of Bonneville's early successes and ultimate financial failure was used as the theme for a romantic history of the early fur trade by Washington Irving, who also wrote a history of Astoria highly favorable to Astor.[26]

Meanwhile, Oregon had acquired new publicists to advance its cause in the United States. Most significant, perhaps, were the efforts of a Boston schoolteacher, Hall J. Kelley, who in 1830 published *A Geographical Sketch of That Part of North America Called Oregon* (Boston, 1830). Compiled from descriptions of the area that he had read quite uncritically, Kelley's book coupled the most fulsome praise of the scenic and health-giving characteristics of the region with an argument that the "settlement of the Oregon country would conduce to a freer intercourse, and a more extensive and lucrative trade with the East Indies." The next year Kelley also published *A General Circular to All Persons of Good Character, Who Wish to Emigrate to the Oregon Territory* (Charleston, MA, 1831).

Such propaganda, given validity by the actual expeditions of Nathaniel Wyeth, another Bostonian, cultivated the germs of what would grow into an "Oregon fever" and would in another decade begin to carry hundreds of Americans westward. The precise motivations of these early publicists of Oregon expansion are impossible to judge today. It seems clear, however, that neither Kelley nor Wyeth represented any organized interest group.

Before major American migration to Oregon developed, missionary interests entered the picture to provide both organization and continuing support. In 1832, according to the *Christian Advocate and Journal*, several Indians from the Far Northwest arrived at the fur trade center of St. Louis, where they reportedly expressed a desire to have the Christian faith introduced or maintained among them. The *Christian Advocate* did not explain how this idea arose among the Indians and whether or not, as has been alleged elsewhere, their representatives actually asked for "black robes," a reference to French Catholic priests who had appeared much earlier in the Far West.[27]

The following year the Methodists decided to support a mission to the Northwest Indians, and the Reverend Jason Lee, with his nephew and a few helpers, joined Wyeth's party bound for Oregon. Once there, they settled in the fertile Willamette River valley, not far from Fort Vancouver, rather than further east in the area from which the Indian appeal had come.

The Methodist group was soon followed by another party led by Dr. Marcus Whitman and sent by the American Board of Commissioners for Foreign Missions (ABCFM), the same group already supporting a mission in Hawai'i. Whitman took up his work east of the great bend of the Columbia near present-day Walla Walla, Washington. Still further east in what is now northern Idaho, Father de Smet and others began Catholic missions from American bases. Though Indian converts were few for some years, the missionaries established thriving agricultural settlements and wrote home glowing reports of Oregon's potential.

The Protestant groups thus brought additional families into Oregon to engage in farming and mercantile occupations. They tried to attract to the area the type of sober, industrious settlers whose example would aid in converting the Indians to similar patterns of living. In 1838 Jason Lee went east to help bring out more settlers, and by 1840 new groups were beginning to arrive by both land and sea. By 1841 the ABCFM mission was able to print the Book of Matthew in the Nez Perce language on a press presumably shipped to Oregon from the Hawai'i mission.[28]

As a result, by the beginning of the 1840s the Americans had turned the tables on the British. Now it was citizens of the United States who predominated numerically, although the area of their settlements lay almost entirely south of the Columbia. In familiar American fashion the new settlers soon began to establish their own form of local self-government. For example, when Lee went east in 1838 he had taken with him a petition signed by thirty-six settlers urging the United States to take "formal and speedy possession" of the Oregon country.[29]

Through all this both the English and Americans were watching each other's moves with concern. The concept of preemptive imperialism was very much alive in both countries. The visit to Oregon of a British naval expedition under Captain Edward Belcher in 1839 aroused new fears among Americans, and a petition signed by some sixty-seven residents was addressed to Congress. It paralleled appeals from McLoughlin and other British subjects for more support from their own government. In Washington the Missouri senators Benton and Linn still found scant support, however, when they called for the formal extension of U.S. sovereignty or at least control in Oregon. A joint resolution to this effect, in 1841, once again failed to pass.[30]

However, the effect of the growing American population in Oregon grew increasingly difficult to ignore. A party of 114 people under Dr. Elijah White in 1842 formed only a part of that year's migration, and in the following year nearly 1,000 Americans reached Oregon. By 1846 the American population there was estimated at more than 5,000 citizens. While seeking the establishment of U.S. rule in the area, and with growing popular support for that action, representatives of these settlers began to take matters into their own hands. The rudiments of a provisional government were created through local initiative between 1843 and 1845.[31]

This action by American settlers faced the representatives of the British Hudson's Bay Company with a serious dilemma. The company had initially been willing to allow American farmers to provide an increasing share of their supply of grain and other provisions. The company had, in fact, at first provided almost the only market for those products. As farming continued to expand, however, it further threatened the operations of a fur trade that had largely been trapped out already in the Columbia River area. Accordingly, the Hudson's Bay Company found it expedient to withdraw the center of its northwest operations to Victoria, on Vancouver Island, in the early 1840s.[32]

AN AMERICAN TITLE

During 1845 and 1846 the Oregon agitation in the United States reached a climax. As more settlers journeyed westward, political factors related to the annexation of Texas helped to precipitate a decision on Oregon as well. A Democratic campaign slogan in 1844 had linked the two, though the portion most publicized in the north was "54–40 or fight."

Following his inauguration, President James Polk first directed Secretary of State James Buchanan to renew an earlier offer to Great Britain to extend the forty-ninth parallel marking the boundary between the United States and Canada on to the Pacific where it would likewise divide Oregon between the Americans and the British. When this overture was rejected by the British minister in Washington, Polk announced that the United States would demand all the territory in question there up to the southern boundary of Russian Alaska. A reluctant Buchanan was directed to serve upon Great Britain the one year notice required for renunciation of the convention of 1827, thus terminating the policy of "joint occupation."[33]

This abrupt step, coupled with strong Anglophobe sentiments expressed in Congress and part of the American press, provoked a reciprocal anti-American reaction in Britain. Loose talk of war could be heard on both sides of the Atlantic, but neither government found such a conflict to be in its best interest. With hostilities pending with Mexico over Texas and the Southwest, there was special reason for President Polk to be amenable to a compromise over Oregon. The withdrawal northward of Hudson's Bay Company activity, moreover, had made possession of the land between the Columbia and the forty-ninth parallel less important now for Britain than before.

On this ground, then, it became possible for Buchanan and the British minister to sign a boundary treaty on June 15, 1846. By its terms the 49° line was extended westward from the Rockies to Puget Sound, with the whole of Vancouver Island left to the British, who also retained certain rights of navigation on the Columbia. Continued uncertainties and near hostilities between American and British-Canadian settlers over the water boundary between Vancouver and the mainland were resolved by an arbitral decision of the emperor of Germany in 1872.[34]

The United States had become a Pacific-bordering nation now, for reasons both varied and changing. Just how great a part Pacific-centered motivations, as opposed to continental ones, had played in bringing about this result is not clear. Norman Graebner has argued that maritime interests defined the extent of the coastal claims to include Puget Sound access in the north and San Francisco, and perhaps San Diego, to the south. It must be noted, however, that the definitive acquisition of Oregon was accomplished at a time when maritime interests were by no means at their strongest in Congress, particularly those concerned with Pacific trade. Many of the most ardent advocates of the "54–40" movement, though they adduced future commercial gains as reasons for expansion, nevertheless came from nonmaritime sections of the country and had neither specific knowledge of, nor pecuniary interest in the Pacific trade. Opposition to the expansion was, in fact, strongest in the northeastern section, which had dominated American enterprise in the Pacific.[35]

One conclusion may safely be reached. The transcontinental expansion of the United States proceeded from drives of its own that did not depend on Pacific and Asian trade prospects to carry it to the coast.

EARLY AMERICANS IN CALIFORNIA

The beginning of American interests in California, or better Alta California, is intertwined with those in Hawai'i and Oregon; yet, there are significant differences in the original situation and in the course of development that followed. In California, unlike Oregon, there were settlements and a form of government of European origin before the first Americans arrived. Alta California was a part of New Spain, though Spanish missions and communities there dated from no earlier than the late 1760s. This meant that the first visitors from New England had to deal with a recognized authority.

Again, it was the Northwest Coast fur trade that brought most of the first citizens of the United States to the shores of California, although the first American ship to touch there was not a fur trader. In 1796 the Boston ship *Otter* touched at Monterey, ostensibly for wood, water, and possibly fresh provisions. While in the vicinity, however, its captain secretly landed eleven fugitives from the Australian penal colony to whom he had given passage. Spanish authorities had refused him permission to land these people. Thus, Yankee relations with the Spanish authorities began here, as elsewhere, with deception and evasion of Spain's stringent and exclusive policies toward foreign merchants.[36]

In 1799 Captain James Rowan entered San Francisco Bay with the *Eliza* and was allowed to purchase provisions. Already Spanish officials in Mexico were growing concerned over the increasingly frequent appearance of Americans on the coast, and officers in California were instructed to observe their activities closely and to deal with them cautiously.[37]

In 1800 two more American ships, the *Betsey* and the *Enterprise*, put in California appearances, and by that year the pursuit of furs had definitely pushed southward to California. Soon thereafter the Santa Barbara Channel area became noted for its supply of sea otter. In the next few years California's usefulness to the Boston fur traders was increased. They hunted otter and seals on the coasts and offshore islands as far south as Baja California. They also made use of whatever unoccupied harbors they could find for refitting and watering places. Along with this a small trade developed with the Spanish Californians, including mission fathers and an occasional official. The Yankees traded what manufactures they had brought along or whatever they could spare from the ship's stores. In return they secured meat, grain, vegetables, and occasionally furs.[38]

The local population was starved for many commodities, and the Americans quickly learned that though their trade was against Spain's laws, *Californios* were prepared to wink at the law. The coast, moreover, was not tightly controlled by Spanish *gardacostas,* although a few Amercans ran afoul of them. To the Americans, it should be noted, this early exchange of goods and occasionally of specie with the Spanish-Mexicans of California was merely a sidelight to their main commerce with the Northwest Coast, Hawai'i, and China.[39]

Shortly after the beginning of the nineteenth century a new aspect of the search for furs touched the California area. This was a collaboration of sorts between Americans and Russians, sometimes with the use of Aleutian or Alaskan natives in the hunt as far south as San Diego and even beyond.[40]

Although the fur trade declined during the 1820s, Americans continued to be attracted to the California coast by other branches of commerce. One of these involved the sale of New England or foreign manufactures in the commodity-starved market that stretched from San Diego to San Francisco. In return, the Yankees received livestock, some grain, provisions, and a little Spanish gold and silver. As American merchants took up residence in Hawai'i, a small trade between those islands and the California coast also developed. Horses and cattle were brought to the islands in return for transshipped manufactures.

In the 1820s the trade in California hides and tallow described in Richard Henry Dana's *Two Years before the Mast* also began. That book helped to put California before the eyes of the American public after it was published in 1840. After Mexico won its independence from Spain early in the 1820s, Mexican officials began to sanction this trade with the Americans, at least tacitly, because it played an important part in supplying the settlements of Alta California with necessary and desirable merchandise.

At some point in this period American whaling vessels began to touch the Pacific coast of North America in search of water, wood, provisions, and a place to repair both ships and men after the ravages of the sea. Toward midcentury the whalers would play a larger part in the California economy, but in the 1830s and 1840s they came only in small numbers when compared with the fleet that visited Hawai'i. At times as many as thirty or forty whale ships were in San Francisco Bay in one year, but their limited stocks for barter were hardly a major factor in the growth of the American commercial stake there. They did, however, provide another source of information about California to the American public, and their limited activity could, and did, serve as a base for some highly exaggerated political rhetoric about future economic possibilities.

AMERICAN SETTLEMENT

A few of the Americans drawn to the California coast by the trade eventually settled there permanently, converted to Catholicism, and married into local families. Alfred Robinson of Santa Barbara and Abel Stearns of Los Angeles were typical of such cases. They were not advocates of American expansion into the area as a rule, though a number of them lent aid of various kinds to other Americans who began to arrive overland between 1826 and the early 1840s.[41]

In 1826 Jedediah Smith became the first of the overland fur traders to reach California's Mexican communities, and after him a handful of adventurers, nearly all fur traders, followed. Some of these remained to become useful citizens of California under Mexican, and later U.S., rule. A few of them, by their misconduct, merely strengthened the Californios' prejudices and fears concerning their energetic and ambitious neighbors to the east. By 1840 there were probably not more than sixty Americans genuinely resident in California, but the following year overland migration increased markedly. In 1845 alone at least 250 immigrants arrived by such routes.[42]

In the beginning many of the newcomers clustered around a fort built by the Swiss-American Johann (John A.) Sutter (or Suter) at Sacramento. There they rested and gathered advice beore moving on to take up land or occupations elsewhere. By 1846 the number of U.S. citizens in California had increased to about 700, and both they and the perturbed Mexican-Americans anticipated further increases in the tide of immigration. It is quite possible that the growing numbers of American settlers would have eventually secured California for the United States even had war and military invasion not forced the issue.[43]

Like the settlers in Oregon, those who moved to California from the United States in the early and middle 1840s seem to have been bent on finding fertile lands and a pleasant climate in which to pursue essentially agrarian occupations. California's soil and climate were extolled by men like Hall J. Kelley and Alfred Robinson in books or reports published in the East. In his writings about the desirability of securing Oregon, earlier mentioned, Kelley devoted considerable space to extensive description and praise of the land to the south. One looks in vain in the statements or writings of the early settlers, however, for any evidence of interest in transpacific commerce. That kind of talk was left chiefly to promoters and politicians in the East who looked for political or economic rationalizations for their expansionist desires.

Public policy in Washington toward California followed a generally passive course down to the mid–1830s. The early trade and first settlements of Americans in this remote region seem to have occasioned remarkably few exchanges between U.S. authorities and those of Spain and then Mexico. In 1833 a consul was selected for the port of Monterey, but the nomination was recalled, and no new appointee was named until December 1837. Not until 1843, with the appointment of Thomas O. Larkin, already a resident of California, was effective U.S. representation attained there. Two appointments to a consular post at San Francisco were made before Larkin's nomination, but they do not appear to have been effective in the performance of the office.[44]

GOVERNMENT INTEREST

An active diplomatic interest in California was demonstrated in 1835, however, in an unsuccesful attempt by the Jackson administration to purchase at least a part of the area. It appears that Jackson's interest in California was part of an attempt to win Northeastern support for a program of national expansion and to balance the Southern drive for the acquisition of Texas. New York and New England might have been expected to react favorably to a program of expansion that would include the acquisition of the valuable harbors of San Diego and San Francisco, and the boundaries mentioned in Jackson's proposal would have included both. Among California's virtues, its strategic location for transpacific commerce with China was often mentioned by politicians like Daniel Webster.[45]

Another factor urging California upon the attention of the authorities in Washington was the recurrent rumor that Britain and France were showing interest in its possible acquisition. In Britain's case there were repeated incidents from about 1837 into the 1840s that appeared to give substance to such rumors. A *History of California,* published in England in 1839, recommended the cession of California to Great Britain in payment of $50 million owed by Mexico to British creditors. The British, its author suggested, might then develop California through a chartered company modeled after the East India or Hudson's Bay models. An Anglo-Mexican convention of 1837 seemed to give plausibility to the scheme by its provision for the conversion of individual British bond claims against Mexico into land grants. The head of the Hudson's Bay Company, moreover, had expressed interest in adding at least part of California to his domains.[46]

Official American interest in California, however, experienced something of a lull during the Van Buren administration and the years after the business panic of 1837. By the time John Tyler became president, however, interest was reviving. Tyler, a Virginian, seemed more sympathetic to expansion projects to the southwest than his predecessor, a New Yorker, had been. Whatever the cause, Tyler's minister to Mexico, Waddy Thompson, was an enthusiastic advocate of the annexation of California. His dispatches told of its fine climate and fertile soil, which were being largely neglected, in his view, under Mexican rule. American possession of the ports of San Francisco, Monterey, and San Diego would, he declared, ensure the nation's commercial supremacy in the entire Pacific. Whaling interests, too, would benefit greatly from the development of bases there under the American flag, while the agricultural potential of the California valleys, he predicted, would make them the "granary of the Pacific." Thompson also raised again the specter of British and/or French designs on the area to strengthen the argument.[47]

Thompson hoped to arrange a transfer of title in satisfaction of American claims similar to the one earlier proposed in Great Britain. His proposal would have included Mexico's cession of California to the United States in return for a payment of some millions of dollars. All or part of this money could then be used by the Mexican government to meet the claims of American and British creditors. In return for British acquiescence in the agreement, the United States would be willing to settle the northwestern boundary at the Columbia River. The proposal, however, aroused no enthusiasm in Oregon, Mexico, or even in Washington.[48]

Whatever prospects existed for this scheme, or any other, for the purchase of California were destroyed in 1842 by the action of Commodore Thomas ap Catesby Jones, USN, in command of the navy's Pacific Squadron. Provided with a strengthened naval complement and instructed to keep an eye on the west coast of Mexico in the event of war, Jones misconstrued a dispatch from the U.S. consul at Mazatlan to mean that war had actually broken out. From Callao, Peru, he sailed northward and seized Monterey in October. This set the stage for some of the *opera bouffe* with which the history of California is strewn before Jones was obliged to haul down the flag of the United States, salute that of Mexico, and depart.

After that no Mexican official of any stripe dared countenance sale of part of the nation to the demonstrably aggressive Yankees. Duff Green, an agent of Secretary of State Calhoun, reported in 1844:

I am convinced that it is impossible to obtain the consent of [the Mexican] Government to the cession to the United States of Texas, California, or any part of the public domain of Mexico whatever. . . . [I]n the midst of a civil conflict where each party is seeking pretences to murder and confiscate the property of their opponents, and where the principle is maintained that it is treason to sell any part of the public domain to the United States, it is worse than folly to suppose that either party can alienate any part of Texas or California.[49]

WAR WITH MEXICO

It was the war with Mexico, precipitated by the Texas question, that finally brought the extension of U.S. rule over California. President Polk's determination to secure the coastal province as part of his Mexican policy is well documented. And if he spoke occasionally of Pacific trade advantages as a rationalization for the step, it appears that the domestic political impact of such an appeal was uppermost in his mind. Polk was no China trader, nor were the men around him in touch with or primarily influenced by either Pacific shipping or whaling interests. Pure expansive nationalism was a more likely motive.[50]

As news of the war reached California, yet another of that province's many uprisings was taking place. This one, the so-called Bear Flag Revolt, was led by Americans who sought autonomy from Mexico and/or incorporation into the United States. Although poorly organized, it might yet have exerted considerable influence in north central California even if the war had not broken out. Because of their growing numbers, and the prospect that many more would soon be arriving, the immigrant American community had become an important force in California. The aggressive policies of their government and the willingness of some of the immigrants to act together gave them a power out of all proportion to their numbers.

The Bear Flag Revolt was not authorized by President Polk, and at first it seemed likely to endanger his California policy. It ended, for example, whatever possibilities might still have existed for acquiring California through peaceful negotiation. In the opinion of one historian of California, the Bear Flag movement "was unquestionably responsible for much of the ill-will among the native inhabitants which later made necessary the forceful conquest of the province. It was never a general movement among the Americans in California, many of whom condemned it out of hand, but was confined to a limited area and carried out largely by trappers instead of by permanent residents."[51] Whatever the original standing of the Bear Flaggers, however, their movement quickly gained a semblance of legitimacy once war broke out, and some of them joined with U.S. armed forces in its pursuit.

At the outset of the war in the spring of 1846, John Frémont was in California with a small force of American troops, ostensibly on an exploring expedition. This soon became a military mission, and Frémont's camp became a nucleus for the organization of American strength in the north. Consul Larkin joined in these military activities, as did some of the other American residents. The motives of Americans in the area appear to have been varied. Some, like Commodore John D. Sloat, who reached Monterey in July with a naval detachment, seem to have worried that a British attempt to seize all or part of California was imminent. Inflamed passions in California easily interpreted any British activity as an aggressive threat. In Washington similar views were used for political effect.[52]

On July 7th Sloat raised the U.S. flag over Monterey and within the next few days similar actions took place in San Francisco and at Sutter's Fort. It appeared that the conquest of California was going to be an easy matter. In the south, however, things did not go so smoothly, and despite the arrival of additional forces overland under General Stephen W. Kearny, some time and sharp fighting were required before American control was assured. Commodore Robert F. Stockton had in the meantime taken command of the Pacific Squadron and played a material role in setting up the new regime.

During the war period overland migration to California continued, augmented now by an increasing flow of Americans arriving by sea via Cape Horn. One party of more than 200 Mormons, led by Sam Brannan, sailed from New York to San Francisco. More of their co-religionists came overland, including a Mormon battalion, and at one point it was rumored that Brigham Young was planning to move his major group to California. Between 1846 and 1848 the American population of California grew from about 700 to more than 7,000.[53]

In mid-January 1847, Frémont and Adres Pico, acting governor of Mexican California, signed a surrender document ending hostilities there. A few weeks later the Treaty of Guadalupe Hidalgo was signed in Mexico ending the war and providing for the cession of California to the United States as one of its provisions.[54] Now the government in Washington would have to confront the responsibilities involved in governing the new possession and develop policies to deal with it. A nation that only two years earlier had possessed no territory fronting the Pacific now controlled a Pacific coastline of some 1,500 miles.

6

AMERICANS IN HAWAI'I I

IN THE ERA OF KAMEHAMEHA I

The American approach to Hawai'i, like that to China or to the Pacific coast of North America, was a matter of private enterprise, without government intervention. In August 1789 Captain Robert Gray reached Hawai'i in the *Columbia* and traded with the islanders on his way from the Oregon coast to China with the first cargo of furs to travel that route under the American flag. Both British and French vessels had preceded the *Columbia* to Hawai'i, and for some years after this first American voyage, British arrivals, notable among them the visits of Captain George Vancouver, continued to outnumber American ones.[1]

Eventually, participation in a variety of trades brought so many more Americans into Hawai'i's part of the Pacific that within a half-century after Captain Cook's arrival, the interests of U.S. citizens in what were then still called the Sandwich Islands were greater than those of any other group of foreigners. The record left by those early visitors was a mixed one, but the conduct of some captains and crews left bitter memories among the Hawaiians.

Until after the War of 1812 the fur trade remained the most important single reason for American visits to the islands. It was a transient interest, and one which gave little or no incentive to the masters of American ships to interfere in Hawaiian politics or to attempt permanent settlement. As for claiming territory for the United States, the priority of the British in discovery and in political contact with the Hawaiian chiefs, if nothing else, put that out of the question.[2]

Fresh water, firewood, fresh provisions, a chance to refit vessels after long Pacific voyages, and what Pacific sailing masters were pleased to call "recreation" of the crews on shore made the Sandwich, or Hawaiian group, attractive and practically unique in the Northeast Pacific. In addition to these obvious attractions, others began to appear before long. Foreign visitors discovered, for example, that some of the light lines made by the Hawaiians from olona and other fibers were useful replacements for those lost or worn out by hard use at sea.

Hawaiians themselves proved to be capable replacements for depleted crews, and increasing numbers of them shipped out on vessels of several nations. The mild island climate was also a welcome respite from the rigors of the North Pacific, making it a pleasant wintering and resupplying resort for fur traders who had failed to fill a cargo in a single trading season. And if the Hawaiians were at times unpredictable in their reception of the visitors in these early years, they were certainly no more so than the inhabitants of the Northwest Coast.[3]

Conditions of trade improved once Kamehameha I introduced an element of stability into the Hawaiian polity by his interisland conquests between 1790 and 1810. After he had established his authority, foreign visitors commented on the safety with which they could anchor, trade, and even lay up vessels for repair. Each Western ship arriving in Hawai'i was welcomed by a personal visit from either Kamehameha or his officials. The king was clearly intent on encouraging trade with the West and with modernizing his island kingdom. Foreigners, a few of them Americans, aided the Hawaiian monarch in extending his control over the islands with Western ships and firearms.[4]

During the last stage of his conquest of Oahu and for some years thereafter, Kamehameha was free from political interference by official representatives of the foreign powers. Yet as late as 1810 he is quoted as terming himself a "subject" of King George of England, apparently in memory of George Vancouver's friendly support and advice. A second factor was clearly the influence of Englishmen John Young and Isaac Davis, two of his closest foreign advisers. Still more significant in this alleged recognition of "subject" status to England was the influence of those who helped him draft a letter of 1810 to the British monarch in which the word "subject" was used.[5]

By 1810 it is certain that most of the foreign visitors to Hawai'i, though not yet most of those resident there, were Americans. In that year, Archibald Campbell, an English visitor who resided on Oahu for more than year, noted the greater number of American vessels touching there. He also noted the presence of some sixty foreigners resident on that one island, and wrote that a variety of "inducements" were offered by Kamehameha and other chiefs who were "always anxious to have white people about them." In general, Campbell regarded most of the transitional foreign residents of Hawai'i at that time as of bad character. In his rush to encourage foreigners to settle in Hawai'i, Kamehameha was clearly unable to distinguish yet between the "good" and the "bad" among them.[6]

By 1812 a maritime commerce of such proportions had developed that Honolulu was gradually emerging as the most important port of call in the islands, where traffic in both island and foreign products was conducted. The appearance of such a trade center in itself illustrates the radical changes taking place in the lives of the Hawaiians as a result of contact with foreigners. Urbanization and commerce were both alien to what had hitherto been an agrarian and subsistence economy and lifestyle. Honolulu had not been one of the most important pre-contact Hawaiian settlements, but its protected, deep-water anchorage made it a favorite for foreign captains. Then, the lure of excitement and of the desirable goods that the outsiders brought with them began to attract Hawaiians there in unprecedented numbers. Kamehameha I, himself, took up residence near the harbor at one period, the better to encourage, supervise, and profit from the trade.[7]

At the time of Kamehameha's death in 1819, however, it was still a relatively small settlement. In 1818 Peter Corney described it as a "village" consisting "of about 300 houses regularly built," with three houses to a family. Judging from Corney's estimate, the population of Honolulu in that year could not have exceeded 500 people. Despite its small size, a French visitor the next year found the town "the center of the activity that gives impetus to change in religion, customs, and commerce." Another 1819 visitor found that there were already contrasts between the people living in Honolulu and those he had observed at Lahaina. In Honolulu people were "eager for amusement and give themselves up to it," life was "varied and tumultuous," the people "fond of agitation," by contrast with placid and "tranquil" Lahaina. The difference he attributed to the intercourse with foreigners at Honolulu, compared with "complete isola-tion" from them in Lahaina.[8]

EARLY COMMERCE

A thin patina of commercial, money economy, centering about the foreigners, slowly began to overspread the day-to-day subsistence economy of the native people, especially in and around the port towns. For those Hawaiian farmers near the ports, new crops and livestock were introduced from the West and avidly taken up to meet foreign demand. Thus, commercial farming slowly be-gan to exist side by side with subsistence farming in those areas able to benefit from the foreign market. Young Hawaiian women began to flock to Honolulu, at least for short periods of time each year, to exchange their sexual favors for the gifts or money that could be earned from foreigners there, and in this they were sometimes aided by male go-betweens. Consumerism and a certain degree of upward mobility began to penetrate Hawaiian society, at least in Honolulu.

Gradually, the control exerted by the chiefs over trade with the West began to loosen. The commoditization of sex, for example, was largely out of their hands, although some apparently tried to tax it. The arrival of Western merchants further accelerated that loss of control. After 1812 there were usually one or more foreigners on shore with supplies of foreign manufactures for sale. In the 1820s certain New England firms set up resident agents at Honolulu, among them James Hunnewell and John Coffin Jones.[9]

No equal commercial role was achieved in Hawai'i by citizens of any other nation in that period, at least partly because of Europe's wartime preoccupations. Both British and Russian naval officers had noted the desirability of establishing a base in Hawai'i, as had the Spaniard Martinez, as early as 1789. But not until the establishment of a Hudson's Bay Company agent in Honolulu in the 1830s did the Americans face strong foreign mercantile competition.[10]

To the original traffic in provisions for fur traders, Hawai'i was able to add another commercial line before 1820. This was the sale of aromatic sandalwood for export, which first developed as a supplement to that in provisions and then blossomed into a full trade on its own primarily between 1810 and 1830.[11]

With the return of peace between Great Britain and the United States in 1815, the expansive energy of American maritime enterprise was released with new vigor, and Hawai'i felt the effects. Both the fur trade and that in sandalwood saw fresh bursts of activity that continued beyond the death of Kamehameha I, whose regime had made much of the trade possible even while he tightly regulated it. American interests in Hawai'i down through this period remained on the same private, individual-venture basis on which they had begun. The year of Kamehameha's death, 1819, witnessed developments that would change this.

URBANIZATION AND CONSUMERISM

The death of Kamehameha I was quickly followed by four events of momentous importance for the people of Hawai'i: the establishment of Honolulu as the center of government; the overthrow of the Hawaiian religion; the arrival of the first whaling ship; and the coming of the first wave of Puritan missionaries. The new political significance of Honolulu, added to the greater economic importance it assumed with the arrival of the whalers, caused the town to grow rapidly from the small village Corney described a year before Kamehameha's death. In the mid–1820s, Andrew Bloxam, botanist on HMS *Blonde,* overestimated the population of this "London of the Sandwich Islands" at 10,000, "of whom there are more than 300 Americans with whom the principal trade consists." It was, he wrote, "getting to be quite a civilized place."[12]

For Hawaiians living in an urban setting the effects of the new influences from the West, and later from the East, were magnified, but few Hawaiians, however remote they might be, could escape them entirely. Mortality and population movement left large areas of the islands uncultivated and sparsely populated. Christianity intruded into even the most remote areas, with over a dozen churches in the Hamakua area of the Big Island alone by the midcentury. From their earliest arrival in 1820 the missionaries set out to eradicate completely the traditional Hawaiian lifestyle. The influx of Western goods gradually wiped out traditional Hawaiian arts and crafts as well, until by the late nineteenth century such items as kapa and calabashes had largely become museum pieces.

The basis of the traditional Hawaiian economy before the arrival of Cook had been the *ahupua'a,* a wedge-shaped division of the land that extended from the mountains down to the seashore, widest where it reached the ocean. Each ahupua'a was largely self-sufficient, since it included all of the economic activities available—from lumbering and other highland pursuits to fishing and seafood gathering on the shores, with farming on the lands in between. Within the ahupua'a goods were exchanged by reciprocal "gift-giving," as in the case of fish for taro, principally within the *'ohana,* or extended family.

The influx of Western "consumerism" brought with it a market economy, based initially on a barter system that was gradually replaced by a monetary one. A Hawaiian could still support himself and his family by a few hours of work per week in his taro patches, but if he limited himself in this way he denied his family the attractive new products of the West. And even then the market economy made demands upon him in the form of forced labor for his *ali'i* (chief) in behalf of the latter's acquisitiveness.

At the same time the support and security furnished by the 'ohana was likewise being undermined by the new developments. The 'ohana was fragmented by the trend toward urbanization. Hawaiian men and women who moved to the towns were isolated from their rural 'ohana, which often were on a different island, while the 'ohana were likewise deprived of many of their youngest and potentially most productive adults. With the possible exception of Oahu, it is likely that the average age of the rural population was markedly higher than that in the towns as a result of urbanization. Given the higher mortality rate characteristic of such migrations from a settled rural lifestyle to an urban setting, it is also probable that many more Hawaiians had actually moved to Honolulu and the other towns than were counted in the population, the others having gone to their graves. Through it all the number of Hawaiians continued precipitously to decline, and observers began to speak of the imminent disappearance of the Hawaiian race.

THE LEGACY OF SANDALWOOD

The exploitation of the commoners by the ali'i only increased after the death of Kamehameha I, judging from the descriptions of conditions in the 1820s. The ravages of the wars of Kamehameha I were now replaced by new scourges, created by the growing emphases on commerce and Christianity. First, there was the pursuit of sandalwood, unregulated after Kamehameha's death, with the ali'i little concerned over the effects on their people caused by the pursuit of their own profit. In their quest for the consumer goods of the West, the ali'i burdened themselves with debts to be paid in sandalwood and ruthlessly exploited Hawaiian commoners in the rape of Hawai'i's forests. Failure to answer the call of the ali'i brought down instant punishment, which included the burning of the homes of the recalcitrant.[13]

The conditions of those who obeyed the orders were described by many visitors, including Sir George Simpson, who wrote that the wars of Kamehameha were "almost immediately succeeded by a still heavier scourge"—the pursuit of sandalwood. By granting to the ali'i unrestricted opportunities to harvest sandalwood, Kamehameha II had, Simpson wrote, surrendered control of the trade to chiefs ''in whose eyes satins and velvets, china and plate, wines and sweetmeats, were infinitely more precious commodities than the lives of serfs,'' with the result that

men were driven like cattle to the hills, to every cleft in the rocks that contained a sapling of the sacred fuel, while, through the consequent neglect of agriculture and the fisheries, the women and children, without the controlling either of social decencies or domestic affections, were left to snatch from each other, the strong from the weak and the weak from the helpless, such miserable pittances as rapacious tyrants and hungry thralls were likely to spare for idle mouths.[14]

It was the sandalwood traders, primarily Americans, who encouraged the appetites of the ali'i for Western vessels, clothing, furniture, and other luxuries, and led them into a burden of debt that was to be satisfied by furnishing the traders with the fragrant wood. The sandalwood of Hawai'i was, however, limited both in quantity and quality and was insufficient to satisfy the burden of debt that the ali'i had been encouraged to entail. When those debts could not be paid, they became a major source of complaint among the foreign trading community and an open invitation to intervention by representatives of their governments.[15]

For the Americans, both Lieutenant John (''Mad Jack'') Percival, in the USS *Dolphin* and Captain Thomas ap Catesby Jones in the USS *Peacock* obtained formal recognition by the chiefs of their debts to U.S. citizens in 1826. In that year the burden of the consumerism of the ali'i was transferred to the shoulders of Hawaiian commoners, both male and female. Late in that year a tax law was adopted that was designed to help the chiefs pay off their sandalwood debts. This law required each able-bodied man in the kingdom to deliver to the authorities before September 1, 1827, a specified quantity of sandalwood, or four Spanish dollars or other equivalent, in exchange for which each man was allowed to cut a smaller amount of sandalwood for himself. Each woman was also required to furnish a mat, 6' by 12', a kapa of equal value, or the sum of one Spanish dollar. Payment of this unreasonable tax was predictably irregular, however, and when Captain W. B. Finch arrived on the USS *Vincennes* in 1829 he found the chiefs still in debt to Americans to the amount of at least $50,000.[16]

THE ARRIVAL OF THE MISSIONARIES

In October of 1819 the brig *Thaddeus* sailed from Boston for Hawai'i bearing a party of seventeen persons sent out by the American Board of Commissioners for Foreign Missions (ABCFM). These determined passengers represented the beginning of the American missionary effort that was to play a major role in the subsequent history of the Hawaiian people. In that same month there were already in Hawaiian waters two New England whaling ships, probably the first ever to use Hawaiian ports. They were the *Equator,* of Nantucket, and the *Balaena,* of New Bedford. Pioneers in the North Pacific whale fishery, these two vessels were followed in succeeding years by dozens and then hundreds of American whalers who would frequent Hawaiian ports.[17]

The convergence of these two new groups of Americans on the Hawaiian Islands created new interests that soon dwarfed those of the earlier traders. Their importance to the United States, moreover, became such that before long they required some form of official cognizance be taken of them, thus creating the first U.S. policies toward the Hawaiian kingdom.

These new American interests also added new forces for change in the life-style of the people of the islands. To the stresses being created for Hawaiians by modernization, Westernization, and urbanization were added after 1820 the influence of the Puritan missionaries who contributed to Hawaiian social disorganization through their manipulation of Hawaiian leaders. The missionaries were the most powerful source of American influence upon the people of Hawai'i for decades after 1820. Arriving only months after the death of Kamehameha I, they found that even more recently the Hawaiian system of *kapu* had been overthrown, idols burned, and much of the traditional religion abandoned, at least by the principal chiefs. This revolution in Hawaiian religious and social life represented, for one thing, the eroding of native beliefs as a result of contact with the culture of the West. The contempt of European visitors for the superstitions and kapu system of the islanders had shaken Hawaiians' faith in them. The impact of this "revolution" upon their entire society paved the way for missionaries in a manner that the latter could only regard as "providential."[18]

Without the guiding hand of Kamehameha I, and without the measure of social stability provided by the old faith, Hawai'i's principal chiefs began to lean more heavily on whites for advice in matters political and social as well as religious and moral. Of the foreigners among them, the chiefs apparently concluded that the missionaries were more honest and more disinterested than most. For their part, the missionaries soon decided that the secular and religious sides of Hawaiian life were inseparable, a belief congenial to their Puritan faith.

Before their first decade in the islands was over, therefore, missionaries were providing advice to the chiefs and kings in matters of law and government, as well as on "civilized" social ethics, Puritan style. They also took the first steps toward building a system of public education based upon a written Hawaiian language. In all these endeavors Hiram Bingham, first leader of the mission, and his colleagues sought to impose Puritan standards of religious and social behavior on the Hawaiians to an extent unmatched anywhere else in the world.[19]

If the founders of the Hawaiian mission felt compelled to voice many complaints against the behavior of their fellow countrymen in Hawai'i, theirs was still an Americanizing influence upon the native people of the islands. This did not mean that the missionaries initially sought or advocated American political influence there, though some of their critics would later charge them with it. That would have interfered with their plans for building a Puritan commonwealth free from outside corrupting influences. They had not been sent out by their government or by a private agency with imperial ambitions. But when faced with the threat of political control by any other major power, the American missionaries in Hawai'i were quick to reveal their national allegiance.[20]

In the meantime, they tried to create an independent, prosperous, peaceful, and Puritan commonwealth capable of maintaining its existence against Western colonial expansion. With the support of some naval officers and even some merchants, mission leaders counseled the chiefs toward the adoption of ''made,'' as opposed to traditional, laws, printed for all to see. This they did with the Bible and the legal and eventually constitutional systems of the United States as guides. A decree of December 1823 ordered a strict Puritanical observance of the sabbath. Another laid the basis for a system of compulsory education in Hawaiian, for which the Puritan missionaries would be the sole suppliers of written materials. Then they influenced a series of chiefly orders that created a miniature code of laws against not only murder and theft, but which also contained Puritanical proscriptions against such things as adultery and fornication.[21]

The Puritan conception of the relationship between pulpit and politics found congenial surroundings in the Hawaiian tradition of government that relied on a kapu system enforced by religion as the means of policing society. In the Puritan view, however, government was the instrument for forcing morality on an unwilling populace in the hope that eventually they would lead moral lives without the necessity for such external pressure. This was the concept that had guided the Puritans during their brief rule of England in the early seventeenth century, and in their early settlements in New England. The idea that government should be a moral instrument was not new with the Puritans, but their definition of immoral behavior pushed beyond any reasonable limits. Puritans were, for example, consumed with the view that idleness was ''sinful''—''the very rust and canker of the soul.'' As one wrote in seventeenth-century England: ''God hates the slothful.''[22]

Puritans also insisted on defining, themselves, the means by which people should pursue ''happiness.'' Happiness was to be sought by the people in pleasing God, not themselves. ''Natural'' man anywhere was the enemy of the Puritans, and, says one scholar, ''the mode of thought and feeling and repression which they wished to impose was totally unnatural.''[23] In short, it would be impossible to find any group more at variance with the views of the Enlightenment or the lifestyle of the Hawaiians than the Puritans.

Their efforts to impose Puritan morality on the Hawaiians brought the missionaries into conflict with other Americans resident and transient in the islands, particularly the whalers. Others, including American naval officers, likewise criticized the tyrannical nature of their regime, and French visitors, perhaps most influenced by Enlightenment views concerning the ''noble savage,'' were especially denunciatory. Even an American missionary of less radical views wrote, after visiting the islands, that the lifestyle the Hawaiian mission was seeking to impose on the Hawaiians was "more like strict old Puritanism than any other national exemplification of religion, which the world at present knows."[24]

The result was that the missionaries did not seek to bring the Hawaiians to modern life through a gradual evolution, based on the culture and institutions that had served the Hawaiians well for centuries. Nor did they seek simply to convert the Hawaiians to Christianity, as less radical missionaries might have done. Instead, they sought to eradicate everything that they saw, and to seek virtually an overnight revolution, thus shattering the remaining links between the Hawaiians of the post–1820 world and the generations that had preceded them, even as other aspects of the Western culture were doing the same. The combination left the Hawaiian people with virtually nothing from the past to which they could cling in confronting the present and future. The missionary Hiram Bingham gloated over the success of the "experiment" in his memoirs, writing:

It was not a matter of wonder that any agreeable substitute, moral, literary, or religious, which should be generally adopted by the people in the place of gambling, or any influence that should speedily put an end to the practice of that vice, while our proposed substitute was openly and diligently, but kindly, urged upon the mass, should be supposed, whether correctly or not, to have nearly abolished the sports of all classes of the people throughout the Sandwich Islands. The experiment was interesting.[25]

By 1822 the mission was operating a printing press that was producing educational materials and religious texts in Hawaiian, which the missionaries had made a written language. The first newspapers, periodicals, printed proclamations, and laws were turned out on mission presses in Hawaiian or English. Control of the output of these presses naturally gave the Puritan missionaries a strong instrument with which to influence an increasingly literate Hawaiian society. This merely supplemented the influence exerted upon the Hawaiians through sermons, lectures, and consultations with both chiefs and commoners.[26]

In addition to their influence in the islands, the missionaries shaped American knowledge and attitudes concerning Hawai'i and the Pacific by a variety of means. They wrote letters home, to families and friends, and they wrote reports to home congregations and to the missionary board in Boston. Some of them wrote books, which were apparently widely read, often by people who then passed on the view of Hawai'i and the Pacific that they contained. Occasionally some missionaries wrote to officers of the government in explanation, solicited and unsolicited, of their conduct in events that touched on governmental relations. Finally, missionaries from Hawai'i, or their children, visited the United States and were frequently called on to address church meetings on the subject of God's (and America's) work in the Pacific. Put together, these represented an influence in shaping American views of Hawai'i and the Pacific quite out of proportion to the number of people involved in the mission.

Like their British counterparts of the London Missionary Society, the American missionaries possessed a strong organization headed by the American Board of Commissioners for Foreign Missions, but supported and maintained by hundreds of individual church groups throughout the United States. Here was the potential for a pressure group able to rival any that then existed among chambers of commerce or Washington-centered bureaucracies. Had it strongly and consistently raised its voice in support of an aggressive program of territorial expansion in Hawai'i or elsewhere in the Pacific the history of U.S. policy in the area might have been far different.

By the 1830s, then, the missionaries' concern for the welfare of their Hawaiian charges extended far beyond purely spiritual matters, and the survival of the mission became mingled in their thinking with the survival of the Hawaiian people and their independence. Under increasing pressure from British, French, and American foreigners in their midst, it began to appear that the islanders might be on the verge of losing control of their lands and economy, if not their political sovereignty. At that point, in 1836, memorials from mission leaders and the Hawaiian king and chiefs were sent to the ABCFM in Boston asking that instructors be sent to the islands to give training in industrial arts and other aspects of the secular civilization of the West. Only with such preparation, went the plea, might the Hawaiians hope to continue to control their own destinies.[27]

The memorials unfortunately ran afoul of a shortage of funds caused by the financial panic of 1837 in the United States, as well as of the conservative reluctance of the board members to see the mission become involved in nonreligious affairs. If missionaries were to become formal advisors or ministers of the Hawaiian monarchs, they would have to leave the mission.[28]

THE WHALERS

As had been the case with the fur traders, the original purpose of the whalers in touching at the Hawaiian group was to secure wood, water, fresh provisions, and recreation. As the volume and regularity of exchange increased, the bargaining position of the Hawaiians improved somewhat, and measures for increasing production of supplies for so many ships were taken under orders from the chiefs. The growing foreign population added to the demand, as did the increasing number of Hawaiians in the port towns who were now divorced from their earlier self-sufficiency. As the urban and maritime market grew in the 1820s and 1830s, the earlier limited forays in market-oriented agriculture by Hawaiian farmers were expanded, although their full development would take place in the heyday of the whaling industry in the 1840s and 1850s and so will be described in the next chapter.[29]

By 1829 the first U.S. commercial agent at Honolulu, John C. Jones, estimated that the value of American commerce passing through Honolulu each year, including both ships and goods, had reached some $5,270,000. This far exceeded the volume of trade or investment in the islands by any other foreign nations at the time, and as the dominance of the Americans in the whale fishery of the northern Pacific increased in succeeding years, the primacy of U.S. influence in this major center of the business grew correspondingly.[30]

It would be no exaggeration to say that from 1830 until at least the mid–1850s the whale fishery was the central force in the money economy of the Hawaiian kingdom. It supported merchandising, shipfitting and repairing, dockside labors, the entertainment industries, and the production of an exportable surplus of supplies and provisions. It also provided, through various levies, including fines, a large part of the revenues of the Hawaiian government.

Hawai'i, then, had already begun to exhibit in the 1820s and 1830s the profound influences of the two major American interests in the islands. It increasingly owed its major financial support and public prosperity to the presence of the whalers, at the same time that the Puritan missionaries were beginning to dominate the government and to use it as their instrument for implementing sweeping and radical changes in the daily lives and culture of the Hawaiian people.

INTERESTS AND INFLUENCES

More than one writer at that time and later found it strangely ironic that these two groups—whalers and missionaries—who were so often at swords' points, should together have acted so powerfully to increase American influence in Hawai'i. When the Hawaiian chiefs turned to the Puritans for advice in controlling unruly seamen and unscrupulous traders, the first printed laws of the Hawaiian kingdom were laid down for all groups to obey, much to the chagrin of the whalers and other American visitors.

In their disputes with whalers, sailors, and merchants, missionary leaders sometimes took their grievances to the representatives of U.S. authority in the Pacific, the naval commanders. The U.S. commercial agent at Honolulu, John C. Jones, was unsympathetic to missionary complaints. Well before 1830, in fact, he and the British consul Richard Charlton were among the most vocal critics and opponents of missionary influence in the Hawaiian government, and leaders of the missionary group were seeking to have Jones replaced. Naval officers, too, such as Lieutenant Percival of USS *Dolphin*, learned to their regret the power of missionary influence.[31]

In Hawai'i, as elsewhere in the Pacific, the meeting and competition of citizens of different foreign nations frequently created mutual suspicions of ulterior motives. British observers, like Consul Charlton for example, viewed the American missionaries as conscious agents of expansionist aims of the United States. Americans worried that the visit of Kamehameha II (Liholiho) and his queen to England in 1823–1824 would lead to the assumption of a British protectorate over the islands, especially in view of past statements the king had made. The deaths of the king and queen in London, however, ended any designs he might have harbored for placing Hawai'i under British control.[32]

Washington had not been totally unaware of events in the mid-Pacific kingdom. Commercial agent Jones was reporting on the importance of the American stake in the trade there and on the mounting debts of the chiefs resulting from the sandalwood trade. The missionaries, at the same time, were busily and voluminously publicizing their activities in the islands. It was partly for these reasons, and partly out of concern over the increasing naval activity of European powers in the Pacific, that a series of visits were made by U.S. Navy ships to Hawai'i in the 1820s, including those of the *Dolphin* and the *Peacock* earlier mentioned. Captain Jones of the latter ship actually went so far as to sign a treaty with the Hawaiian leaders that, though not acted upon by the U.S. Senate, nevertheless served as the basis of Hawai'i's relations with the United States for years.[33]

The 1830s brought sharp increases in international rivalry in Hawai'i and much of the rest of Polynesia. It does not appear, however, that U.S. policy toward these island groups was strongly influenced by considerations of a strategic or political nature at that time. The protection of the lives and property of American citizens continued to be the chief function of U.S. naval officers in their dealings with Hawaiian authorities. Naval commanders were enjoined to respect the authority of native governments and to maintain friendly relations with them. If American influence in Hawai'i grew, it was because of the private activities of Americans there—whalers, missionaries, merchants, and later the sugar planters—each pursuing their own interests and not as appointed or conscious agents of a national policy of expansion in Hawai'i.[34]

The aggressive actions of the French in the Pacific toward the end of the 1830s, however, stirred both the British and Americans in the area to considerations of national policy. Content to pursue their commercial or missionary activities free from regulation by Washington, the Americans nevertheless preferred to seek protection, even the control that might accompany it, from their national government rather than face the prospect of French domination of the islands and of their interests there. Between 1836 and 1839, especially, French activity in Hawai'i alarmed both Hawaiian leaders and American missionaries.

HAWAIIAN RESPONSE

Under the pressure of threats from French and British naval commanders, sometimes supported by the American commercial agent Jones, the Hawaiian government was compelled to accept a series of unequal treaties or agreements limiting its control over foreigners resident in the kingdom. Both the chiefs and their foreign advisors came to realize the necessity of making their form of government correspond to Western legal norms if they wished foreign powers to recognize Hawaiian sovereignty. In this situation they turned principally to American advisors and American political principles, finding in the missionaries, in their opinion, the most nearly disinterested part of the foreign community.[35]

Accordingly, the Hawaiian government first asked Reverend Lorrin Andrews to serve as advisor in such matters. Andrews, however, was unwilling to leave his duties at the mission academy in Lahaina to step into a wasp's nest. The kingdom then asked the Reverend William Richards to look for a suitable person in the United States while he was on a home visit. When he returned in 1838 without finding an advisor for the chiefs, Richards was, himself, appointed to the post of advisor on foreign affairs to the Hawaiian king and chiefs.[36]

Richards and his successors rendered vitally important services to Kamehameha III, and the store of experience and learning on which they drew came from an Anglo-American heritage. Both Richards and Dr. Gerrit P. Judd, who succeeded him as advisor to the king and then as chief minister, continued to be missionaries and Americans at heart, even as they served the Hawaiians. This was reflected in their attitudes toward those of other religious persuasions and other nations. Both men were accused by fellow Americans, as well as by the British and French, of serving their own and their co-religionists' interests at the expense of others, including the Hawaiians.[37]

Richards's functions were advisory and instructional in nature, but they were apparently closely attended by the principal chiefs, and his advice was frequently followed on economic as well as political matters. In 1839, partly as a result of missionary advice, a declaration of rights and code of laws were proclaimed, and in 1840 the chiefs adopted a written constitution for the monarchy. In both, the convictions of American advisors concerning personal rights and limited executive authority were clearly shown. Though the chiefs still retained their decision-making role, one Hawaiian historian contends that that role became less firm in defending traditional ways with the passing of the older chiefs of Kamehameha's time.[38]

Reform of internal institutions was not enough, however, to assure the maintenance of Hawaiian sovereignty. At the beginning of the 1840s New Zealand, the Marquesas, and Tahiti succumbed to European domination, and fears increased in Honolulu that Hawai'i's turn could not be far off. The one hope for continued freedom seemed to lie in securing from the three powers most interested—the United States, Britain, and France—a common recognition of Hawai'i's independence, even a tripartite guarantee of it, if possible. Some such recognition might have been inferred from the appointment of consuls to reside in the islands or by the signing of specific treaties with the monarchy, but that was an imperfect recognition at best. Determined to remedy the situation as best it might, the Hawaiian kingdom now began a series of efforts to negotiate formal recognition of its independence.

THE PURSUIT OF DIPLOMATIC RECOGNITION

The quest of the Hawaiian kingdom for recognition of its independence by Western powers began in earnest in the 1840s. Two ineffectual attempts at obtaining such recognition from the United States were made early in the decade by Thomas J. Farnham and Peter A. Brinsmade. Neither man was fully accredited by the Hawaiian government, and both had private motives for their actions that would have made them unsuitable as diplomats even if they had possessed such accreditation.[39]

In 1842 Sir George Simpson, governor of the Hudson's Bay Company for North America, visited Hawai'i and impressed the governing authorities with his abilities and his interest in their affairs. Simpson was asked, at his own suggestion, to approach the British government on behalf of Hawai'i, but he also suggested that William Richards be sent to the United States to seek recognition and that Richards be empowered to negotiate treaties with Britain and France.[40]

Following Simpson's suggestion, the Hawaiian government appointed Richards and Ha'alilio, the king's secretary, as commissioners to the United States, Great Britain, and France, with the object of securing from those countries formal recognition of Hawai'i's independent political status. Simpson was to assist the Hawaiian commissioners in London after they had first visited Washington.

Arriving in Washington in December 1842, Richards and Ha'alilio found American officials, especially Secretary of State Daniel Webster, quite uninformed on matters concerning Hawai'i. Moreover, Webster was preoccupied with other concerns and not deeply interested, at first, in the mission on which the two representatives from Honolulu had come. In vain they cited the major roles played by Americans in raising Hawai'i to the status of a literate, Christian nation, and the importance of the islands to American commerce. Webster temporized and suggested they obtain recognition from Great Britain first.

Eventually, however, the intervention of friends from both the mercantile and mission fields succeeded in gaining the attention of members of Congress, notably Massachusetts representative Caleb Cushing, and through them access to the secretary of state. Still, Richards felt that Webster was uninformed, uninterested, and merely putting them off. Only when Richards suggested to a congressional acquaintance that Hawai'i might put itself under British protection if recognition could not be obtained from the United States did he finally get some action.[41]

The two Hawaiian commissioners met again with Secretary Webster and later with President Tyler. They found the administration suddenly more interested in their mission, and at the end of December 1842, they received a statement of U.S. policy toward Hawai'i. While it did not constitute formal recognition, the declaration went some distance toward meeting the desires of Kamehameha II and the chiefs. The statement by Webster read, in part:

The United States have regarded the existing authorities in the Sandwich Islands as a Government suited to the condition of the people, and resting on their own choice; and the President is of opinion that the interests of all the commercial nations require that this Government should not be interfered with by foreign powers. Of the vessels which visit the islands, it is known that a great majority belong to the United States. The United States, therefore, are more interested in the fate of the islands and of their Government, than any other nation can be; and this consideration induces the President to be quite willing to declare, as the sense of the Government of the United States, that the Government of the Sandwich Islands ought to be respected; that no power ought either to take possession of the islands as a conquest, or for the purpose of colonization, and that no power ought to seek for any undue control over the existing Government, or any exclusive privileges or preferences in matters of commerce.

Entertaining these sentiments, the President does not see any present necessity for the negotiation of a formal treaty, or for the appointment or reception of diplomatic characters. A consul or agent from the Government will continue to reside in the islands.[42]

Then, in a special message to Congress that accompanied copies of the correspondence between the State Department and the Hawaiian envoys, Webster added, speaking in the name of the President:

Considering, therefore, that the United States possesses so very large a share of the intercourse with those islands, it is deemed not unfit to make the declaration that their Government seeks nevertheless no peculiar advantages, no exclusive control over the Hawaiian Government, but is content with its independent existence, and anxiously wishes for its security and prosperity. Its forbearance in this respect, under the circumstances of the very large intercourse of their citizens with the islands, would justify the Government, should events hereafter arise, to require it, in making a decided remonstrance against the adoption of an opposite policy by any other power.[43]

This material was sent to Congress at the same time as that dealing with recent events and American interests and policies in China, including information concerning Britain's recently concluded Treaty of Nanking. While the attention of Congress was thus directed toward the Pacific in the debate over a first diplomatic mission to China, there also arrived news of the French seizure of the Marquesas Islands and their establishment of a protectorate in Tahiti. As if this were not enough, there occurred in early 1843 the "seizure" of the Hawaiian Islands by Lord George Paulet, Commander of HMS *Carysfort.*

At few moments in the entire nineteenth century was American attention so strongly attracted to the Pacific area and to the varied interests of their countrymen there. It is not surprising, then, that the first forthright statements of national policy concerning China, Hawai'i, and, in a sense, Oregon should have emerged within a matter of months.[44]

The attitude taken by the United States toward Hawai'i was something of a disappointment for Richards and Ha'alilio. While the statement of policy might possibly strengthen the defense of Hawaiian independence, the American refusal to enter into a formal treaty of recognition provided a poor precedent for obtaining such recognition from London or Paris. The subsequent action of Congress in voting to send a commissioner to Honolulu, in addition to a consul, was more promising. Yet it was a crisis in Anglo-French relations, produced by French action in Tahiti, and Lord Paulet's unauthorized seizure of Hawai'i that made it possible for the Hawaiian representatives to secure treaties with the European powers.

The United States neither assisted in this achievement nor joined in it. The British government appears to have been deeply disturbed by French and American reactions to Paulet's seizure of Hawai'i, especially since it came at a time when Britain was condemning France's similar action in Tahiti. A powerful promissory faction within the British foreign policy establishment was also making its influence felt in matters dealing with the Pacific islands.[45]

The international discussion of Hawai'i's future became involved with questions of claims against the island monarchy by various British and French subjects, and it was not until late November 1843 that the two governments could agree on a joint recognition of the independence and territorial integrity of Hawai'i. Both powers hoped to induce the United States to join them in this act of recognition and in a common pledge not to consider annexation of Hawai'i in the future. In this they were disappointed. President Tyler replied to an inquiry by the British and French ministers in Washington in May of 1844 that participation in such a pact would violate the traditional policy of the United States against entering upon such international commitments. Apparently this was a rationalization based on Jefferson's famed injunction against "entangling alliances." It could also be considered an extension into the Northeast Pacific of the Monroe Doctrine. Secretary of State Calhoun told all concerned that it was the policy of the United States to recognize Hawai'i's independence. There was no promise of future action.[46]

AMERICANS IN HAWAI'I II

POSTTREATY PROBLEMS

The treaties and statements of 1843–1844 did not fully resolve all the international problems of the Hawaiian kingdom. Special privileges of an extraterritorial type had been written into agreements forced on the Hawaiians by the naval representatives of Britain and France between 1836 and 1839. Though the United States had not been a party to these, its general most-favored-nation policy, indicated in the Thomas ap Catesby Jones agreement of 1826, indicated that its citizens might expect to receive the same privileges accorded other foreigners. The Hawaiian commissioners in 1842–1843 had tried to secure the removal of the most objectionable parts of the French treaty, forced on the kingdom by Captain Laplace in 1839. In this they were unsuccessful, and, in fact, relations with Great Britain and the United States were embittered in the 1840s by the insistence of their representatives in Honolulu, with support at least from London, upon strict interpretation of the unequal provisions of the treaties.[1]

George Brown was the first U.S. commissioner (not minister) to Hawai'i, and he arrived at Honolulu in 1843. His instructions from Secretary of State Webster specifically stated: "It is not deemed expedient at this juncture to fully recognize the independence of the islands or the right of their Government to that equality of treatment and consideration which is due and usually allowed to those Governments to which we send and from whom we receive diplomatic agents of the ordinary ranks." Acting on this and on Webster's warning to be wary of foreign intrigues, Brown behaved in such an overbearing, arbitrary fashion as to antagonize the king and Hawaiian officials. They severed relations with him, and the king asked for his recall.[2]

At the beginning of the Polk administration a new commissioner, Anthony Ten Eyck, was appointed to succeed Brown, and he, too, managed to alienate the government of Kamehameha III by tactless and bullying behavior. Neither of these men was a diplomat by training, or a merchant, or familiar with Hawai'i and the Pacific before his appointment. They represented a tendency of the time to fill minor posts abroad with the offscourings of American politics or those with political connections, instead of men with some knowledge of their task.

The intrigues of foreigners and the prominence of some of them, especially Americans, in the government of the king stimulated rumblings of discontent among portions of the Hawaiian population in the 1840s. Despite Hawaiian pleas for the removal of these foreigners, however, their help was needed and their influence continued, although fears were growing that the very independence that men like Dr. G. P. Judd, a former missionary, and Robert Crichton Wyllie, an English physician and merchant, were trying to uphold was endangered.[3]

ECONOMIC CHANGE

One fundamental cause of the growing foreign influence in the Hawaiian government sprang from the increasing complexity of the kingdom's economic ties with the outside world. Commissioner Brown reported to Washington shortly after his arrival in Honolulu that U.S. vessels and cargoes worth more than $8 million had been in Hawaiian ports within the preceding nine months of 1843 and that the trade was steadily growing. Hawaiians lacked the commercial experience and connections to meet the needs of such an extensive and complicated traffic, and most of the business transacted with foreign whaling and merchant vessels was now conducted by foreign merchant firms, chiefly American owned.

Moreover, as sugar planting developed, along with other varieties of large-scale agricultural production for export, foreign management and capital became even more deeply involved in the internal economy of Hawai'i. All of these changes raised fundamental questions about property rights, land tenure, and personal legal status that called for more precise legislation, experienced jurists, and firmer administrative organization, which in turn seemed to necessitate foreign counsel. In each case it was American influence that, although not alone, predominated.[4]

From the 1820s into the 1850s the most important form of money-economy business (excluding the Hawaiians' basic subsistence economy that still survived) was the supplying and equipping of whaling and merchant ships stopping at island ports. Plantation revenues still played a minor role at that time.

Of lesser importance, at least down to the immediate period of the California gold rush, was Hawai'i's growing role as a distributing center for trade with various parts of the American Pacific coast. Goods shipped to Oregon or California ports were frequently consigned to agents of such Boston firms as Bryant and Sturgis, Marshall Wildes, and others for transshipment to their destinations.

The Hudson's Bay Company established commercial contact with Hawai'i from its base at Fort Vancouver, on the Columbia, and in 1834 the company opened an agency in Honolulu. After the establishment of American control of Oregon and California, with merchant communities of a permanent character at San Francisco and other coastal ports, this part of Honolulu's commercial role diminished in importance.[5]

RECIPROCITY OR ANNEXATION?

For many years the establishment of a reciprocally advantageous trade relationship between the United States and Hawai'i was a subject of discussion in mercantile and then in government circles in the islands. This gave rise to talk of a possible reciprocity treaty with the United States, or even of annexation. As time went on, negotiation of a reciprocity treaty was frequently advocated or opposed on the grounds that it might aid or hinder the prospects of a political union. Annexationists, from the beginning, were to be found among the Americans in Hawai'i. The Hawaiians steadfastly clung to their monarchy and independence.[6]

The view taken varied, of course, with the hopes or fears of those on either side of the annexation question. In 1849 the eagerness of Hawaiian officials for reciprocity met with American desires to regularize commercial relations, and a treaty of amity and commerce was drawn up. Actually, two separate treaty drafts were signed, and the United States Senate combined the preferred provisions of each into the final document. Designed to run for ten years, this first treaty provided for most-favored-nation treatment on tariff arrangements, with certain special provisions dealing with the rights of American whalers in Hawaiian ports and of U.S. citizens resident in the island kingdom. The 1849 treaty at last marked full and clear diplomatic recognition of the government of Hawai'i by the United States.[7]

During the negotiations that led up to the 1849 treaty, both Commissioners George Brown and Anthony Ten Eyck took very srong stands in seeking extra-territorial privileges for Americans in Hawai'i. In both cases they seem to have been influenced, in part, by members of the American community in Honolulu who opposed the government and its missionary advisors. It is an interesting case of men on the scene developing policy attitudes quite out of tune with those of their government at home. Conflicts of this sort are not uncommon in the history of international relations, but they seem to have plagued U.S. relations in the Pacific to a remarkable degree.

At midcentury Hawai'i experienced two more demonstrations of the precarious nature of its independence. In August 1849 a French naval squadron under Rear Admiral Legoarant de Tromelin sailed into Honolulu harbor and supported demands being made upon the Hawaiian authorities by French consul Guillaume Patrice Dillon.[8] The French forces seized the fort at Honolulu and the king's yacht and made peremptory demands upon the government before withdrawing.

The United States took no direct action at the time, though President Zachary Taylor restated the special interest of the United States in Hawai'i, and America's opposition to any foreign attempt to take control there, as part of his annual message to Congress in December 1849. Two years later President Millard Fillmore repeated these sentiments, with the usual references to the magnitude of American commercial and whaling interests in the islands and "the consideration that they lie in the course of the great trade which must at no distant day be carried on between the western coast of North America and eastern Asia."[9]

In an effort to settle the outstanding difficulties with France, and also to strengthen the commitment of the major powers to Hawai'i's independence, Dr. Judd was sent on a mission to Paris, via Washington and London, late in 1849, taking with him the two young princes in line for the Hawaiian throne. Negotiations with the French proved generally unsatisfactory, but Judd did derive some comfort from new American expressions of opposition to any foreign interference with Hawai'i's sovereignty.[10] After an interview with Secretary of State Clayton at the end of May 1850, Judd wrote in his private journal:

Mr. Clayton said that he should notify France and England that his Govt. will not look with indifference upon any act of oppression committed or any attempt to take the Islands. . . . The U.S. do not want the Islands but will not permit any other nation to have them. I asked if the U.S. would go to war on our account. He replied yes—that is they would send a force and retake the Islands for the King and if that made a war they would carry it out.[11]

It must be noted, however, that successive administrations in Washington refused to pledge that the United States would never consider annexation of Hawai'i. President Fillmore was apparently ready to make such a pledge, but he left office before any agreement could be drawn up. The British and French ministers in Washington were delighted with Fillmore's change of view, but the advent of the expansion-minded Franklin Pierce brought a reversion to the previous policy.[12]

When Hawaiian fears of French designs were renewed by the appearance of another of that country's warships bearing new demands, Hawaiian officials approached both British and American representatives in search of protection from France should it be needed.[13] A proclamation placing the Hawaiian kingdom under the "protection and safeguard of the United States of America until some arrangements can be made to place our said relations with France upon a footing compatible with my rights as an independent sovereign" was actually signed by Kamehameha III and presented to the U.S. commissioner Luther Severance to be kept secret unless and until it might be needed to prevent a French seizure. Lacking instructions from Washington in the matter, Severance could only give private assurances that the United States would defend its flag in Hawai'i if it should be necessary to raise it. He made plans with Captain William

H. Gardner, of USS *Vandalia,* then in port, for action in the event of a French attempt to raise its flag over the islands.[14]

FILIBUSTERS

Curiously enough, it was concern over possible aggression against Hawai'i by Americans that swept through the islands in 1851. The California gold rush had brought a mixed bag of rough characters to the Pacific, along with more reputable citizens. Disappointed in their hopes of striking it rich, some of these men wandered about the Pacific for a time, creating disorder and unease wherever they went, sometimes as far away as the coasts of China and Australia. In 1850 and 1851 consuls and missionaries in various parts of the Pacific island world reported the presence or passage of drifters bound to or from the gold fields of California or Australia. While not all these persons were Americans, some groups raised real fears of a seizure of power in Hawai'i and possible forced annexation to the United States between 1851 and 1854.[15]

Reports of French designs on the Hawaiian group and the high-handed actions of de Tromelin and Dillon were picked up by the San Francisco press. The *Alta California* suggested on April 22, 1851, that though matters had apparently quieted a bit, "the French will again persist and the King's government refusing will be obliged to seek an alliance . . . with the United States, or throw them under our protection, or yield themselves up and become a part of our Union." Then, in a simile that was often used by expansionists in reference to both Cuba and Hawai'i, the editorial concluded, "The pear is nearly ripe; we have scarcely to shake the tree in order to bring the luscious fruit readily into our lap."

Expansionist sentiment also flared over rumors reaching California that Secretary Webster had refused to accept an alleged offer to place the islands under U.S. control.[16] In June 1852 Senator John B. Weller of California offered a resolution, passed by the United States Senate, that called upon the president to provide information as to whether or not such an annexation proposal had been received from Hawai'i. The administration twice rejected the request, fueling sharp criticism of its "English policy" from certain members of Congress, not all in the opposing party.[17]

Meanwhile, repeated rumors were reaching Honolulu that filibustering expeditions were actually being planned in California in late 1851 and 1852. The arrival of a suspicious-looking group in November 1851 aboard the clipper *Game Cock* was feared to be the opening of a campaign to seize the kingdom, and efforts were made to put the islands in a defensive posture. More valuable to the defense of the realm, probably, was the presence of cruising U.S. and British naval units. Upon inquiry at the State Department, the French minister in Washington was informed that federal authorities in California had been instructed to take steps to prevent filibustering against Hawai'i from U.S. soil. The threat, if threat there really was, passed, but it led to a serious effort to provide for the annexation of Hawai'i to the United States that actually reached the treaty stage.[18]

THE ANNEXATION TREATY OF 1854

The Whig party, which had won election of the Taylor-Fillmore ticket to office in 1848, had taken an anti-expansionist stand in its successful campaign against James K. Polk. Yet such a prominent Whig as William H. Seward, senator from New York, expressed feelings shared by others in that party when in 1852 he urged that an inquiry be made into the possibility of acquiring the Hawaiian Islands for the United States.[19] Talk of annexation was also heard in Hawai'i, but the American community in the islands appears to have been as divided in its sentiments as was the interested population in the United States. Most missionaries appear to have opposed annexation at first, and even later many approved of it only if absolutely necessary to avert some other foreign rule.

Both Dr. Judd and Richard Armstrong, for example, at first rejected the idea of annexation before coming to regard it as a lesser of possible evils. And some of the merchants showed little relish for inclusion in the tariff structure of the United States if it would harm their interests. Relatively few appear to have been much disappointed when the instrument of cession entrusted to Commissioner Severance during the French crisis was returned to the Hawaiian authorities, ending, at least for the time being, the prospect of a loss of sovereignty.[20]

The Democrats, trumpeting an expansionist program, were victorious in the American presidential campaign of 1852. Franklin Pierce announced that his administration would not be "controlled by any timid forebodings of evil from expansion."[21] While it is unlikely that he had Hawai'i specifically in mind in making this statement, events quickly put into his hands an opportunity to act there. Through most of 1853 there was intense political agitation in Honolulu, centering about efforts to remove the powerful influence of Dr. Judd from the cabinet. In this agitation the question of annexation was frequently raised, though in an equivocal manner. Some advocated a change in the cabinet, or in the constitution, in the hope that this would forestall annexation. Others insisted that removal of Judd, and the same constitutional changes, would hasten it. One small group of Americans memorialized the king to the effect that annexation would be desirable as a means of avoiding revolution. Talk of filibusters from California appeared once more, apparently raised by foreigners opposed to American annexation, but a few hotheads among the Americans also seem to have spoken of the possibility and may even have tried to encourage it.[22]

As earlier noted, the British and French ministers in Washington inquired late in 1853 as to the intentions of the United States toward Hawai'i, accompanying this with a new proposal for a tripartite guarantee of Hawaiian sovereignty. The proposal was rebuffed, as an earlier one had been, and Secretary of State William L. Marcy, while disavowing any plans to initiate annexation proposals, stated: "I will not conceal from you that it is highly probable that the Government as well as the Congress and People of the United States would be disposed to receive them" if they should come from Hawai'i.[23] He warned again that the United States would resist British or French efforts to take possession of the islands, and he asked the American ministers in London and Paris to determine how far the two powers were likely to go in resisting an American annexation.

The newly appointed U.S. commissioner to Hawai'i, David L. Gregg, became convinced, after reaching his post in December 1853, that a proposal of annexation would soon be made by the Hawaiian Crown, if only to forestall the ambitious revolutionary plans of a portion of the American community in Honolulu.[24] Gregg wrote in his diary that Judd had told him confidentially that Kamehameha III "had long been tired of the trouble of reigning and had frequently wished to propose annexation to the U.S."[25] This idea had been rumored for some years now, and it had reached the ears of interested parties over much of the Pacific and in the capitals of the major powers.

In February of 1854 Kamehameha III did direct that inquiries be made concerning the official U.S. attitude toward and terms for annexation. In response, Commissioner Gregg received authority from Washington to negotiate a treaty of annexation. By August of that year, Gregg and Foreign Minister Wyllie had completed a draft treaty that provided for the annexation of Hawai'i to the United States as a state "as soon as it can be done in consistency with the principles and requirements of the Federal Constitution." Annuities amounting to $300,000 were to be paid to the Hawaiian ruler and to the principal chiefs as designated by the king. In case of "emergency" the treaty was to be implemented at once.[26]

Prince Alexander Liholiho, the heir apparent, opposed this treaty, as did the British and French representatives in Honolulu and many, if not most, members of the Hawaiian and foreign communities. Foreign Minister Wyllie, born a British subject, and Judge William L. Lee, an American, joined with the king and crown prince in prolonging the negotiations in hopes that the immediate difficulties of the kingdom would pass. Through most of 1854 an agitated condition existed in Honolulu, however, fueled by business depression, talk of a violent uprising, and rumors of filibusters. At one time four foreign war vessels were in the port simultaneously, their commanders in touch with their national representatives on shore. All offered assistance, if needed and requested, to maintain order in the event of violence. In Washington both British and French representatives made known their governments' opposition to annexation of Hawai'i by the United States.[27]

Then, in December 1854, King Kamehameha III died. His young successor to the throne was an outspoken opponent of annexation, and one of his first official acts as monarch was to end the negotiations. This was a fortunate turn, for to have the treaty signed by the king and then rejected by the United States Senate would have been humiliating to the Hawaiians and damaging to American interests in Hawai'i. In retrospect, Secretary Marcy told Gregg that there was strong opposition in Congress to the proposal of statehood for Hawai'i, to the royal annuities, and to certain other aspects of the annexation proposal. Some of this was partisan politics, and some was based on deeper principle. Included, certainly, was the reluctance of Southern senators and representatives to add another free state to the union, and the determination of the Hawaiian authorities to accept no other status. It does not appear, however, that the expressed displeasure of Britain and France, alone, would have defeated the treaty. With an ongoing war in the Crimea against Russia, active intervention by those nations was highly unlikely, and Marcy and Pierce knew it.[28]

SUGAR AND RECIPROCITY

The basic conditions that gave Americans an initiative in influencing the Hawaiian kingdom's foreign relations centered in the powerful ties of economic and strategic interest that were still growing between the islands and the United States, especially its Pacific coast. The gold rush had mightily affected the money economy of Hawai'i, and the collapse of the boom market at San Francisco, coupled with a peaking of whaling activity, had much to do with the attitudes of some of those who had advised Kamehameha III to consider annexation by the United States. With the collapse of the annexation plan of 1854 and the accession of Kamehameha IV (Alexander Liholiho) to the throne, the political influence of Americans within the Hawaiian government was diminished. But new economic factors and a growing sense of strategic relations in the Pacific continued to maintain U.S. interest in the island kingdom. If there was a threat to Hawaiian sovereignty in the 1850s and after, it clearly came from the huge republic to the east.

One economic interest in the islands in which American initiative and capital were strongly involved was sugar planting. In the 1850s and 1860s this was a growing enterprise, limited, however, by problems of labor supply and marketing. For labor the planters found their first answer in the Hawaiian people, through the influence of their chiefs. Later, as the native population continued to decline while labor needs increased, workers were imported, especially from Asia. The principal market for Hawai'i's sugar was the United States, and at midcentury the American tariff laws made it difficult for any but the most efficient foreign producers to sell there profitably. Under the tariff law of 1846, foreign sugar paid a duty of 30 percent *ad valorem*. The planters and the Hawaiian government, therefore, were eager to secure relief from this tariff and offered in return to reduce Hawai'i's import duties on products from the United States.[29]

In 1855 U.S. commissioner Gregg recommended negotiation of a reciprocity agreement, ostensibly as a means of encouraging the maintenance of Hawaiian prosperity and independence. Hawai'i's chief justice, William L. Lee, traveled to the United States to conduct negotiations, and he was encouraged by the favorable attitudes of Senator Gwin of California and Secretary of State Marcy. President Pierce, however, doubted the constitutionality of granting special tariff favors to one country, even when made on a reciprocal basis. If it were necessary to extend the same privileges to other sugar-producing countries, he warned, both Hawaiian and domestic U.S. producers might be overwhelmed by the influx of cheap sugar from the Caribbean.[30]

Thus, Pierce singled out the objection that for two decades would stand as a principal barrier to any reciprocity treaty. Others, however, pointed out at the time that the proposed treaty would be much more valuable to Hawai'i than to the United States and might even lower American tariff revenues.

In the 1855 negotiations reciprocal free lists were worked out by the representatives of the United States and Hawai'i, the latter receiving strong support from Pacific coast traders who stood to profit from enhanced markets in the islands, especially for flour, fish, coal, and lumber. Judge Lee also raised the question of U.S. protection of Hawai'i from foreign intervention or filibusters, but obtained only a general statement of policy from Secretary Marcy. Marcy was willing to give specific assurance that the United States would do its legal utmost to prevent filibustering expeditions from American soil, but he refused to enter into a bilateral, or multipartite, nonintervention treaty or to offer a formal pledge of armed protection.[31]

The 1855 treaty, more popular in Hawai'i than in the United States, was not approved or even brought to a final vote in the Senate, and during the following years of civil conflict in the United States the issue could not be revived.

In 1863 the diplomatic rank of the U.S. representative in Honolulu was raised to that of minister, recognizing the progress of the kingdom as a civilized nation, and also denoting its increased importance to the United States. The action may also have been at least partly designed to forestall, in some way, the rise of British or French influence in the kingdom while the United States was helpless to intervene because of the Civil War.

During the latter 1860s and the 1870s further economic changes in Hawai'i made a reciprocity treaty with the United States more important than ever to the islands. As noted previously, a decline of whaling activity set in rapidly and almost totally collapsed. From 373,450 barrels of oil in 1852, the North Pacific whale fishery declined to about 63,000 barrels in 1860, and to less than 20,000 in 1872.[32]

The collapse of Pacific whaling brought about the extinction of most Honolulu businesses specializing in whaling items. Merchants formerly engaged in them had either to shift their investments or go out of business. A new base had to be found for the money economy of the kingdom and to furnish the public revenues on which the government had come to rely. The market economy was no longer merely a facade over the basic subsistence economy of the people. It was indispensable to the prosperity of the kingdom.

After a few years of generally depressed business conditions, a new base was found in the rise of sugar as the mainstay of Hawai'i's economy. Exports of sugar, which in 1855 amounted to 289,908 pounds, had reached 1,444,271 by 1860; 15,318,057 in 1865; and 23,129,101 by 1873. By the last date sugar had become a million dollar industry in the islands. It accounted for three-fourths of the value of Hawai'i's exports and a similar proportion of its public revenues.[33]

A number of auxiliary enterprises sprang up around this major agricultural industry, the majority of them in the hands of U.S. citizens or Hawaiian subjects of American ancestry. Commercial agencies, or factors, developed to market the sugar crop and to provide capital and conduct purchasing operations for the plantations. Some of the machinery used in the sugar mills and fields was manufactured locally, and the factors had a hand in financing that business. Shipping among the islands and between them and North America was improved and expanded, with slowly increasing reliance on steamships. In all of these and other sugar-related activities, American enterprise predominated, though with notable competition from British- and German-owned firms. Another tie to the American market developed during the 1860s with sugar refineries in the San Francisco Bay area, which processed the raw product from the islands.[34]

At the end of the 1860s a combination of factors in both the United States and Hawai'i led to a serious depression in the sugar business. This gave new impetus to the effort to secure a reciprocity treaty with the United States. Another influence in the same direction was an increase in California imports of sugar from Java, China, and the Philippines, when Hawaiian producers refused to enter into binding agreements with Pacific coast refiners. For a time these refining interests tried to hinder the reciprocity movement in an effort to put additional pressure on Hawaiian planters to give them exclusive marketing contracts.[35]

Important as reciprocity or annexation might appear to Americans in the Hawaiian Islands, however, the issue still did not appear to be of great consequence to many in Washington in the years after the Civil War. A new reciprocity agreement was drawn up in 1867 under instructions from Secretary of State Seward, but it too failed to win congressional approval, even though considerations of political and strategic importance were now added to the economic arguments. Reciprocity, it was argued, would bind the islands closer to the United States and thus frustrate supposed British or French ambitions for their control. One group argued that reciprocity would inevitably hasten annexation. Others insisted that by meeting the immediate needs of Hawai'i's business leaders, reciprocity would probably delay annexation or forestall it altogether.[36]

There was comparatively little argument, at first, about the possible strategic significance of Hawai'i to the United States as a naval and shipping base on transpacific routes, but the idea was there. U.S. minister to Hawai'i Edward McCook wrote to Secretary Seward in May 1867: "When the Pacific railroad is completed and the commerce of Asia directed to our Pacific ports, then these islands will be needed as a rendezvous for our Pacific navy, and a resort for merchant ships, and this [reciprocity] treaty will have prepared the way for their quiet absorption.''[37] Kept alive from session to session of Congress by extensions of the time for its approval, the reciprocity treaty of 1867 still failed to pass.

The Ulysses S. Grant administration at first showed even less sympathy than that of Andrew Johnson for a treaty with Hawai'i. Later, however, the issue was revived, and the strategic location and significance of the islands were given stronger emphasis by the new U.S. minister in Honolulu, Henry A. Peirce. This point, together with Hawai'i's apparent turn toward closer relations with Great Britain and its Pacific possessions, helped turn the trick. A state visit to Washington by Hawai'i's new king, Kalakaua, in 1875, dramatized Hawaiian-American relations, and in that year, at last, a reciprocity treaty was signed and then approved in the following year.

The fourth article of the treaty included this provision:

It is agreed on the part of His Hawaiian Majesty, that, so long as this treaty shall remain in force, he will not lease or otherwise dispose of or create any lien upon any port, harbor, or other territory in his dominion, or grant any special privilege or rights of use therein, to any other power, state, or government, nor make any treaty by which any other nation shall obtain the same privileges, relative to the admission of any articles free of duty, hereby secured to the United States.[38]

Washington had clearly in mind events transpiring elsewhere in the Pacific islands and in eastern Asia at that time.

STRATEGIC INTERESTS

In 1873 Major General John M. Schofield and Brigadier General B. S. Alexander visited Hawai'i on a confidential mission for the War Department to report on the potential strategic and commercial value of Pearl Harbor, on the island of Oahu near Honolulu. The mission coincided with negotiations for the reciprocity treaty, with the involvement of certain Americans in events in Samoa, and with continuing agitation for and against federal subsidies to Pacific shipping lines.[39]

During negotiation of the 1875 reciprocity treaty, in fact, certain men in Hawai'i conceived the idea of offering to the United States special privileges in Pearl Harbor as an inducement to approve the treaty. The same idea surfaced in Washington. Hawaiian opposition prevented any such grant at that time, but when renewal of the agreement came up for consideration in the following decade, exclusive American use of Pearl Harbor became an American condition for reciprocity, and it was incorporated in the new treaty.

By that time the growth of sugar production had so bound the Hawaiian kingdom to the United States, economically, that it was virtually impossible to refuse this further limitation on its sovereignty. At the same time, understanding of the strategic importance of the islands for the protection of American shipping and defense of the Pacific coast had reached the point where such a safeguard seemed essential, if only to keep any other power from establishing itself there. Neither the navy nor the War Department had any plans for military construction or development of the harbor at that time, however, and no effort would be made even to dredge the opening to it for more than thirty years thereafter.

This shift of emphasis from the protection of American lives and property to considerations of perceived national political and strategic interest was the most significant development in U.S. policy toward Hawai'i in the late nineteenth century. Hindsight demonstrates that the reciprocity treaty of 1875 was far more valuable to the planters in Hawai'i than it was to all but a few business interests in the United States. Over all, the treaty meant a net loss in tariff revenues to the United States, at a time when such revenues were still the principal source of federal revenue, and, thereafter, in the face of opposition from U.S. sugar producers, it became clear that considerations of political and strategic rather than economic advantage were ultimately responsible for the renewal of reciprocity in 1887.[40]

By that time a new spirit of expansionism was abroad in the United States, especially in sections of the media. To some it seemed a revival of the old Manifest Destiny idea, especially after the trauma of the Civil War and the political and economic reconstruction of the nation that had followed. Once again, as in an earlier period, recurrent rumors of foreign, i.e., British, French, and, later, Japanese, designs on Hawai'i were advanced as reasons for vigorous reassertion of a primary American interest there. Hawai'i was the "key to the dominion of the American Pacific," trumpeted Secretary of State James G. Blaine in 1881, and the United States, he promised, would "unhesitatingly meet the altered situation by seeking an avowedly American solution for the grave issues presented" if another power should seek to introduce a hostile influence there. Statements of this sort were still buttressed by references to the dominant role of Americans in Hawai'i's economic life, with the historic part played by American missionaries in introducing the arts of civilization in the islands a further rationale.[41]

One of the most eloquent and influential expansionist speakers and writers was Captain Alfred Thayer Mahan, of the United States Navy. In an article entitled "The United States Looking Outward," which he wrote for the *Atlantic Monthly* of December 1890, Mahan related Hawai'i to the military security of the United States and that of the future isthmian canal, which, he held, was vital for the future development of the nation. U.S. national security, he pointed out, was threatened by the political unrest in the Caribbean republics, in Central America, and in Hawai'i. Then, within two years of publication of Mahan's article, political unrest in Hawai'i entered a new and critical phase.[42]

THE DECLINE OF THE HAWAIIAN KINGDOM

Through the last half-century of its existence, the Hawaiian kingdom continued the decline that had begun with the death of Kamehameha I. Measures urged on the government by its foreign advisors for the improvement of the Hawaiians, whether sincerely motivated or not, only worsened their condition. Thus the "feudal system" that many missionaries claimed was a hindrance to Hawaiians' efforts to improve their condition was eliminated and fee simple ownership of land was instituted. At first limited to Hawaiians, such fee simple ownership of land was soon extended to foreigners, as well, in 1850. The Puritan revolution was now complete: Divorced of everything else from their past, the Hawaiians had now also been separated from their attachment to the land under the guise of granting them ownership of it. And, as Andrew Lind wrote, "once the conception of private property had permeated the masses and individual title had been secured, the sale of land to the more commercially minded foreigner was inevitable."[43]

A more serious problem for the continued viability of the Hawaiian monarchy has been documented by Lilikala Kame'eleihiwa in her book, *Native Land and Foreign Desires*. This was the rapid shrinkage of the land directly under the control of the king. This shrinkage not only led to reduced revenues for the sovereign but also curtailed the traditional basis of the power of any king—the ability to show generosity in the temporary grant of lands to his supporters. During Kamehameha I's time all the lands of the islands were under his control, but during the reigns of his successors, Kamehameha II and Kamehameha III, the lands under the direct control of the king shrank as a result of the schemes of Kaahumanu and others. In the course of aggrandizing themselves, Kaahumanu and her allies weakened the monarchy and contributed to its eventual collapse.[44]

With most of the land either owned by individual ali'i after the new land laws, or under the control—as government land—of the leading ali'i around the king, the legalization of fee simple land titles for foreigners set in motion for land what Kamehameha's death had provided for sandalwood. Just as the ali'i had denuded the Hawaiian forests of sandalwood in the early 1820s to obtain Western goods, now the same greed caused them to dispose of their lands to foreign buyers for, in many cases, a mere fraction of their real worth. As a consequence, beginning with the early 1850s more and more of Hawai'i's land passed not only from the hands of the king and government, but also from the hands even of Hawaiians.

If not inevitable, the process was at least a natural outcome of the conditions that existed in Hawai'i in the 1850s and 1860s. By 1853 the Hawaiian population had declined to barely 71,000. No matter what one accepts as the population of the islands at the time of Cook's arrival, it is evident that there were, at most, one-fourth as many Hawaiians in 1853 as seventy-five years earlier and perhaps only one-tenth as many. Moreover, by the early 1850s perhaps 50 percent of the Hawaiian population had abandoned their ahupua'a to live in the emerging towns or in close proximity to them. From the accounts of visitors to the islands during this period, it is apparent that the only areas being farmed with any enterprise by the Hawaiians were those near the ports of call of the whaling ships. Everywhere else, Western visitors wrote of abandoned farms, deteriorating irrigation systems, and neglected orchards.

In their farms around the thriving whaling ports, however, Hawaiian farmers were strikingly energetic and productive, more similar in the eyes of Western visitors to their European and American counterparts than to their fellow Polynesians. As one wrote: "It was a novelty in Polynesia to see persons along the road, bringing wood, charcoal, and provisions of various kinds, to supply a market; in short, a subdivision of labour, and regular system of industry, in accordance with the customs of Europeans."[45] Lieutenant Charles Wilkes likewise wrote: "One cannot but be struck with seeing the natives winding their way along the different thoroughfares, laden with all kinds of provisions, wood, charcoal, and milk, to supply the market and their regular customers. Indeed, there are quite as many thus employed as in any place of the same number of inhabitants in our own country."[46]

Others commented on the productivity of the Hawaiian farms around Honolulu, and on the great variety of fruits and vegetables they produced for the markets in the city. In addition to carrying them to the markets, Hawaiian men also hawked their wares directly to the residences of the town. Clearly, if a stimulus to industry existed for Hawaiian farmers, such as the whalers provided, they were capable of producing and marketing an array and quantity of goods that amazed Western visitors.[47]

The collapse of the whaling industry in the 1860s and 1870s, however, eliminated the incentive to industry produced by that market, even as it was creating a crisis for the economy of the kingdom. The replacement of whaling by sugar as the mainstay of Hawai'i's economy brought a profound change for most Hawaiians involved in agriculture—from the independent farmer toiling on his own small piece of land to the regimented laborer on a large, foreign-owned plantation. Visible aspects of the transition in the economy could be seen on the island of Maui in the decline of Lahaina, dependent on whaling, and the rise of sugar-oriented Wailuku.[48]

The precipitously declining Hawaiian population could not, however, furnish the number of workers required by the plantations, especially after the sugar industry received a spurt from the reciprocity treaty of 1875 with the United States. As Lawrence Fuchs has written, the effect of reciprocity was to cause sugar to reach "out everywhere, surging into rice lands, coffee lands, taro patches, and small Hawaiian kuleanas. In 1875, there were twenty plantations; five years later there were sixty-three."[49]

Three results flowed from this reciprocity treaty of 1875, however, that spelled doom in large letters for the Hawaiian people and their government. For one, it tied Hawai'i's rapidly expanding economy even more closely to that of the United States, making Hawaiian prosperity more dependent than ever on access to that market. For another, it meant that the relatively small oligarchy of white sugar planters and their bankers and factors began to exert even more influence on both Hawai'i's economy and government. And third, the expansion of the

Hawaiian sugar industry meant that the importation of foreign laborers to work on the plantations would now turn into a flood.

The search for cheap plantation labor to supplement the dwindling number of Hawaiians had already begun in 1850 with the formation of the Royal Hawaiian Agricultural Society, which began to import Chinese laborers in 1852—293 of them. The expansion of the sugar industry after reciprocity led the sugar planters to search for laborers all over the world. By the time of annexation in 1898, Fuchs estimates that 45,000 Chinese; 15,000 Japanese; 13,000 Portuguese; 1,400 Germans; 600 Scandinavians; and 600 Galicians had been brought to Hawai'i to toil on the plantations.[50]

The effect was catastrophic for the Hawaiians. Even though their population had been dwindling, they had still constituted a majority in Hawai'i before the 1870s. But by the time of the overthrow of the monarchy in 1893 the Hawaiians were a minority in their own land. Moreover, many of the workers who were being imported almost immediately entered into competition with the Hawaiians as industrious small farmers. Unlike the white Americans and Englishmen who came to Hawai'i to prosper in business or the professions, leaving Hawaiians to till the soil, the Chinese and Japanese immigrants were mainly of peasant origin, and many of them quickly began to grow rice and other crops, even taro, in competition with the Hawaiians. Even the manufacture of poi, the staple Hawaiian food, had largely been taken over by the Chinese by the 1890s.[51]

The dwindling number of Hawaiians and the kingdom's increasing reliance on the sugar industry could not but exert an influence on the monarchy. One area of contention between the Hawaiian monarchy and the white residents of the islands was the constitution of the kingdom. A constitution promulgated in 1852 had severely weakened the traditional power of the king by creating a two-house legislature, the lower house of which was democratically elected. When he came to the throne, Kamehameha V refused to take an oath to that constitution at his coronation and he immediately set out to revise it.

The new constitution promulgated by Kamehameha V in 1864 was based on his belief that the Hawaiian people were not yet ready for universal manhood suffrage, and that there should be a property qualification for both voters and members of the legislature. Kamehameha V also believed that the ''prerogatives of the crown ought to be more carefully protected . . . and that the influence of the crown ought to be seen pervading every function of the government.'' He wanted the powers of the privy council to be reduced, and the powers of the lower house, especially of the legislature over financial matters, to be curtailed. The result of all this was that the powers of the king were greatly increased from what they had been in the constitution of 1852. In a sense the constitution of 1864 represented a coup d'etat by Kamehameha V through which he reclaimed at least some of the royal power that had been lost in the earlier constitution.[52]

The constitution of 1864 remained in force for twenty-three years, during which time it was a constant target of opposition from the white businessmen in the kingdom. At this point, however, the Hawaiian kingdom was still strong enough to assert its sovereignty even in the face of their opposition.

Kamehameha V remained a bachelor throughout his life, intending that his heir should be his sister, Victoria Kamamalu. She, however, died in 1866, and the king did not name an heir even when his health began to fail. This very able king—the last of the Kamehameha line, and the last king to resemble the earlier monarchs—died in 1872 at the age of only forty-three, and with him went much of the charisma associated with the Kamehameha name.

Two "elected" kings followed, the first of whom was William Lunalilo, who reigned for only thirteen months, 1873–1874. In that short time, however, Lunalilo managed to do immeasurable harm to the Hawaiian kingdom. Confronted with a relatively minor, and almost *opera bouffe*, mutiny by the royal guard in 1873, the king responded by disbanding the kingdom's only army, leaving just the band. As a result of Lunalilo's rash action, Hawai'i had by 1874, for the first time since Kamehameha I, no army at all, only a small palace guard that existed mainly for ceremonial purposes and not to fight. Thanks to Lunalilo, the Hawaiian kingdom was now unable to defend itself or even to maintain order in Hawai'i if there were outbreaks of violence.[53]

When Lunalilo died there were two contenders to succeed him. One of these was Queen Emma, the widow of Kamehameha IV, the other David Kalakaua, who had been one of the two final candidates for the throne in 1872 before losing out to Lunalilo. Both candidates had strong backers in 1873, and their campaign for the throne was a bitter one, accompanied by riots and damage to property. It was, one observer noted, "only prevented from assuming a dangerous form by the timely interference of an American and English man-of-war."[54] Peace was restored only by the landing of marines and sailors from a British and two American warships, accompanied by a Gatling gun, with the city of Honolulu virtually occupied by and under the protection of Great Britain and the United States. With peace restored, Kalakaua was installed as king and took oaths in support of the 1864 constitution.[55]

In the process, however, a dangerous precedent had been set in the necessity to rely on marines and sailors from foreign ships to restore order—a situation that owed its origins to Lunalilo's rash decision to disband the Hawaiian army. The inability of the Hawaiian monarchy to maintain order even in its own capital, not to mention its defenselessness before any foreign enemies, did not bode well for the future of a kingdom that was bobbing in a sea of domestic and international intrigue in the 1880s and 1890s.

Kalakaua, who ruled from 1874 to 1891, made strongly nationalistic Hawaiian speeches, tried to revive much of the old culture, and appointed more Hawaiians to cabinet offices than had any of his predecessors. His reign was a renaissance of Hawaiian culture, much to the dismay of surviving missionaries and their descendants. Still, the Hawaiian population continued to decline despite everything the monarchy did, and the Hawaiian economy continued to be as fragile as ever—dependent now primarily on sugar for its prosperity. And for profits from sugar, Hawai'i was largely dependent on the U.S. market, especially after the reciprocity treaty of 1875.

The white elite was concerned with what they chose to view as evidence of Kalakaua's "racism." Kalakaua and the foreigners jockeyed for power between 1876 and 1887, and the government was a scene of confusion. During those years no cabinet remained in office for more than two years. In his efforts to gain revenue independent of the legislature, Kalakaua sold opium licenses— which was appalling to the sons and daughters of missionaries, as was his revival of ancient Hawaiian culture.[56]

To counteract the king, prominent whites in Hawai'i organized a secret society called the Hawaiian League and gained the support of an all-white rifle company called the Honolulu Rifles—which had supposedly been organized to serve the Hawaiian kingdom as a kind of unofficial substitute for the army that it lacked. "The rebel group," Lawrence Fuchs says, "included the best and most efficient soldiers in the kingdom. Interested businessmen gave money to outfit and arm this newly organized unit, which many members of the league joined. Soon there were three haole rifle clubs, a fourth made up of Portuguese immigrants, and a German company." As matters approached a showdown between the king and the white elite, the only real military force in Hawai'i was not under the command of his officers, but was instead under the control of his enemies.[57] Gavan Daws has written that "Kalakaua was uncomfortably aware that the only well-organized military company was the Honolulu Rifles, whose members at that moment were drawing a bead on his crown."[58]

By 1887 the white elite was powerful enough to stage its own coup d'etat at the expense of the Hawaiian monarchy. In that year Kalakaua was forced to agree to what has been called the Bayonet Constitution, since it was thrust on him under the threat of force. The additional powers that had been given to the king by the constitution of 1864 were now swept away. Fuchs reports that the new constitution "made the King subordinate in theory as well as in fact to the propertied haoles of Honolulu."[59]

Hawaiians held protest meetings and counterrevolution was in the air. Robert Wilcox, part-Hawaiian, led a movement to dethrone Kalakaua in favor of his younger sister Liliuokalani and to enact a new constitution. This attempted coup failed, however, and its failure revealed the impracticability of attempting to maintain royal power by force when only the monarchy's enemies were armed and trained.[60]

8

OCEANIC INTERESTS

SHIPPING

One major change in the nature and extent of U.S. interests in the Pacific area in the second half of the nineteenth century was a decline in America's share of commercial shipping in that ocean. The eclipse of the whaling industry in the 1860s meant that in many parts of the Pacific where American ships and sailors had been the most frequent visitors before the Civil War, they became less common, even rare, in the 1870s and 1880s. More than this, the vast merchant marine that had carried the American flag and American goods to all quarters of the globe in earlier years now entered into a period of diminution that was both relative and absolute.

Between 1865 and 1875, for example, America's share in the shipping of its own foreign trade dropped from 47 percent to 30 percent, and for a time even the actual tonnage on the seas showed a decline. This general trend continued down to World War I, by which time only about 8 percent of the foreign trade of the nation was being carried in American bottoms.[1]

The decline was less marked on the Pacific than on the Atlantic, partly because the long voyages with bulky cargoes like California grain or Oregon timber could continue to use wooden sailing ships competitively. The cost of providing coal to widely scattered island or coastal bases made steam shipping too costly for such traffic. Coal production did develop in Washington Territory, in British Columbia, Japan, and Australia, but output there down to 1900 did not support an extensive American steam-powered oceanic fleet. Iron manufactories or major centers of shipbuilding were similarly late to develop on the American Pacific coast, although abundant supplies of timber supported some shipbuilding enterprises on the Oregon coast and in Puget Sound.

The reasons given for the comparative decline of American maritime activity overseas have been numerous, varied, and disputed. Certainly one of the most important was the fact that the shift from wood and sail to steel and steam deprived American shipbuilders and shippers of a major advantage they had previously enjoyed over their competitors—namely, lower construction costs because of abundant domestic timber. Yet, federal law still forbade the substitution of cheaper foreign-built ships for domestic vessels in American registry.[2]

American maritime labor costs had commonly been higher than those of competing maritime nations, and this margin had increased as the expanding domestic economy offered better-paying jobs than seafaring could provide. Even the United States Navy had to rely on aliens to fill its crews. Investment capital also found less risky and more profitable employment in domestic fields, and most of the firms that once had specialized in Pacific shipping and/or trade now turned their energies to manufacturing, transportation, or real estate investments at home in the second half of the nineteenth century.[3]

Instead of fulfilling the dreams of Benton, Perry, Seward, and other earlier prophets of a future "American lake" whitened by American sails, the nation's shipping seemed to be fading from the Pacific. Yet the dollar value of U.S. imports and exports in major Pacific markets continued to show increases. Carried in foreign ships, handled by foreign agents, even insured by foreign firms, this growth in value kept alive some interest in Pacific-bordering lands as markets and suppliers. Even so, the growth in value of Pacific trade failed to keep pace with that of the domestic economy or even of transatlantic commerce.

Transpacific commercial activity in the 1870s and 1880s, then, was of proportionately less value to the United States than it had been in the years before the Civil War. From an economic determinist point of view, then, one might assume that the influence upon national policies exerted by those actually involved in Pacific foreign trade and investment would be correspondingly diminished.

Yet, "hope springs eternal," and there continued to be advocates of aggressive governmental action in the Pacific who adduced economic reasons to justify their calls. Perhaps earliest among these were promoters of steam navigation lines, who sought the support of the United States government. Some of them sounded very much like Senator Thomas Hart Benton at his most orotund with their descriptions of the vast commercial empire in the Pacific that merely awaited the adoption by congress of this or that project or policy. Men interested in Fiji, Samoa, Australia, the west coast of South America, or even in expanded transpacific contact with China and Japan at various times urged more governmental action on this basis.[4]

In April of 1885, for example, John A. Kasson, one of the early advocates of an American imperial role in the Pacific, wrote from his post as U.S. minister to Germany:

I venture to add an expression of my sorrow, bordering upon a sense of shame, that the blindness, weakness, and timidity of a long continuing so-called American policy has made our flag on the Pacific Ocean insignificant, and has led foreign nations to ask for our view, if asked at all, after the fait accompli, instead of before it. The Pacific Ocean should have been an American sea, traversed by American ships not only to Japan and China, but to the new Australian world, touching at numerous islands having American plantations, and covered by the American flag. Instead of this . . . we have now everywhere the flag of the three embattled nations of Europe, still grasping for the insular fragments left unappropriated and exposing every American interest of the present and the future on the Pacific to embroilment in their wars.

Kasson then went on to suggest that Europe might yet seize the Sandwich Islands, to the detriment of American interests.[5]

There is particular relevance, then, in the tart report of Commander William T. Truxton, who in 1870 was sent with USS *Jamestown* on a tour of Micronesia in response to the appeals of several Americans for the defense of alleged American interests there. Though the new U.S. minister to Hawai'i, Henry A. Peirce, had written of the great potential economic and strategic value of that region, Truxton reported that the "Phoenix, Gilbert and Marshall islands all put together would not equal in extent an average-sized American farm, and their whole trade, shared between British firms and Godeffroy and Sons, could not exceed fifty thousand dollars a year." Moreover, "they lay on no important trade route, and would soon lose their value as whaling grounds." Truxton estimated that it would take "ten years and at least a million dollars" to make an exhaustive survey of them.[6]

What Truxton pointed out with regard to Micronesia might with candor have been applied to other island areas as well. The number of Americans in the region, Hawai'i excepted, was inconsequential, their character, except for missionaries, often dubious, and the extent of their business interests meager in the extreme from a national standpoint. There seemed, moreover, little reason to expect that such interests had any reasonable prospect of important growth even with the most favorable of government policies to support them.

The decline of whaling was already obvious at the time of Truxton's report. The Civil War had taken a frightful toll, with at least fifty whaling ships destroyed or captured by Confederate raiders. The risks were too great for most concerns and many ships were sold to the government or transferred to other flags. Between 1860 and 1865 the tonnage of registered whaling ships dropped by nearly 50 percent, from 166,841 tons to 84,233. A brief, but slight, revival after the war was aborted by the destruction of thirty-four vessels in an early freeze of the icepack in the Arctic Ocean in 1871 and a similar disaster in 1876. By 1880 there were only 38,408 tons of whaling ships registered. Nantucket, the pioneer port of Pacific whaling, sent its last vessel out in 1869.[7]

Naval patrols continued to sail among the islands, partly to protect the few traders, whalers, and missionaries, and partly also to help curb the outrages upon island peoples committed by blackbirders and other seagoing outlaws like the notorious "Bully" Hayes. In the 1880s commercial or consular agents were briefly appointed to posts at Butaritari in the Gilberts and Jaluit in the Marshall Islands. Beyond that public policy refused to go, except for a quite unusual involvement in Samoa that began in the 1870s.[8]

SLOW GROWTH OF TRANSPACIFIC STEAM NAVIGATION

One of the great disappointments of the 1850–1900 period was the failure of American steamship lines to appear and expand as rapidly as optimists had expected. In the earliest days of experimentation with the application of steam power to navigation, Americans had shown considerable interest and initiative in the field, but after a promising beginning the United States fell behind Great Britain except in the development of river steamers. The iron, steel, and machine industries developed more slowly in America than did those of its transatlantic rivals. American talent and capital continued to be devoted to that branch of shipbuilding in which nature had best fitted the nation to excel—in the manufacture of wooden sailing vessels. In fact, at the time when the oceanic steamer was coming into its own, Americans developed the famed clipper ship, and its success and appeal to marine traditionalists helped fasten a preoccupation with wood and sail upon the republic for a longer period than might otherwise have been the case.[9]

Americans interested in securing patronage or capital for the development of steam lines, or for experiments in new improvements in steam navigation, generally found it necessary to seek support and encouragement abroad. When William Wheelwright tried to promote a steamship line on the west coast of South America around 1840, he found that he had to look for capital in Great Britain rather than in his native land. And when Representative T. Butler King of Georgia reported a bill from the House Naval Affairs Committee in 1848 to establish a transpacific steamship line under navy control, he was unable to secure the votes necessary to pass the measure.[10]

Repeatedly, over the next few sessions of Congress, steamship line subsidy bills were proposed without success. Some of the opposition sprang from objections to government support of monopolies or to the use of federal funds for the profit of private firms, even though there was precedent for both. The absence of a powerful maritime community committed to steam and steel, or to subsidized experiments in new forms of marine design and engineering, is quite clear. Even in the Navy Department such advocates of a conversion to steam as Matthew C. Perry found it difficult to make headway against tradition-bound officers and lobbyists.[11]

Despite this, Robert Bennett Forbes appears to have introduced the first American steamship into China waters about 1850. British vessels had already operated there for some years. By 1860 Americans had secured an important place in the river and coastwise shipping of China, and even some British concerns there were purchasing American-built river steamers.[12] For some years after 1860–1861, Russell and Company controlled the Shanghai Steam Navigation Company, serving the Yangtze River and some coastal ports. Then they sold their interest to a Chinese firm supported by that government. Clearly, American enterprise was capable of pursuing its interest in this field, as in others, without government policy consultations or subsidy when it wished to do so.[13]

In 1853–1854 an American paddle-wheel steamer of new design, the *Golden Age,* sailed from the United States to Liverpool and thence to Australia. From Australia she made a rapid voyage to Tahiti and then to Panama. The speed with which the ship's cargo of mail and gold was able to travel from Sidney to London, via Panama, aroused much comment. Although the experiment lent some prestige to the maritime industry of the United States, it was a financial failure. For this, the high cost of coaling at Tahiti was principally blamed. One result, however, was that the potential value of Pacific island bases as coaling stations began to receive more attention from both commercial and naval interests.[14]

Though Congress had after much debate approved subsidies to shipping lines on the route to California and Oregon at the end of the 1840s, it was not until 1867 that a transpacific steamship line began operation under the flag of the United States. The Pacific Mail Steamship Company suffered financial difficulties from the start and was under constant political attack from opponents of the whole subsidy principle. Originally granted $500,000 a year on condition that it sail from San Francisco to China via Hawai'i, the company asked to be relieved of the expense of the longer voyage via Hawai'i even before it began operations. Later, it requested and secured a large increase in the subsidy.[15]

The methods used by Pacific Mail in lobbying for congressional support eventually earned it the censure of that body, and the entire subsidy was dropped. More than that, the experience was used thereafter by opponents of subsidies as an argument to deny other American steamship lines the support they needed to compete with subsidized foreign rivals. Pacific Mail did manage to receive another subsidy in the 1890s, and even without government support the company survived past World War I, but American maritime policy clearly was not supportive of an aggressive transpacific steamshipping industry. Shipbuilders, shipowners, shipping and trading firms, and maritime labor groups were hopelessly divided in the policies they sought of the federal government, and American industries failed to keep pace with those abroad.[16]

The general discredit cast upon the subsidy system by the Pacific Mail experience helped defeat proposals for government aid to other steamer lines. A brief experiment in support of a California, Oregon, and Mexican Steamship Company, which also began service between the coast and Hawai'i, became involved in the adventures of William H. Webb and his United States, New Zealand, and Australia Mail Steamship Line, with the result that both lines went down in a welter of economic and political problems.

Webb's attempt to build a rather elaborate Pacific scheme around a subsidized line from San Francisco to New Zealand and Australia via Hawai'i and Samoa ran afoul of congressional opposition to subsidies in 1871–1873. Despite the support of President Grant and certain businessmen in San Francisco and Honolulu, Webb could not secure from Congress the legislation needed for the success of his schemes. Even though the government of New Zealand passed a subsidy measure in Webb's behalf and sailings actually began, the line could not prosper without additional subsidy. When neither the United States nor the Australian colonies proved willing to provide these, the project was abandoned.[17]

The establishment of an American claim to Midway Island in 1867 sprang from Pacific Mail's desire for a mid-Pacific coaling station. The large sums subsequently spent on fruitless efforts to create a useable harbor at Midway only discouraged rather than encouraged further federal enterprise of that sort in the Pacific islands.[18]

AMERICAN COASTAL SHIPPING

Far more important to the nation than transpacific shipping was the growth of trade and passenger traffic, including steam navigation, along the Pacific coast of the Americas. With the Oregon treaty, the Mexican cession, and the gold rush to California, American interest in coastwise navigation on the eastern shore of the Pacific grew enormously. In 1849 the first regular steamers were operating between Panama and California. In 1856 an American firm completed a railroad across the Isthmus of Panama, and in the following year an American-owned line began serving the west coast of Central America and Mexico. Five months later another line was operating northward to Oregon.

Both the rail line promoters and coastwise shippers received one form or another of federal government support. The Bidlack Treaty of 1846 with Colombia gave the United States certain rights to ensure security of passage across the Isthmus of Panama. The shipping lines received federal subsidies based on their contracts to carry the mail. Between the time of the California gold rush and the end of the 1850s, the Pacific Mail Steamship Company alone received federal subsidies amounting to a total of $3,750,000, at a peak level of $700,000 per year, for carrying mail and troops between Panama, California ports, and Oregon.[19]

The first major American steamer to sail the eastern Pacific was the *California,* which left New York in October 1848 and traveled around Cape Horn. The ship had been designed for coastal trade and mail carriage, and it sailed without a full passenger load before the discovery of gold in California was announced to the nation by President Polk. When it reached Panama, on the Pacific coast, it found many eager passengers waiting, and the *California* began playing its important role in the early gold rush.

This first American steamship on the Pacific coast had trouble, however, finding supplies of coal, dry docks, or machine shops. *California* was almost stranded at

Monterey on its maiden voyage due to lack of fuel. In 1854 work began on a government dry dock and machine shop at Mare Island, in San Francisco Bay, and for years after that the yard did more work on private than on government ships. When coal was available it often cost as much as thirty dollars per ton on the coast and once reached fifty dollars, far above normal Atlantic or Gulf coast levels. The discovery of coal deposits in Washington and British Columbia helped ease this situation in later years and gave added support to the growth of coastwise steam shipping.[20]

THE ISTHMIAN ROUTES

The rise of steam navigation along the Pacific coast of the Americas and across the great ocean revived active discussion of a possible transisthmian canal. As early as the 1820s citizens of the United States had shown interest in such a route, and by the 1850s its relationship to potential intercoastal shipping of the now transcontinental republic was clear. The strategic significance of such a canal was being discussed by military men in France and Great Britain, as well as in the United States. In this early period Dutch and American companies were created to build such a canal, but neither succeeded in attracting sufficient capital or governmental support.[21]

French expansion in the Marquesas, Tuamotus, and Tahiti aroused greater interest in that country in an isthmian canal. Speculations arose as to the strategic and economic possibilities of those islands because of new shipping routes that might center on Panama. Those prospects took on new reality once Ferdinand de Lesseps had succeeded with his Suez Canal in the 1860s. Frenchmen, Britons, and Americans who favored more vigorous national policies in Samoa, Fiji, or other island groups from time to time began to refer to the value of an isthmian canal for enhancing the value of national claims that might be established in the Pacific.[22]

The California gold rush found thousands of Americans and Europeans seeking out the various passages across the narrowest parts of the Americas in their rush to the Pacific coast. Various road, trail, and waterway passages were utilized, from Darien in New Granada (Colombia) to the Mexican Isthmus of Tehuantepec. By 1856 a U.S. firm had built a railroad across the Isthmus of Panama, and a mixed riverboat-road route was opened by rival interests across Nicaragua. During this period a sometimes hectic diplomatic struggle took place between the United States and Great Britain for control or major influence over parts of Central America. Mention has already been made of the Bidlack Treaty. The Clayton-Bulwer Treaty of 1850 between the United States and Great Britain was intended by its American negotiators to forestall British expansion in the area. Once gold rush traffic between the American coasts arose, however, the treaty's terms began to appear in Washington as mainly a barrier to America's own hopes for preeminent influence in Central America and to any future plans for an American-owned canal.[23]

The end of the gold rush, the completion of the Suez Canal, and the opening of the American transcontinental railroad combined to diminish some of the interest in isthmian routes. That interest was revived after the American Civil War, however, especially when a French company began efforts in the late 1870s and early 1880s to construct a canal across Panama. Once again Americans began to make references to the strategic disposition of certain Pacific islands with regard to the new trade routes that the canal would supposedly produce. Both Congress and the press voiced strategic concerns for defense and communication between the Atlantic and Pacific coasts as reasons for national interest. In part, the American interest in gaining a hold in the Samoan group was rationalized on that basis. The Navy Department and actual business firms were not strongly involved in this advocacy.[24]

In March 1880 President Rutherford B. Hayes sent Congress a special message in response to publicized concern over the French company's announced project for Panama. In his message Hayes said, in part:

The policy of this country is a canal under American control. The United States cannot consent to the surrender of this control to any European powers. If existing treaties between the United States and other nations, or if the rights of sovereignty or property of other nations, stand in the way of this policy . . . suitable steps should be taken by just and liberal negotiations to promote and establish the American policy on this subject. . . .

The capital invested by corporations or citizens of other countries in such an enterprise must in a great degree look for protection to one or more of the great powers of the world. No European power can intervene for such protection without adopting measures on this continent which the United States would deem wholly inadmissable. If the protection of the United States is relied upon, the United States must exercise such control as will enable this country to protect its national interests and maintain the rights of those whose private capital is embarked in the work.

An interoceanic canal across the American isthmus will essentially change the geographical relations between the Atlantic and Pacific coasts of the United States and between the United States and the rest of the world. It will be the great ocean thoroughfare between our Atlantic and Pacific shores and virtually a part of the coast-line of the United States. Our mere commercial interest in it is larger than that of all other countries, while its relation to our power and prosperity as a nation, to our means of defense, our unity, peace, and safety, are matters of paramount concern to the people of the United States.[25]

In the language of international relations these were strong words, and Congress backed them up with a resolution declaring it in the interest of the United States that its consent be a condition precedent to the construction of any ship canal across the isthmus. Efforts then began to secure abrogation of the Clayton-Bulwer Treaty through a new agreement with Great Britain, and to secure a treaty with Colombia requiring U.S. approval before that nation permitted a ship canal to be built across its province of Panama. Neither of these efforts was at that time successful, and the French canal company, led by Ferdinand de Lesseps, went ahead with its work until fiscal and engineering difficulties halted it in 1888.[26]

After that a new American firm was created, with at least tacit approval from Washington, to complete the canal, but it failed to attract from within the United States enough capital to proceed with the project. As the end of the nineteenth century approached, then, American strategic and commercial interests in an isthmian canal continued, but they had yet to arouse enough support in the business and financial community, or in the federal government, to push the project through to completion. In fact, with the decline of American overseas shipping and the further improvement of transcontinental land communications, commercial demand for a canal seemed to decline.

RELATIONS DOWN UNDER

The period of the gold rushes to California and Australia for a time brought closer relations between the United States and the British Australasia colonies than had previously existed. From that period on there was some increase in American interest and influence in Australia particularly, although the relationship never became of major importance on either side. The competing nature of their agricultural economies and the orientation of Australia's trade toward Britain and other British possessions prevented that. New Zealand was even more strongly British oriented, and its major exports also competed with those of the United States. American trade, moreover, became increasingly transatlantic oriented in the second half of the century. Under these circumstances it is rather remarkable that any appreciable common interests developed at all.[27]

A few Americans played some part in the growth of coach and rail travel within Australia and in the development of early telegraph lines. Cobb & Company, founded mainly by Americans, was a pioneer in overland transport from gold rush days into the twentieth century. Americans also seem to have had some influence in the development of better hotel services, notably in Victoria, in post–gold rush years. The Chaffey brothers, Canadians by birth, took to Australia the fruits of their experience in irrigation engineering in California and did much to open up the valuable Riverina areas of Victoria and South Australia.[28]

The growth of steam navigation connections between the United States and Australia or New Zealand, which might have helped to develop closer ties, was, however, retarded by American indifference—both public and private—and by British opposition. After the failure of Webb's 1870s effort there was no notable American attempt to create a regular steamship service between the United States and Australia for the remainder of the century. Wooden sailing ships, built and registered in the United States, maintained a higher rate of participation in trade between the United States and Australasia than they did in transatlantic or Asiatic commerce through this period. Most notably, they carried Oregon lumber and later tinned kerosene for export to Australia. For years the term "Oregon" was used there to describe a type of lumber, mainly Douglas fir, that played a significant part in Australian construction. Tinned petroleum products, of course, preceded the day of ocean-going tankers.

All this trade was, however, but a minor part of the dwindling overseas shipping business of the United States.[29] In 1900 only ninety out of 2,784 vessels registered as entering the ports of New South Wales were from the United States, and some sixty-four of these appear to have been British ships. Out of 2,714 ships departing the colony that same year, only sixty-seven were bound for American ports.[30] While this may not be an accurate measure of the importance of trade between Sydney and the United States, it does give an idea of the relatively small part played by American vessels in Australia's foreign trade at that time. British and other foreign ships brought more American produce to Australia and New Zealand in the late nineteenth century than did those of the United States.

Australia's trade with the United States, moreover, was largely a one-sided affair, as was that of New Zealand. Only in 1850–1851 was there an excess of Australian exports. Thereafter the balance was steadily in favor of the United States, with grain, lumber, farm machinery and other metal manufactures, and tinned petroleum products far exceeding in value Australasia's exports to the United States. This provided additional motive for colonial and British government efforts to discourage expansion of such a disadvantageous trade or to open wider markets in the United States.

The wool lobby in Washington and the competitive advantages of American grain and meat producers prevented a reversal of the export-import ratio. In 1901 the first published figures for the Commonwealth of Australia showed the United Kingdom provided 57 percent of its total imports, the United States only 13 percent. The British took 50 percent of the exports and the Americans only 6 percent, and this was a year when U.S. imports from down under were unusually high.[31]

In the later years of the nineteenth century, mutual influences of a political sort were exchanged between Australia and the United States. As the colonies progressed toward unification and self government, the examples of American experience on a similar course and of American models of federal and state government were consulted and considered by the founders of the Commonwealth of Australia. By the same token, American reformers were much impressed by the Australian ballot system and borrowed it. The American Henry George had some considerable influence on Australian thinking in the field of labor politics and theory in the 1880s and 1890s, more, in fact, than he did in his own country.[32] Taken as a whole, the ties between the United States and Australasia were not broad enough to demand major policy decisions or even the establishment of better communications.

PACIFIC ISLAND CONTACTS

U.S. trade with the Pacific islands grew unevenly through the later years of the nineteenth century, although, as previously noted, that growth was neither large nor rapid. In the late 1860s a handful of American traders could be found in major island ports and on some remote atolls. Apia, Lauthala, Suva, and Papeete had American consular representatives then, though even their numbers tended to shrink as France and Britain (and later Germany) assumed control of the island groups and began to favor their own nationals and to discourage foreign consular appointments.[33]

There simply was no American colonial policy in the 1870s and 1880s either in Congress or in the executive branch, although occasionally voices might be raised in favor of one or another expansive move. Usually these advocates were of what might be called the "preventive imperialism" type, urging American acquisition of this base or that to prevent its seizure by someone else. European expansionists, in turn, cited the talk of unauthorized American expansionists and the record of the 1840s as evidence of the need for them to "get there first."[34]

In the late 1850s the actions of Henry Owner, an American commercial agent, in the leeward islands of the Society group, especially at Raiatea, aroused French and British suspicions. His negotiations with island chiefs apparently were aimed at securing some sort of American protectorate or privileged position in trade. Owner had neither instructions nor support from Washington, and his actions were repudiated there. They served, however, to feed increased concern by the two European powers over the status of those and other islands.[35]

In the late 1860s and early 1870s alleged American designs on the Fiji group were cited by British and Australian settlers there. They pointed to the claims of John Brown Williams, American commercial agent, and to the vigorous support given to those claims by certain commanders of U.S. Navy ships. Gradually inflated over the years following his first claim against the Fijians in the 1840s, Williams's demands had now reached a total of nearly $44,000. Chief Thakombau, held to represent Fijian authority, was forced to agree to pay this amount by an American naval commander. Since such payment was obviously impossible except through some sort of land cession, members of the British community regarded it as evidence of an American plan to seize control.[36]

Nearly a decade of turmoil in Fiji passed before a new attempt was made to compel the alleged king of the Fijians to pay his debts. This time Thakombau was rescued by an Australian syndicate, the Polynesian Company, in which George R. Latham, then U.S. consul in Melbourne, was an active member. The syndicate undertook to pay off the American claims in return for extensive land and trade concessions. This, in turn, was viewed by some in Britain and the colonies as still another American plot.[37]

On another occasion, officials in Western Australia were exercised over a purported American design to claim the Lacepede Islands off the northwest coast of Australia, and other rumors persistently cropped up in widely separated parts of the Pacific.[38] It would not be fair to dismiss all of these as insincere efforts by foreign expansionists to justify designs of their own. While in retrospect it can be seen that no expansionist policy in the Pacific was possible in the United States in the years after the Civil War, it was by no means obvious either to foreigners or to some Americans at the time that the spirit of Manifest Destiny had been laid to rest.

AMERICANS AND THE LABOR TRADE

A traffic in island laborers, commonly referred to as "blackbirding," scourged the islands of eastern Polynesia, Melanesia, and a part of Micronesia in the closing third of the nineteenth century. In theory, native inhabitants of some islands were hired to work on coconut plantations in Samoa, sugar plantations in Queensland and Fiji, plantations and mines in Tahiti and New Caledonia, and even plantations and guano deposits in Peru and its offshore islands. Some of the most ruthlessly exploitative practices in the trade were those of Peruvian and Chilean labor hunters. Yet the bulk of the business appears to have been in the hands of British subjects, and the principal official efforts taken to curb its abuses were taken by British consular and Royal Navy officers.[39]

A few Americans, such as the notorious William H. "Bully" Hayes, did participate in the kidnapping of islanders and other abuses associated with the trade. The United States government, however, appears to have assumed little responsibility for the suppression of their activities. Navy histories seem to skip over it altogether. Naval officers on patrol among the islands found it difficult to implement orders to investigate and arrest American blackbirders in areas where their legal authority to act was at best unclear. The escape of Hayes from Commander Meade of USS *Narragansett* at Apia in 1872 illustrates the difficulty of such law enforcement.[40]

As long as the islands were outside the jurisdiction of any Western power, policing the area and securing witnesses or prisoners were next to impossible. Moreover, since the nationality of the blackbirders varied, nothing short of complete international agreement and cooperation among naval patrols could be fully effective. The United States did not have a strong history of such cooperation. Though attempts to end the slave trade on the Atlantic had begun early in the century, full cooperation even there, especially with the British, had been blocked by national pride, naval jealousies, and slaveholders' interests, until the Slave Trade Treaty of 1862 was negotiated under the pressured conditions of the American Civil War.

Legislation against the coolie trade in the Pacific passed Congress after mid-century, and some forthright action followed, chiefly in the western Pacific. U.S. representatives also expressed misgivings about the importation of laborers by the Hawaiian kingdom and pressed that government to safeguard the interests of those brought to its shores. Yet a bill to suppress the labor trade in the South

Pacific failed to pass Congress in 1872. British efforts to arrange cooperative naval action in the Pacific on the model achieved in 1862 for the Atlantic failed, however, when the United States insisted on including traffic in Asian laborers as well as Pacific islanders.[41]

The only sure and effective way to deal with the problem of jurisdiction was to assume control over an island group and place in it officials vested with power to make arrests and mete out judgment. It was in this fashion that British control over Fiji served its purpose, and that control did much to curb the evil traffic there and to bring an element of stability to political and economic affairs at the expense, however, of Fijian sovereignty.

There is little doubt, moreover, that British control in Fiji and other islands after 1874 was employed to the detriment of German and American commercial interests previously established there. In this situation Washington proved as unwilling to risk unpleasant relations with Britain over the interests of a few settlers or traders as it had earlier in the case of New Zealand. The British had acted similarly, as can be seen, in recognizing American hegemony in Hawai'i. The Germans, for their part, put the lesson by for future reference when Chancellor Bismarck's prejudice against colonial adventures might be overcome, which did happen in the early 1880s.[42]

THE GUANO TRADE

In the 1850s the United States government took specific steps to advance the interests of its citizens engaged in the search for and exploitation of deposits of guano fertilizer. Support for such policies came from both Northern maritime and Southern agrarian groups, the latter being concerned over declining fertility in the farmlands of the Southeast states. Between 1850 and 1855 diplomatic efforts were made to develop American claims in the Lobos Islands off the coast of Peru and in the Galapagos Islands of Ecuador. International jealousies stemming from both South American and European sources frustrated these attempts.[43]

In 1856 Congress passed a statute which read, in part: "Whenever any citizen of the United States discovers a deposit of guano on any island, rock, or key, not within the lawful jurisdiction of any other government, and takes peaceable possession thereof, and occupies the same, such island, rock, or key may, at the discretion of the President, be considered as appertaining to the United States." A later section of the same measure added that nothing in it should be "construed as obliging the United States to retain possession of the islands, rocks, or keys, after the guano shall have been removed from the same."[44]

Over the next quarter-century some seventy different claims were filed under this act, though it is clear that a number of duplicate claims resulted from faulty calculation of island locations. Edwin Bryan has concluded that in all only forty-eight separate islands were actually involved. For years these claims confused the question of title to the islands, even after the original American claimants had departed and, in a number of cases, guano exploitation was taken over by British or Australian firms. Some atolls near the equator, such as the Phoenix group, were shown for years on British Admiralty maps as U.S. possessions and on American maps as British.[45]

The whole tangled story of the "guano war" that pitted American interests against both foreign and domestic rivals is a case study in the low state of business ethics that prevailed in the post–Civil War years. Presidents, State and Navy departments, and minor functionaries pushed claims that were often dubious and occasionally fraudulent. It illustrates the way public policies can be influenced by very small, self-interested groups, when there is little public knowledge of the subject and no strong countervailing interest.

A principal cause of the waning American interest in the guano islands was the development of techniques for the production of synthetic nitrogen fertilizers, which reduced the need for natural deposits. No interest in the strategic potential of the guano islands appeared in the late nineteenth century. Renewed interest in the islands would have to await the day of transoceanic aviation in the twentieth century. Then, in an atmosphere of growing tension among the Pacific powers, steps were hastily taken in Washington to resurrect and reexamine the claims made under the Guano Act of 1856.[46]

MISSIONARIES, TRADE, AND INTERNATIONAL POLITICS

Missionary activity among the Pacific islands spread out from Hawai'i after the middle of the nineteenth century, extending what was, in essence, another form of American interest into the Marquesas, Gilbert, Marshall, and Caroline island groups. In 1852 the American Board of Commissioners for Foreign Missions cooperated with the now independent Hawaiian Missionary Society to send missionaries to Kusaie and Ponape in the eastern Carolines. A few years later work in the central Pacific was extended to the Marshalls and the Gilberts. In 1853 work earlier attempted in the Marquesas was resumed with French toleration, but hardly supported.[47]

In the Micronesian islands the early missionaries found themselves pitted not only against the old ways and beliefs of the islanders but also against the selfish interests of sailors, blackbirders, and island traders of several nationalities. In spite of these difficulties, their activities spread to a number of islands before the end of the century and left lasting marks in some of them. Occasionally, beginning perhaps at Ponape in 1870, the missionaries were aided by timely visits of American warships. But generally their achievement was their own, and the respect with which they were regarded by the island peoples frequently demonstrated this.

Among the most devoted and successful missionaries in these areas were native Hawaiians, trained in their home islands under the American-founded mission, and often sent out in the company of American ministers. In some areas, such as in the Gilberts, the Hawaiians persevered where their Caucasian colleagues or mentors did not. At times the influence of either group made them virtual rulers among island peoples.[48]

Their very influence, and the opportunities it afforded them to influence island trade and political attitudes, led some of the Hawaiian missionaries to grief. In the early 1880s British naval officers and German copra firms referred to some of the Hawaiian missionaries as agents of the United States. One such missionary, in the Gilberts, lent color to the charge by taking up residence within a compound maintained by San Francisco copra agents. Another tried to negotiate the cession of Butaritari to the Kingdom of Hawai'i in the early 1880s, a project kept alive for a decade or more.[49]

Convincing evidence of the importance of the missionaries is provided by the testimony of German colonial officials who served in later years in Micronesia. Dr. Georg Irmer, quondam German administrator in the Marshalls, wrote of them: "It is especially due to their sacrificing energy that in the island territories the wild cannibals and bloodthirsty reef pirates have been made peaceful men. The Americans did not limit themselves to prayers, singing and tea drinking. In the Marshall Islands, in my time, there were no young people who had not learned to read and write in the American Mission school on Kusaie."[50] After German missionaries had taken over in some of the islands from the Americans, R. Deekin, in his *Die Karolinen,* wrote: "It will naturally take a considerable time before our missionaries suceed in spreading the German spirit and doing away with the preference of the natives for the Americans. This result can hardly be expected before the next generation."[51]

In the second half of the nineteenth century, coconut oil, or more commonly copra, the dried meat of the coconut, came to be the chief cargo sought among the islands of the central Pacific and southern Polynesia. The Germans held a commanding position in the copra business.[52] By the end of the century the American stake in the central Pacific was confined almost entirely to mission activities. Tangible interests in the area were overshadowed, however, by the expansive colonial rivalry among the powers in the Pacific that developed in the 1880s. The United States government took no action to oppose the Europeans. Earl Pomeroy noted: "It was not then the policy of the American government to press the rights or interests of American missionaries in the face of European claims to sovereignty in the western Pacific, even though missionary influence in Micronesia was at its height in the 1880s, on the eve of German penetration."[53] Though U.S. naval units were ordered to Ponape and other islands to investigate missionary complaints in the 1880s and 1890s, foreign officials and foreign missionaries subsequently displaced Americans or circumscribed their activities without intervention by Washington.[54]

In 1885 Germany took over the Marshalls, with Spain's agreement. The following year the Spanish seized Ponape, under papal sanction, precipitating violent disputes with the American Protestant missionaries and their converts. Several years later USS *Alliance* appeared at Ponape amid another crisis, but thereafter took an interest in plans for the future status and development of Alaska.[2]

After the Crimean War ended, the idea of a possible sale of Alaska continued to appear in Russian thinking, and it was still alive when the American Civil War ended. During the latter war, American public sentiment toward Russia had grown friendly as a result of wartime visits of Russian naval squadrons to San Francisco and New York, visits which had been widely, though erroneously, interpreted as gestures of the czar's friendship and support for the Union. On the American side there was some sentiment expressed that the elimination of European control over the soil of this bit of the Americas would be a solid gain for republican institutions and for the security of the United States. There were also, by 1867, some business interests on the Pacific coast interested in possible profits from Alaskan ventures.[3]

In 1866–1867 a San Francisco syndicate, acting through Senator Cornelius Cole, attempted to negotiate with Russian officials an exclusive agreement for fur trading in Alaska. At the same time the Washington territorial legislature was petitioning the federal government for support in securing from Russia by negotiation ''such rights and privileges . . . as will enable our fishing vessels to visit the ports and harbors of its possession,'' at least for obtaining fuel, water, provisions, and shelter in emergencies.[4]

When Secretary of State Seward sought discussions with the Russian minister, Baron Stoeckl, in Washington on the latter petition, he met a skeptical response. Once Stoeckl had returned from a visit to St. Petersburg early in 1867, however, the Russian minister offered a different proposal to the United States. The Russian government, he told Seward, might be willing to accept an offer for the purchase of the entire province of Alaska.

The proposal found an eager listener in the secretary of state, who conferred quickly with President Andrew Johnson on the possible terms of a sale. Too eager to consummate the purchase to make good bargainers, Johnson and Seward offered the Russians $7 million, to which another $200,000 was added for reasons that have never been made absolutely clear, though the money was apparently designed to assist with passage of the treaty and the necessary appropriation through Congress. Then occurred the famous episode of drafting the treaty after midnight and signing it at an ungodly hour in the morning of March 30, 1867.[5]

After the treaty was signed, it required more than a year to secure congressional approval for the appropriation. In the debates that preceded Senate approval (April 1867) and House approval (July 1868), the desirability of the acquisition of Alaska received a belated airing. For the first time real public attention was given to the actual or possible interests of the United States in this part of the Pacific's eastern shore. Many of the issues raised were more related to partisan politics than to carefully considered economic or strategic questions.

Senator Charles Sumner of Massachusetts, chairman of the Foreign Relations

Apia in the 1840s and 1850s. They were never, however, more than a minority of a minority, overshadowed in wealth and influence first by the British and later by the Germans. Still, there may have been as many as fifty of them by 1870, some of whom asked their government to assume a more active role there.[12]

Lieutenant Charles Wilkes, with the United States Exploring Expedition, reached Samoa in 1839. He concluded with certain of the chiefs a treaty (unratified) for the protection of American citizens and commerce, appointed a British subject provisional commercial agent for the United States at Apia, and reported favorably on the harbor of Pago Pago on the island of Tutuila.[13]

Thereafter, occasional American naval patrols touched at Samoa, increasing in frequency after the Civil War. They were on routine trips through Polynesia and did not raise significant policy questions. In 1853 a regular U.S. commercial agent was appointed to Apia, but for some time the post was neither lucrative nor important enough to attract able, or even regular, appointees.[14]

In the tight little foreign community at Apia, however, personal and national jealousies found ample opportunity for intrigue, as Robert Louis Stevenson was to report most memorably in later years. Americans, like Englishmen, were at times capable of conceiving their own ambitions as matters of national interest, memorializing Washington or buttonholing visiting naval commanders with their versions of threats to those interests from foreign powers. The success and the haughty manner of German representatives, first of the Godeffroy firm and later of the Deutsche Handels und Plantagen Gesellschaft fur Sudsee Inseln (known for obvious reasons as the ''long-handle firm''), united Britons and Americans in opposition, even though the two latter groups could disagree violently on occasion.[15]

As their property interests increased, foreigners in Samoa as elsewhere in the Pacific came to favor the establishment of a stable, unified government for the greater security of their lives and investments. Though the Samoan was a marvelously sophisticated political type, the traditional society seemed quite incapable of producing the kind of unified administration that foreigners regarded as normal. Repeated efforts of British, German, and American private citizens and officials to persuade the Samoans in this direction only served to confuse the picture. These efforts, in truth, were commonly designed to serve the interests of the foreigners rather than those of the Samoans, and the latter were aware of the fact and tried to turn them to their own advantage. In the end it was the changing interests of the Germans and Americans that did most to precipitate a crisis that threatened to plunge the powers into war over Samoa.

STEAMSHIP INTERESTS

The specific American interest that threatened to embroil the nation in Samoan troubles stemmed largely from a proposal that arose about 1870 to establish a steamship line from San Francisco to Australia via Honolulu and some Samoan port. William H. Webb, the chief promoter, gained the ear of President Grant and also interested influential citizens of New York, San Francisco, and Honolulu in his scheme. In 1871, while his petition for a mail subsidy for the proposed line was before Congress, Webb seems to have sent Captain Edgar Wakeman, an ex-merchant skipper, to Samoa to seek out a good harbor where the ships of his line might safely anchor and take on coal.[16]

Wakeman was enthusiastic about Pago Pago. He also reported a rumor that Theodor Weber, German consul and head of the Godeffroy firm there, was advocating establishment of a German protectorate over Samoa. Wakeman suggested that an American establishment there might meet with favor among those, both Samoans and foreigners, who were opposed to the idea of German control. His report was forwarded by Webb to the Navy Department, which referred it to the Department of State.

Through Webb's efforts and the urgings of American businessmen in San Francisco and Honolulu, Commander Richard W. Meade sailed with USS *Narragansett* in 1872 from Honolulu to Samoa. There he signed with chiefs of the island of Tutuila a treaty granting Americans the exclusive right to establish a coaling and naval base at Pago Pago. With no specific instructions other than a formal request from the United States minister to Hawai'i, Henry A. Peirce, Meade became convinced that the treaty was in the national interest of the United States, would meet with the approval of the Samoans, and would forestall an imminent German takeover of the islands. Meade's work was not disavowed by the State Department, but the Senate took no action on his treaty.[17]

At the same time that Webb's steamship promotion was proceeding, the Central Polynesian Land and Commercial Company (CPLCC) was being incorporated under the laws of California. The moving spirit in this organization was a British subject named James B. M. Stewart who had come to San Francisco, probably via Honolulu, from Tahiti, where he and his brother had earned a highly questionable reputation. The personable and smooth-talking Stewart managed to involve several of the most prominent business and civic leaders of San Francisco and Hawai'i in his highly speculative scheme for Samoa. Though it does not appear that Webb was originally involved in this enterprise, Stewart or his agents did make contact with the steamship line entrepreneur, and the CPLCC's fortunes came to depend on the establishment of the proposed ship line.[18]

Stewart's general proposal was to operate a commercial establishment on the islands of Tutuila and Upolu that would market the produce of extensive lands (more than could possibly have been secured there to cultivate) for which very dubious "titles" had been secured. Samoan landowners had been induced to agree to the land cessions by elaborate promises of future wealth. Webb's line would presumably use the company's base as a stopping, loading, and refueling station, and would ship the tropical produce, bring in supplies, and perhaps even attract the needed development capital.

This elaborate set of promises collapsed when Webb failed to secure the necessary congressional support for his line. The CPLCC was declared bankrupt in Samoa, and its land claims were ultimately voided. The mysterious Stewart slipped quietly away into the shadows. Several of the San Francisco investors tried to save something from their investment by buying up the California charter. Later, they tried to convert the old land claims into bonds payable by the Samoan government, but all was in vain. The whole fly-by-night venture might have been forgotten but for the involvement of other Americans in the international rivalries in Samoa a few years later.

This whole issue of speculations and dubious land titles was one of the vexing subjects that had kept foreigners appealing to their governments for support in Pacific island groups since the 1820s or 1830s. In Hawai'i, Fiji, New Zealand, and Tahiti, individual foreigners had tried to impose their concepts of property rights on island chiefs and colonial officials. In Samoa the conflicting interests of foreigners, their governments, and the native people reached a critical stage in the 1870s and provoked repeated interventions throughout the remainder of the century.

GOVERNMENT INTEREST

Official involvement by the United States in Samoa sprang from the agitation surrounding the Webb-CPLCC schemes and contemporaneous consular reports of German and British meddling in Samoan affairs, presumably to the detriment of the interests of Americans. In 1873 the Grant administration sent a special agent to Samoa to investigate the general status of American interests there and to make recommendations. "Colonel" A. B. Steinberger seems to have owed his appointment, in large part, to the influence of steamship promoter Webb, but Steinberger's own motives in seeking the position are not clear. He had not been in Samoa previously and had no financial interests there at the time.[19]

Steinberger's first visit deeply interested him in Samoan affairs and in the opportunities there for a far-sighted man. He seems to have become genuinely concerned with helping the Samoans develop a stable political regime, although he soon became aware of the difficulties presented by Samoan tradition, by the welter of conflicting foreign land claims, and by the influence and ambitions of the German faction in particular. He certainly made some friends in Samoa among both Samoans and foreigners. Steinberger conducted his first mission in capable fashion, and his report to Washington earned praise from Secretary of State Hamilton Fish. But his recommendation that the United States guarantee protection of Samoa was another matter.[20]

President Grant had submitted to the Senate the treaty signed by Commander Meade that gave the United States special and exclusive privileges at Pago Pago. The Senate, as noted, had shown no inclination to approve the treaty. With this in mind, Grant refrained now from supporting Steinberger's proposal and a petition from certain Samoan chiefs that sought a U.S. protectorate (both Britain and Germany received similar petitions at one time or another). Steinberger's report was sent to Congress for its information, but without recommendation. If Webb had hoped that congressional interest would be aroused by the protectorate appeal, with corresponding support for his steamer line and other schemes, he was doomed to disappointment once again.[21] No other American interests, save those of the naval bureaucracy, nationalistic pride, or personal jealousies, remained to bind the United States to Samoa.

Steinberger nevertheless returned to Samoa in 1875 with a message and presents for the chiefs from the president of the United States. He did not immediately reveal the fact that the appeal for U.S. protection had been, in effect, rejected by Washington. Under the aegis of presumed official support from his government, he busied himself in assisting the Samoan chiefs to form a new government in which Steinberger consented to accept the role of prime minister.

By this time the "Colonel" had managed to arouse the jealousy and suspicion of both the American and British consuls in Apia, and they set themselves, successfully, to frustrate Steinberger's plans. His proposal to suspend land transfers, and possibly to revoke some of the more questionable ones, earned him more enemies. Finally, with the connivance of the British and American consuls, the would-be prime minister of Samoa was seized and deported aboard a British warship. The political affairs of Samoa eventually returned to their normal chaotic state. Thus, a major effort that might have enabled the Samoans to create a viable political structure under their own control was frustrated.[22]

At the time of his deportation, evidence was found that Steinberger had been secretly involved in negotiations with the German Godeffroy firm. It is still unclear, therefore, where his major aims were directed—whether toward serving the interests of the Samoans, of the United States, of the Germans, or simply his own. Probably it was a combination of all these. He can by no means be described, however, as a purposive instrument of American national policy sanctioned by the State Department or by Congress when he tried to set up a regime at Apia.

A sequel to the "Steinberger government," and to the attention it drew to a possible American interest in Samoa, was the mission of a Samoan chief, Mamea, who came to the United States in 1877–1878 to appeal again for protection. The best Mamea could secure, however, was a simple treaty of amity and commerce that tendered the good offices of the United States in the event of future Samoan difficulties with foreign nations.[23]

This, of course, carried no guarantee of American intervention. The treaty did, however, make special mention of the U.S. privilege of visiting and using the harbor of Pago Pago, though that privilege, as Secretary Fish stated in a response to a British inquiry, was not then regarded as exclusive. The new treaty was approved by the United States Senate. Robert M. Watson has written in his *History of Samoa* that the treaty was "extraordinary for two reasons. It was Samoa's first treaty; it was also America's first departure into the realms of such foreign affairs as might lead to complications with other governments."[24]

INTERNATIONAL RIVALRIES

The "good offices" clause of the 1878 treaty did contain a potential for such involvement, and that fact was not entirely overlooked in Washington. Concern over this issue had been a factor in the Senate's failure to act on Meade's treaty in 1873. The provision was, however, similar to that generally incorporated in treaties of amity and commerce since the early days of the republic. It would require a German expansionist of the 1870s or 1880s, or a dogmatist of today, therefore, to find in it evidence of American imperial ambitions in the islands. The causes of subsequent American embroilment in Samoan affairs were already present, however, in the heightened rivalries of the major powers in the Pacific and in the sympathy now aroused in the United States for the poor, beleaguered Samoans.

This sharpening of international competition among the Pacific islands in the final quarter of the nineteenth century was a reflection of economic and political changes taking place in Europe. The unification of Germany and its rapid rise thereafter as an economic power and rival to Great Britain gave political as well as economic significance to the agricultural and commercial activities of the German Handels und Plantagen Gesellschaft, the "long-handle firm."[25]

Latecomers in the scramble for colonies, the Germans found little that remained by now of value and were determined not to be shut out of the few opportunities that existed. British distaste for their activities in Samoa was communicated to Americans in the Pacific and at home in a variety of ways. And Americans in Samoa found the "arrogant" manners and bustling efficiency of the German agents quite as offensive as did the British, even though the Americans had much smaller interests at stake. The feelings voiced by Robert Louis Stevenson in his *Footnote to History,* however, helped create sympathetic reactions among Americans who had no financial interests at all in Samoa, or in the Pacific.

There is thus a strange irony in the fact that when a major clash over Samoa threatened to develop in the 1880s, it was the Americans, rather than the British, who challenged the Germans. The only major national concern in Samoa that Washington could allege was the navy's tepid interest in the port of Pago Pago, originally developed by and for a steamship line that Congress had refused to support and that had, as a consequence, ceased to exist. The emotional desire to protect Samoan freedom (a hallowed general principle) from German "bullying" had more to do with the final commitment of the United States in Samoa than any mercantile or missionary stake.[26]

So tense had relations become among the foreign powers mainly interested in Apia that a diplomatic meeting was called at Washington in 1887 to seek a peaceful solution. British, German, and American representatives met as equals, though their tangible interests or the numbers of their citizens in Samoa were hardly on a par. Britain appeared willing to recognize the preponderant German influence and was willing to withdraw claims to power there in return for compensating German concessions elsewhere.[27]

It was the United States that objected to turning the islands entirely over to Germany. The American stand was based, officially, on the Samoans' right of self-government, which was quite in accord with previously stated U.S. policy. What was new was the degree of commitment apparently involved in the stand taken in this case. It was radically different from the laissez-faire attitude adopted toward previous European actions in New Zealand, Tahiti, or Fiji, where the interests of Americans had been involved. This new position may have owed something to the supposed importance to the United States of Samoa's location in reference to a "pathway of a commerce which was just in its infancy" and to a future isthmian canal. At least such ideas were abroad in the country at that time.

No accord could be achieved between the American and German positions in 1887, and so the Washington conference adjourned with the Germans still holding the upper hand but increasingly frustrated by a tripartite consular regime in Apia and an ineffective Samoan "kingship" over all the islands.

Two years later matters in Samoa had reached such a pitch of mutual irritation, with consuls constantly meddling in Samoan politics and calling upon their governments for diplomatic support and naval protection, that a military crisis at Apia was averted only by an act of God. In March 1889 six warships out of seven then bristling at anchor in the harbor were destroyed by a hurricane. Three were German and three were American, with Britain's HMS *Calliope* the only one to escape to the open sea.[28]

The disparity between the losses in lives and property thus incurred and the stakes they were presumably defending was so marked that the governments of the powers sobered at the thought of what might have happened had the hurricane not intervened. Once again the German chancellor Bismarck agreed to a meeting, extending invitations this time to convene in Berlin. The Germans could afford to be pragmatic, since their position was based on tangible interests. The Americans again were adamant, standing on ostensibly moral principles. And so a tripartite rule over the Samoan islands was created, with a compromise Samoan king, neutral European officers, and the three consuls "in charge."[29]

In 1889 Congress authorized $100,000 to establish a naval base on the island of Tutuila, and Rear Admiral Lewis A. Kimberly purchased land at the harbor of Pago Pago in 1891–1892. Down to 1900, however, the Navy Department found no reason to proceed further despite arguments that Samoa was of strategic importance to the defense of a future isthmian canal and a general antipathy toward growing German influence in the islands.[30]

In the decade that followed its establishment, the three-headed condominium proved quite as unwieldy as the British and Germans had contended it would be. By 1899, with Samoans fighting Samoans, and German economic influence stronger than ever, Washington was finally willing to agree to a partition of the islands that would give the United States control of Tutuila and the excellent harbor at Pago Pago, plus a few smaller islands, for which it now had less real need than before.

Captain John A. C. Gray, who once headed the American administration in Samoa, noted: "The partition of Samoa was, on the whole, a diplomatic defeat for the United States, which had hoped for many years that Samoa would emerge as a small, independent nation, and when the United States government found itself responsible for an island dependency, it had no program and no machinery for its management."[31] From the standpoint of Pacific policy, indeed of national foreign policy in general, the United States thus involved itself in an international entanglement, even a colonial relationship, in a region remote from its shores, where the tangible interests of its citizens were of very limited extent or promise. It was an ominous precedent.

As the Samoan case demonstrates, arguments on strategic or sentimental/ moralistic grounds could be advanced in behalf of a "forward" policy even where tangible interests were extremely limited. It was especially difficult to refute such arguments when the presumed benefits of such a strategy were to be reaped in the future, as in the case of shipping lines yet to be established or an isthmian canal yet to be dug. In Samoa, moreover, one of the strongest arguments presented to Congress was founded upon political friction with European powers and a measure of national pride. A kind of preventive imperialism—"We have no wish to intervene, but if we don't they will"—was an argument familiar to Americans from their days of continental expansion.

The humanitarian side of the old Manifest Destiny spirit also showed itself on occasion in the Pacific. In Hawai'i, in Samoa, and in Fiji, individual Americans expressed a feeling that if the island peoples must fall under the control of a "civilized" power, they would be better off under American rule than any other. Consuls, merchants, and even missionaries on occasion stated this as if it were a matter of gospel. Their belief was capable of giving moral fervor to a campaign for what others might see as simply a lust for territorial aggrandizement.

Finally, reluctance to recede in the face of foreign pressure from a commitment once assumed, however casually or unwisely, was another aspect of this political motive. Should the reluctance of Congress to embrace expansive schemes weaken, there was plenty of evidence in the Samoan experience that expansionism had not lost its appeal for Americans, and that the Pacific was an area in which it might well seek other outlets.

OVERTHROW OF THE HAWAIIAN MONARCHY

With the passage of the McKinley tariff, the price of Hawai'i's sugar crop dropped abruptly, and the value of sugar properties in the islands plummeted. One estimate in 1892 placed losses traceable to the McKinley act in the vicinity of $12 million. No clearer demonstration could have been given of the dependence of Hawaiian sugar and Hawaiian prosperity upon the American market, and political and economic uncertainly quickly followed. To some in the islands, annexation offered the only real solution to the problem in which Hawai'i now found itself.[32]

In addition to the political unrest brought about by disturbed economic conditions, the death of King Kalakaua in January 1891 brought new complications. Liliuokalani, who succeeded her brother on the throne, was determined to restore the power of the Hawaiian monarchy and to lessen the influence of foreign, propertied interests in the political affairs of the kingdom.

Against any such reversion to "absolutism" was ranged much of the foreign community, and some of the American group revived talk of annexation with even greater earnestness. A semisecret "Annexation Club" was created in 1892, with Lorrin A. Thurston, lawyer, legislator, and descendant of a mission family, as one of its leaders. This group began considering possible replacement of the monarchy, and Thurston visited Washington to learn the sentiment of the Harrison administration toward any such change. The United States minister in Hawai'i, John L. Stevens, was completely in sympathy with the annexation group, and they counted on his support when the time should come to put their plans into action.[33]

In January 1893 a combination of circumstances that centered about the queen's proposal to promulgate a new constitution on her own initiative touched off a virtually bloodless coup. At a critical moment, U.S. forces were moved ashore from USS *Boston*, then in Honolulu harbor. Ostensibly landed to protect American lives and property, the manner of their deployment was clearly designed instead to discourage armed resistance by proroyalist forces if any occurred. Queen Liliuokalani, on advice of her counselors, then surrendered her authority "until such time as the Government of the United States shall, upon the facts presented to it, undo the action of its representative and reinstate me in the authority which I claim as the constitutional sovereign of the Hawaiian Islands."[34]

This had been the approach successfully taken by Kamehameha III at the time of the British seizure of the kingdom in 1843. By it the queen sought to place the responsibility for the coup on Minister Stevens, rather than on any of her own actions or those of her subjects. Stevens opened himself to the charge by recognizing the provisional regime, headed by Sanford B. Dole, prematurely and without authorization from Washington. The tactic had worked for Kamehameha III in 1843–1834, but it would not do so fifty years later. Both the times and the circumstances were different.

CLEVELAND NIXES ANNEXATION

For a time, however, it appeared that the queen's hope for restoration of her rule might be realized. Though an annexation treaty was quickly brought to completion, the outgoing Republican Harrison administration could not secure Senate approval of it with a change of administration and party control pending.

Very shortly after taking office as president in March 1894, Grover Cleveland, a Democrat, withdrew the treaty from Senate consideration pending further executive investigation.

It was not the terms of the treaty itself that Cleveland wished to reconsider so much as the circumstances that had brought it into being. Suspicion had spread in the United States that the provisional government in Hawai'i represented a small, self-interested minority, not the people in general. It was also suspected, in Cleveland's party at least, that the U.S. minister and naval commander at Honolulu, perhaps with the connivance of the Republican administration of Benjamin Harrison, had been improperly involved in the overthrow of an officially friendly government. Both by principle and partisan interest, Cleveland and his secretary of state Walter Q. Gresham felt compelled to investigate the circumstances of the overthrow of Queen Liliuokalani.[35]

Former Democratic representative James H. Blount of Georgia was sent to Hawai'i as a special agent with full power to investigate the situation and make recommendations to the president. The appointment did not require Senate approval. Blount's record of previous opposition to the Hawaiian sugar planters and to imperialism, in general, plus a partisan interest in condemning actions of the preceding Republican administration, may have influenced his judgment.[36]

There was evidence enough to warrant Cleveland's misgivings, however. Upon reaching Hawai'i Blount quickly terminated the brief protectorate created by Minister Stevens, refused the hospitality offered by both Stevens and Hawai'i's new provisional government, and set about conducting hearings in an atmosphere charged with emotion and factionalism. He soon accumulated an abundance of evidence that seemed to indicate Liliuokalani should be restored to her throne.

The problem for Cleveland now was how to accomplish such a restoration. President Dole and the new regime in Honolulu refused to step aside for Blount, or for Albert S. Willis, the new U.S. minister who succeeded Stevens. The uncertainty that then characterized the president's policy gave it the appearance of secrecy, and this brought growing criticism from Congress and sections of the press. The intransigence of the queen, moreover, helped to frustrate any effort to restore her rule for a critical period, as she at first insisted that the death penalty be imposed on those who had plotted her overthrow.

Cleveland was unwilling, and possibly unable, to use military force to restore Liliuokalani to the throne. His attorney-general advised him that such a step would require the approval of Congress, and it was increasingly clear that a strong section of Congress and the American public would not support the use of the army or navy to "haul down the flag" and restore a monarch to her throne. Finally, in December of 1893, Cleveland turned the whole matter over to Congress without recommendation as to the course that should be pursued.[37]

Congressional investigations and debates on the Hawaiian question ran through the first half of 1894, generating much heat but remarkably little light. They revealed sharply divided sentiments as to the legality, propriety, and desirability of the extension of U.S. control over the islands. Pure partisanship dominated part of the discussion, with Republicans defending Harrison and Stevens and upholding expansion. The Democrats, on the other hand, generally sided with Cleveland and Blount, but there were important defections from both parties on the issue.

Most of the arguments over imperialism that would be brought forth later in connection with the Spanish-American War and in the election campaign of 1900 were given preliminary airing at this time. Annexation of noncontiguous territory, for example, was assailed as a violation of traditional and sound national policy by one group and upheld as its logical extension by another. In the long run it became clear that neither side possessed a clear popular mandate on the issue. A two-thirds majority could not be mustered in behalf of an annexation treaty in the Senate, but Congress would also not authorize a forcible restoration of the queen. As a result, the Republic of Hawai'i, established on July 4, 1894, lived until 1898 as an independent nation, reminiscent of the Republic of Texas nearly a half-century earlier.[38]

During those intervening years agitation for annexation continued, both in the United States and in Hawai'i. In the islands the dependence of the fledgling republic upon its economic ties with the United States seemed to much of the Honolulu business community, at least, to make annexation essential, even inevitable, if stable and orderly growth were to continue. American and Hawaiian-American capital continued to dominate the economy, accounting for at least two-thirds of the investments in sugar and merchandising. Even those properties owned by non-American aliens were deeply involved with markets and sources of supply in the United States.

The U.S. election of 1896 returned a protectionist Republican administration to the White House and raised again the specter of possible American tariff discrimination against Hawai'i's major export product, with new fervor thus imparted to the annexationist cause there. Happily for its advocates, the McKinley administration also proved to have a strong expansionist element.

There was no unified "voice of business" calling for annexation, not even in Hawai'i. Some Honolulu businessmen opposed it for reasons of nationalist sentiment that was tied to countries other than the United States. Another group feared the effect of American immigration laws on their supply of cheap Asian labor. Still others anticipated a possible inflow of mainland capital and competition. And in the United States beet and cane sugar producers, some refiners, and others argued against incorporation of Hawai'i into the union. It can probably be safely said that the great majority of American businessmen were quite indifferent to the admission of Hawai'i, except as their feelings were swayed by nationalist, racist, or other than economic motives.[39]

ANNEXATION ACHIEVED

In addition to the economic arguments for annexation, further support for the cause developed in 1897 out of difficulties between the Hawaiian republic and the government of Japan. Fearful of a rapid rise in the numbers of Japanese resident in the islands, Hawaiian authorities refused to permit a party of immigrant laborers from that country to land in March 1897. The Tokyo government promptly protested the action, alleging violation of rights under an immigration treaty of 1886. In May the Japanese warship *Naniwa* arrived at Honolulu bearing representatives of that government, of the press, and of the immigration contractors.

Rumors of Japanese plans for invasion or coercion of the Hawaiian authorities quickly developed, and they were used by partisans of annexation to stress the need for action by Washington if Japanese seizure of the islands were to be forestalled. The *Japan Times* even cited European rumors of an alliance between Japan and Spain to thwart American expansion. This purported threat continued to be used by annexationists right down to the day of annexation despite Japanese disclaimers of belligerent intent.[40]

In June 1897 President McKinley sent to the Senate a new treaty providing for annexation of the Hawaiian Islands by the United States. Its terms mostly followed the draft of 1893, except that it dropped the indemnity to the queen provided in the earlier treaty.[41] The Japanese minister in Washington presented a formal protest against the treaty on the grounds that it might disturb the status quo in the Pacific, endanger the treaty rights of Japanese in Hawai'i, and interfere with the settlement of problems then in process of negotiation between Japan and Hawai'i over immigration, voting rights, and other matters.

The government of Japan, as foreign minister Count Okuma made clear to U.S. minister Buck in Tokyo, was quite aware of the manner in which a supposed Japanese threat to the island republic was being used to further the annexationist cause. Reassured, however, that the rights of Japanese would be respected in the event of annexation, the Tokyo authorities withdrew their protest in December 1897, even though Japanese press criticism of the American action continued.[42]

The State Department had taken an interest in Hawai'i's importation of labor for many years, and on occasion the U.S. representatives had exerted some effort to prevent the creation of too strong a foreign influence in the islands by this means. Now, during the troubled months of the summer and autumn of 1897, U.S. minister Harold W. Sewall was instructed to keep a close watch upon the Japanese-Hawaiian negotiations in Honolulu. In the event of an attempt by the Japanese to use force, Sewall was authorized to announce a provisional protectorate by the United States and to call on the naval commander in the area for support. Theodore Roosevelt, assistant secretary of the navy at the time, advocated immediate annexation even at the risk of war with Japan.[43]

Despite the urgent economic and strategic questions thus raised, sufficient congressional support to approve the annexation treaty could not be obtained through the remainder of 1897. All the old negative arguments on constitutional grounds were revived, and the influential domestic sugar lobby again brought its influence to bear in opposition. A sharpening debate on the fundamental question of imperialism, its morality, and its compatibility with American institutions raged about the question of Hawai'i's annexation well before the war with Spain began or the question of the Philippines appeared.[44]

The war with Spain in the Pacific and the resultant American presence in the Philippines influenced American positions and policies elsewhere in the Pacific. New emphasis, for example, was placed on the strategic position of Hawai'i. No longer were the islands viewed merely as an outwork of defense for the North American continent. Now they were valued as a way station on a vital sea route to Manila.

During the war the leaders of the Republic of Hawai'i, with a keen eye on the possibility of annexation, offered the facilities of their islands to American war vessels and troops, despite the unneutral character of such a policy. Friends of Hawaiian annexation in the U.S. Congress could then argue, as they did, that Hawai'i must now be taken into the union, partly because of its demonstrated strategic usefulness, but also because it might otherwise face the danger of Spanish retaliation. Far-fetched as the latter rationale might appear, the events of the war did provide the extra emphasis on Pacific military strategy needed to carry the annexation proposal through Congress.[45]

In the face of continued strong opposition, supporters of annexation decided in March 1898 to abandon the treaty route for the method once employed to annex Texas—a joint resolution of Congress. Reported first in the Senate on March 16, the resolution was put aside during the excitement attending the outbreak of war in Cuba, and it was not finally voted on by the Senate until July 6. Approval had already been accorded by a wide majority in the House on June 15. On August 12, 1898, the flag of the United States was raised over Iolani Palace in Honolulu.[46]

10

AN IMPERIAL POWER

IRONIES

In a period of some eighteen months in 1898–1899 the United States assumed sovereign control over Hawai'i, Wake Island, Guam, the Philippines, and the eastern islands of Samoa in the Pacific, and Puerto Rico in the Caribbean. Cuba became for a time an occupied country and a protectorate. Even in an age accustomed to flag-raisings and the expansion of colonial empires this was still something of a major coup. What made it more remarkable was its achievement by a nation that was itself a former European colony and had more than a century of anticolonial rhetoric in its political tradition.

The expansion of the 1890s sprang, however, from roots deep in the American past, combining idealism with the crassest of material motives. Familiar, or once familiar, domestic ideas interacted here with momentary domestic political alignments and with developments on the international scene to produce the Spanish-American War and the emergence of the United States as a self-conscious world power and administrator of an overseas empire.[1]

It is ironic that the Pacific was the principal scene of this outburst of expansive energy. The tangible economic, political, and cultural ties of Americans across the North Atlantic vastly exceeded their interests of a similar type in the Pacific and Asia. In none of the new possessions, with the exception of Hawai'i, were the traditional justifications for America's Manifest Destiny relevant. There were no large groups of American settlers in Samoa or the Philippines, no American merchant or missionary communities in Guam or Wake to ask for protection. And any prospect of incorporating the new Pacific possessions into the union as states was considered remote or impossible by imperialists and anti-imperialists alike.[2]

In only a minor degree, then, can this American thrust across the Pacific be attributed to political or economic changes in the area itself, except for the threat of great power encroachments on China. Even in that regard the policy makers of 1898 knew little about the area and the actual interests of Americans there, as their own words make clear. They could, therefore, speculate the more airily about future possibilities. They paid little or no attention to the attitudes or desires of the native peoples of the area. As a result, many of their expectations about the costs or consequences of the steps they were taking, or urging others to take, proved grossly in error in subsequent years.

EARLY RELATIONS WITH THE PHILIPPINES

The acquisition of the Philippines was without a doubt the most important result of the Spanish-American War for subsequent American relations and policies in the Pacific. This accepted, it is remarkable that one can find so little evidence of American interest in the archipelago before the coming of the war. Burdened by restrictive Spanish regulations, Manila had not become a major center of international trade before 1898.[3]

The first commercial contact between the United States and the Philippines came as early as 1796, when one of the ships owned by Elias Haskett Derby of Salem touched at Manila and loaded sugar, pepper, and indigo. Thereafter, American visits occurred with increasing frequency as more ships sailed into the western Pacific. A fairly frequent, but small, trade developed despite Spanish regulations, with American purchases of Philippine hemp, rice, coffee, tobacco, hardwoods, and other Philippine products, in exchange for sales of textiles, hardware, and other products of the United States, Europe, and other parts of Asia. As in the rest of America's Asian trade, the balance of trade was generally in the favor of the Philippines, with specie often used to make up the difference.[4]

U.S. customs records show a value of $234,568 for imports from the Philippines in 1822, followed by a fairly steady increase until 1857 when the figure exceeded $3.5 million. Growth thereafter was irregular, though in 1872 the figure reached $7,781,629, and in 1884 topped $12 million. In 1897, however, the total was only $4,383,740. These figures do not include Philippine products carried in American ships to other foreign ports for sale. By 1855 Manila was exporting more to the United States and Great Britain than to Spain. Thereafter the trade volumes varied, but they were never large as a percentage of America's Asian or total trade.[5]

If the United States had become a significant factor in the foreign trade of the Philippines, the reverse was clearly not the case. America's total commerce with the Philippines made up less than one-half of one percent of her foreign trade. This, moreover, was in a period during which foreign trade was dwindling to a mere tenth of the total national business of Americans. The offices of American companies in Manila gradually closed as the century went on, and by 1898 it has been estimated that there were fewer than thirty Americans in all the islands of the Philippine group.[6] Clearly it was not the presence of significant American economic interests in the Philippines that dictated their seizure by the United States and their retention after the Spanish-American War.

THEODORE ROOSEVELT AND DEWEY

On the contrary, to a remarkable degree the military intrusion of the United States into that archipelago in 1898 appears to have sprung from the will and activity of a small group of influential men strategically placed in government and society, possibly constituting America's first modern foreign policy elite. For that reason it is important to study their roles and motivations.

Theodore Roosevelt, assistant secretary of the navy under President McKinley, had been looking for, even hoping for, a war to "tone up" American society for some time. In 1891 he had eagerly anticipated a possible conflict with Chile over a minor naval-diplomatic contretemps. In 1897–1898 he looked forward to war with Spain and did his best in the short time he was in that office to see that the navy was prepared for it. As early as September 1897, he was advocating and planning operations in the Pacific against Spanish units. It was largely through his efforts that Commodore George Dewey, whom he regarded as an aggressive-minded officer, was placed in command of the Asiatic Squadron in 1898 with orders to take offensive action against the Spanish Philippines if war broke out.[7]

Roosevelt's personal objectives in advocating this line of action appear to have been to strengthen the navy, to help in achieving the defeat of Spain, to raise the fighting spirit of the nation, and in some way to enhance the long-term strategic position of the United States among the powers in the Orient.[8]

When the declaration of war with Spain did occur, Dewey sailed with his squadron for Manila. He possessed very limited information as to the strength and disposition of the Spanish forces there, and even less as to the ultimate aim of his mission or the national policy it was designed to serve. Although he had been ordered to destroy the Spanish fleet as a potential threat to the United States, Dewey had no clear knowledge of what he was supposed to do next. Nor did anyone in the McKinley administration.[9]

As the American flotilla steamed toward its historic rendezvous with the Spanish at Manila Bay, Emilio Aguinaldo, a leader of Filipino nationalists, was arriving at Hong Kong. Aguinaldo, then in exile from his homeland, had been in Singapore when he was contacted by Edward Spencer Pratt, the American consul-general there, at the suggestion of a British subject, Howard W. Bray, who had formerly resided in the Philippines. Bray's idea, adopted by Pratt, was that the Filipino dissidents and the Americans might find mutual benefit in combining forces against the Spaniards. Pratt notified the State Department and Commodore Dewey of this view.[10]

Dewey encouraged Pratt to send Aguinaldo on to Hong Kong. Interestingly, the State Department, on the other hand, very promptly warned Pratt to make no promises to the Filipino leader concerning future American policy. That understood, the department gave its blessing to cooperation, and Aguinaldo traveled on to Hong Kong in a U.S. naval vessel only to find that Dewey had already sailed for Manila. Both Pratt and the consul at Hong Kong later denied that they had promised Aguinaldo that the United States would turn the islands over to the Filipinos when the war was over. At the same time, neither they nor virtually any other Americans at the time had any expectation that the United States would take control of the Philippines as a colonial possession. That attitude they must have conveyed to Aguinaldo.[11]

The Filipino leader, however, later contended that he had received definite assurances of American support for Filipino independence as an inducement to gain his aid against the Spanish. Even Dewey, according to Aguinaldo, gave such assurances before the latter stepped ashore to take a position of leadership among the rebel forces already around Manila.[12]

As U.S. troops began to land in the Philippines in the summer of 1898, the aims of the Americans began to appear more and more questionable to the Filipinos. Yet their repeated inquiries as to the future policies of the United States in the islands received no clear answers. The reason was simple. No one at Manila or in Washington really knew.

AND THE AMERICANS STAYED

There was no apparent reason for Dewey to remain at Manila Bay after he had eliminated any potential threat to the United States by destroying the Spanish fleet there. Conceivably he could have sailed away from Manila, leaving the port in the hands of the Spanish. According to H. H. Kohlsaat, McKinley once remarked, "If old Dewey had just sailed away when he smashed that Spanish fleet, what a lot of trouble he would have saved us."[13] Yet the president himself seems to have had a hand in ensuring that the results of the naval action would be lasting.

Four days before Dewey's first official message reporting his victory reached the White House, General Nelson Miles, of the War Department, was already recommending that an army expeditionary force be sent "to occupy the Philippine Islands." The next day, McKinley endorsed the proposal with a cryptic note that added, "The above is only carrying out verbal instructions heretofore given."[14] A week later Major General Wesley Merritt was appointed to command the occupation force.

It should be noted that neither Dewey nor the Navy Department were pushing for such a military occupation. On May 7, Secretary of Navy Long wired Dewey that additional ammunition he had requested was being sent to him, and possibly army troops "unless you telegraph otherwise. How many will you need?"[15] This was three days after McKinley had approved the sending of an army force and while the War Department was already busy with plans for its embarkation at San Francisco. It would appear that the two military bureaucracies were more in rivalry than cooperation at that point.

Dewey replied that he could take Manila at any time, but to hold it "and thus control Philippine Islands would require, in my best judgment, well-equipped force of 5,000 men. . . . Spanish force is estimated 10,000 men. The rebels are reported 30,000 men."[16]

That some had a broader, more accurate conception of the responsibilities being entered upon is indicated by General Merritt's proposal from San Francisco that at least 14,000 troops be placed under his command, regulars, not militia. When the War Department hesitated to accept this estimate, General Merritt insisted that his demands were not excessive, "when the work to be done consists of conquering a territory 7,000 times from our base, defended by a regularly trained and acclimated army of from 10,000 to 25,000 men, and inhabited by 14,000,000 people the majority of whom will regard us with intense hatred born of race and religion."[17] Only Merritt, it appeared, recognized that his mission would involve not only the conquest of the Spanish forces but of the Filipinos as well. This amazing bit of intelligence and foresight failed, however, to deter the McKinley administration or the War Department bureaucracy.

The importance of all this uncertainty as to the nature and purpose of the military expeditions sent to Manilla lies in the fact that later the very presence of the U.S. forces there would be one of the strongest arguments used in the campaign to keep possession of the islands. "Don't haul down the flag" was more important than the hope of commercial gain in winning popular and congressional support for retention of the islands. Dewey's assumption, moreover, that possession of Manila would represent control of the entire archipelago came to be accepted in Washington. Thus, after the fall of Manila and the signing of an armistice, it became relatively simple for many Americans to assume that their nation was in possession of the whole of the Philippines and that there was no acceptable alternative to continuing that control.[18]

In fact, however, at the time of the signing of the armistice with Spain in August 1898, such authority as existed in the Philippines outside of Manila was in the hands of Filipinos or a few Spaniards. Meanwhile, more and more American troops kept arriving, until they numbered far more than had originally been requested. Nevertheless, neither the Filipinos nor American military leaders on the scene had yet any instructions as to the future American mission in the islands, and they could obtain no response from Washington to their inquiries on that score.

The simple fact was that in the absence of any preconceived plan for governing the Philippines, no one knew what U.S. policy was or should be. For weeks the only policy was drift, despite what later apologists for McKinley have tried to prove. Certainly the interests or views of the Filipinos had not been assessed or even considered. Not even the most ardent advocates of annexation had devised plans for the governance of this distant, alien people. As charges of "imperialism" or "colonialism" were hurled at the administration in the

Very shortly after taking office as president in March 1894, Grover Cleveland, a Democrat, withdrew the treaty from Senate consideration pending further ex-ecutive investigation.

It was not the terms of the treaty itself that Cleveland wished to reconsider so much as the circumstances that had brought it into being. Suspicion had onies from her. Their antipathy, however, was tempered by the distance of the Philippines from their own shores and by their lack of significant, established, commercial, or strategic interests there. Some of the opposition also stemmed from the possible effect of the war upon Spain in Europe and on the prestige of monarchies in general. Before the outbreak of the war, representatives of the major powers at Washington submitted a mild statement expressing a hope that matters could be settled without hostilities. That was as far as the Continental powers were willing to go, without British cooperation, in opposing the American action.[24]

The German government, especially, had demonstrated a keen interest in the Philippines, and that interest has been credited with having considerable influence on the American decision to retain them. The late but aggressive expansion of the German Empire had already clashed with American interests in Samoa. Captain Mahan voiced suspicions of the kaiser's policies, and Theodore Roosevelt, Senator Lodge, and others shared them. Influential American citizens and officials, including Commodore Dewey, were prepared to take offense at the appearance of a powerful German naval squadron in Manila Bay during the Spanish-American hostilities.[25]

Both Germany and Japan already had extensive commercial interests in the central and western Pacific, and they were eager to strengthen those interests by the 1890s with political control of islands not previously claimed by other major powers. In 1898, moreover, Berlin had reason to believe that the United States would probably not attempt to retain control over the Spanish possessions after the war. The Germans were encouraged in this belief by the American ambassador to Germany, Andrew D. White, who, when questioned by the German government in July 1898 stated his personal belief that the United States would not only be uninterested in retaining the Philippines but would be at least not opposed to German acquisition of them.[26]

While the Spanish-American War was still in progress, the Germans were negotiating with Spain for purchase of at least part of the latter's Pacific island holdings. By September 10, 1898, a tentative agreement had been reached regarding the Caroline Islands, even before the Spanish-American peace negotiations got underway in Paris. Uncertainty and growing puzzlement over American objectives caused any final agreement between Germany and Spain to be held in abeyance, helping to account for the presence of German naval units at Manila shortly after Dewey's victory. On the other hand, the presence of those German naval units helped to convince some in Washington that Germany intended to take the Philippines if the United States did not.[27]

Attention is given to the position of Germany here for two reasons. First, friction between Dewey and von Diederichs, the German naval commander at Manila, gave rise to an oft-repeated story that the Germans were trying to "muscle in" on the Philippines right then and there.[28] The expansionist and often anti-German press spread this story. Second, during the negotiations at Paris representatives of an American missionary group already established in the Caroline Islands, and certain persons interested in a possible international cable station in that area, both argued for the retention by the United States of at least part of Spain's holdings in Micronesia. They were outmaneuvered, however, by German pressure on Madrid for fulfillment of their tentative agreement of September 10 concerning the Carolines.[29]

The ultimate result of this contest of interests was to leave the United States in possession of the Philippines, with Germany holding the other Spanish Pacific islands in such a fashion as to make the strategic arguments for American retention of Guam and the Philippines absurd. A string of German, later Japanese, islands lay across the route from Hawai'i to Manila, making the Philippines a "heel of Achilles" for American defense, as Theodore Roosevelt later termed it.[30]

After the annexation of Hawai'i, a gesture toward closing the tremendous geographic gap between the new American possessions in the Pacific was taken when uninhabited Wake Island was formally claimed for the United States on January 17, 1899, by Commander E. D. Taussig of the Navy gunboat *Bennington*. Given the size and terrain of this tiny islet, there seemed little likelihood that it could contribute greatly to American strength in the Pacific, and there were at that time no plans to make it do so. Denial of access to any other power once again surfaced as an argument, chiefly naval, for territorial acquisition.[31] The Spanish-held island of Guam, in the Marianas, was another and potentially more important coaling station and supply base seized in 1898. An American warship en route to Manila with ammunition and reinforcements for Dewey was ordered to capture Guam and disarm its Spanish garrison.[32]

AN ISTHMIAN CANAL AND PACIFIC STRATEGY

When the war with Spain broke out, the new battleship *Oregon*, the most powerful and modern unit in the United States Pacific Squadron, was ordered to sail from San Francisco some 18,000 miles around Cape Horn to reach the Atlantic-Caribbean theater of war. That event, and the subsequent difficulties of attempting to conduct simultaneous naval operations in two oceans, and to defend two coasts, dramatized the need for an interoceanic canal.

Captain Mahan had been insisting for years upon the necessity of such a canal for the defense of the continental United States and for the promotion of foreign trade. His followers, Theodore Roosevelt and Henry Cabot Lodge among them, took up the cry, and in 1896 the Republican party platform stated that a "Nicaragua canal should be built, owned and operated by the United States." The Nicaragua route was stressed at that time because a French concession still existed for one via Panama.[33]

In December of 1898 President McKinley cited the new urgency given the canal question by the enlarged responsibilities of the United States in the Caribbean and Pacific. The administration began negotiations with Great Britain to remove the old Clayton-Bulwer Treaty of 1850, now an obstacle to an American owned and controlled canal. That agreement, originally signed by the United States as a means of thwarting a supposed British design to dominate the entire isthmian region, now stood in the way of what was deemed an American strategic necessity. Somewhat reluctantly, the British government agreed to replace the old treaty with one acceptable to the United States. Negotiations began in Washington and continued into the new century before being resolved on terms acceptable to the United States.

The decision to build an isthmian canal increased American strategic interest in Samoa in the face of growing German economic and political interests there. In 1898 the German government proposed to the British Foreign Office that in return for their joint recognition of American claims in the Philippines the United States might be asked to recognize uncontested German power in all Samoa and that of the British in Tonga. British reluctance to enter into the bargain prevented an official proposal to Washington.[34]

The strained condition of German-American relations in 1899 made some definite settlement over Samoa desirable. Negotiations began in both Apia and Washington that ultimately produced the agreement dividing the island group between Germany and the United States. Great Britain was satisfied by German concessions to British interests in Tonga, Niue, the Solomons, and Africa. The wishes of the Samoans were not taken into consideration. Under the agreement, the United States received the island of Tutuila, with its port of Pago Pago, the Manu group to the north, and Rose atoll to the east.[35]

For administrative purposes American Samoa was placed under the control of the Navy Department, virtually by default and without guidance as to the policies or procedures to be followed. This condition, probably intended to be temporary, continued for a half-century with relatively little change. Naval officers assigned to the Samoan station met problems of local policy mostly by interfering as little as possible with the traditional authority of the *matai*, holders of family titles. There was no appreciable demand from American private interests to create a major commercial base at Pago Pago, or to exploit the meager resources of the American-held islands. Where American Samoa was concerned, there appeared to be neither private interest nor public policy in the United States.[36]

INDIVIDUAL, GROUP, AND NATIONAL INTERESTS

The transpacific territorial expansion of the United States occurred before serious public debate over the reasons for it could take place. After the fact, the argument over causes and motivations grew long and often bitter, and it has not ended to this day. Americans a century later are still attempting to understand the intricate patterns of motivation that underlay the expansions of 1898.

Though President McKinley described the annexation of Hawai'i as the consummation of American policy there, rather than an aberration, many Americans and foreigners questioned the consistency with the nation's past of this new assumption of rule over alien peoples in noncontiguous areas. A whole series of debates resulted over Hawai'i, over the Philippines and, inevitably, over the relationship of all this to American interests and relations in East Asia. There was not one single confrontation between expansionists and anti-expansionists; there were many different arguments, on varying grounds and involving different areas. Since the debates in most cases took place after the fact of intervention, the emotional cry "don't haul down the flag" was probably more important at the time than more rational constitutional arguments as a guide to action or inaction.

Many of the most ardent and publicized expansionists were politicians and bureaucrats (the latter especially from the Navy and State departments). They also included journalists, freelance writers, academic figures, and clergymen. The principal leaders of the American business community were conspicuously absent from the group.

Read today, the speeches and writings of that time seem poorly documented and frequently erroneous as to precedents, existing world conditions, and future prospects. Yet, at the time, the debate engaged some of the best minds of the nation and offered exciting visions of international prestige and power. Pursuit of empire appealed to a generation of young men born to wealth, yet not keenly interested in the world of creating it. They found the idea of "public service" appealing, but not the dirty business of politics.

The opponents of expansion in 1898–1900 were generally no better informed about the Pacific or the world in general than were its advocates. They appealed to a different set of national ideals and constitutional principles. They shared many of the racial views of the expansionists but lacked the necessary data with which to attack the ill-founded economic and strategic arguments of that group.

The questions of national interest and policy raised in those discussions at the turn of the century have since been the subject of continued debate, scholarly research, and polemic literature. It may therefore be useful to examine both the motives behind and the after-the-fact rationalizations of the Pacific expansion. For purposes of convenience they will be grouped under the headings: political-strategic, economic, and humanitarian, recognizing, however, that no one of these categories commonly appeared in isolation from the others.[37]

POLITICAL-STRATEGIC EXPANSIONISM

The "large policy" advocated by Henry Cabot Lodge, Theodore Roosevelt, and others must be given first consideration, if only because of the publicity given its proponents by historians. These men and their influential friends waged a strenuous campaign to win to their side at least President McKinley and congressional leaders, and to commit the nation to an aggressive foreign policy. The essence of their message was that the United States had, by area, population, and now industrial might, become a great power and should therefore act as other great powers did.

There was a strong element of social Darwinism in their argument. Both Lodge and Roosevelt, for example, spoke at times of the battle for survival among nations and "races" and the principle of natural selection that was involved in these struggles. The United States, Lodge declared, must continue to grow, if not in territory then in political and economic power, or it would slip backward in the race among nations. "National progress," to advocates of the large policy, demanded expansion of American interests outside the nation's borders to include military bases and possibly even colonial possessions, though the latter were seldom mentioned.[38]

Their ideas were often inconsistent, changing with the passage of time and the vagaries of opportunity. As time passed the large policy developed a more consistent content, at least partly through the influence of Captain Mahan. The number of bases to be sought in the Caribbean and isthmian regions increased, for example, while those in the Pacific seem to have been limited before the war with Spain to an Alaska-Hawai'i-Isthmus of Panama perimeter, with a position in Samoa later added. Mahan, despite the statements of certain later writers, does not appear to have seen the need for or the defensibility of a Philippine base until after Dewey's seizure of Manila Bay in 1898.[39]

Mahan's primary interest was in the navy and its expansion, and in remarkably influential books, articles, and speeches he equated the national interest with naval power. Insisting that all great nations needed powerful navies to protect their far-flung commerce, Mahan went on to point out that overseas bases were indispensable if a powerful navy were to carry out its function. It was the transport and protection of America's commerce that was his central theme, not the development of that commerce. Disposal of growing agricultural and industrial surpluses, the advancement of civilization, and the attainment of national greatness were all bound up, in his mind, with the expansion of the navy.[40]

When it came to the question of how the great power status of the United States was to be asserted in the 1890s, expansionists did not suggest that Europe, the North Atlantic, or even Africa were proper scenes for such activity. The focus of their attention was on Caribbean bases and the Pacific. In the Pacific their interest focused first on Hawai'i, which had figured in American strategic considerations since well before the days of the large policy. The strategic location of those islands in the northeastern part of the great ocean—where no other land mass had similar relation to the defense of the Pacific coast—had been apparent to British and French naval officers in the 1830s, to Captain Wilkes in the 1840s, and to Brigadier General Schofield in the 1870s.[41]

Theodore Roosevelt expressed his view of the strategic implications after the overthrow of the Hawaiian monarchy in 1893: "We did not create the Hawaiian Islands; they already exist. We merely have to face the alternative of taking them ourselves and making them the outpost for the protection of the Pacific Coast or else of seeing them taken by any powerful nation with which we are at war, and at once transformed into the most dangerous possible base of operations against our Pacific cities."[42] Roosevelt also expressed concern over the post–1893 growth of Hawai'i's Asian population and the Japanese government's expression of a special interest there.[43]

Where Samoa was concerned the expansionists were refreshingly vague. References to markets there and to responsibilities to the "delightful people" of the islands who had put their trust in American protection went along with unsupported claims by such nonexperts as John Hay that the harbor of Pago Pago was "indispensable" to the United States.

Beyond the islands of the eastern Pacific no definite territorial ambitions seem to have moved the expansionist group before the autumn of 1897, if then. The future importance of East Asian markets for American commerce figured prominently in their speculations, but they did not commonly result in suggestions that American colonies should be planted in the western Pacific or on the Asian coast. Even talk of possible naval or maritime bases in the western Pacific, an idea broached by Dr. Peter Parker in the 1830s and by Commodore Perry in the 1850s, was not revived until after May 1898. There was, then, no concerted government effort to search out records of American activities and prior rights in the islands of Polynesia or Micronesia such as took place after World War I and on the eve of World War II.[44]

This point needs emphasis because of later statements that the navy had been actively planning a campaign in the Philippines and the establishment of a power base in the western Pacific long before the Spanish-American War. Though the Navy War College considered contingency plans for a war with Spain as early as 1894, the Philippines did not enter into planning until the following year, and then American naval action in the area was viewed simply as a means of diverting Spanish ships from the Atlantic and Caribbean. In 1896 Lieutenant William W. Kimball authored a plan that envisioned seizure of Manila to serve as a bargaining chip in peace negotiations, though for what goal he did not specify.[45]

In September of 1897 Theodore Roosevelt, recently appointed assistant secretary of the navy, mentioned the Philippines for the first time in a public utterance, and then only as a place where Spanish naval forces would have to be rendered powerless in the event of a war with that country. There is no evidence that either Roosevelt or his friend Captain Mahan had previously considered how a naval base might be established there, or how such a base might serve the interests of the United States. Serious consideration of such a prospect would have dictated that attention be given to the strategic importance of the Micronesian islands that lay between Hawai'i and the Philippines, and there is no evidence that either they or the Navy Department did so.[46]

The strategic rationalizations for American retention of the Philippines, therefore, came largely after the seizure of Manila, not before.[47] Although hastily assembled, short on accurate data, and weak in argument, they proved heady stuff for media publication and popular consumption. The idea of a geopolitical elite, moving men and machines about on the great oceanic board, delighted one group. The spectacle of the American flag waving over distant bases and islands, bringing order and healthier and cleaner lives to "native" peoples, pleased others. And the vision of Americans facing up to the Old World powers and giving a new model to the old, exploitative imperialism of Europe was a clincher. In this sense strategic, or better, pseudo-strategic, arguments helped to prepare Americans to take up the burdens of empire in the Pacific.

It is a strange irony that Cuba's struggle for freedom should have set loose the expansive force that took the U.S. flag across the Pacific. Yet without that catalyst American acquisition of the Philippines, Wake, or Guam at that time or later is difficult to imagine. Even the annexation of Hawai'i would at least have been delayed and might never have become politically palatable to Washington without the war with Spain to push it through Congress. There lies the one real argument for the importance of military strategy factors as motives for the expansion of 1898–1899.

ECONOMIC RATIONALIZATIONS

The explanation of American expansion in the Pacific in the 1890s on economic grounds has been the subject of both scholarly and doctrinaire study for many years.[48] Most of the argument in 1898 was founded, however, on imagined prospects rather than present realities. At times it partook clearly of the kind of fantasy that had marked American speculations about Asia's markets since the day of Samuel Shaw. And, as in earlier times, the Pacific was seen merely as a zone of transit to those Asian markets. Most of the argument, moreover, was advanced by men not concerned with or experienced in the responsible management of business firms. They were politicians and publicists, some of them writing for so-called business journals, who introduced "commercial" arguments to help win support for less tangible aims.

Captain Mahan, for example, began a noted article, "The United States Looking Outward," by asserting the need for a great navy to protect a far-flung commerce that did not yet exist but must surely be in prospect. And some, like the Reverend Josiah Strong, who urged the humanitarian, Christian mission of the United States to extend its rule, also spoke of the incidental economic blessings that such expansion would doubtless bring to all concerned.[49]

These arguments were not new in the 1890s, but during that decade and the following one they appeared more frequently than probably ever before. There seems also to have been a stronger tendency now to call for positive government action to *promote* American commerce and investment abroad, in place of the chiefly *protective* policy toward existing private interests that had previously prevailed.

The depression of 1893 and the slow economic recovery thereafter spurred some to look to the expansion of foreign markets for "surplus" American goods and "surplus" American capital as one, or even as the only, way to achieve a return to sustained prosperity. Asia appeared to many of them to offer the best prospects for this. Prominent intellectual leaders like Brooks Adams wrote some of the most fascinating and perhaps influential essays supporting this argument, essays that were filled with brilliant insights and sweeping generalizations based on very limited factual information.[50] Adams's oversimplifications and erroneous assumptions strongly appealed to Roosevelt and his circle when they could be used to support the views of the large policy school.[51]

Underlying such arguments lay a series of assumptions that were questionable, at best. One was that the per capita level of consumption within the United States and industrialized Europe would probably remain fairly constant. Thus, any continued growth of production would inevitably surpass the limits of domestic consumption in the capitalist nations. A statement from the Department of State in April 1898 put the argument this way: "It seems to be conceded that every year we shall be confronted with an increasing surplus of manufactured goods for sale in foreign markets if American operatives and artisans are to be kept employed the year around. The enlargement of foreign consumption of the products of our mills and workshops has, therefore, become a serious problem of statesmanship as well as of commerce."[52]

A second assumption seems to have been that the expanded fields abroad for American manufactures and capital would have to be sought in underdeveloped lands rather than in other industrialized nations. For would-be experts of the time it seemed illogical that markets for manufactured goods could be found in countries that were themselves engaged in exporting those manufactures. A similar argument was applied to capital exports. Thus, if American neophytes were to compete with more experienced European producers and salesmen for those foreign markets not already surrounded with preferential barriers, obviously some help from their government would be required. New importance was thus attached to the consular service and diplomacy as handmaidens of business. There were new attempts to upgrade American legations abroad, both in rank and in the quality of personnel. In 1881, and again in 1897, the State Department ordered the preparation of more frequent and detailed consular reports and their publication for the benefit of the business community.[53]

As it turned out, however, a rising standard of consumption within the United States in the twentieth century proved the first of these assumptions false. The second was contradicted by the entire history of American foreign trade, both before and after the 1890s. The bulk of that trade continued to be with industrialized nations, or regions possessing adequate purchasing power, and not with Asia or Africa. As American capital began to venture abroad in larger amounts it sought the greater security of developed or nearby countries rather than remote ones, however great the need for capital in the latter. American industrialists and financiers voted with their dollars, and only a minor proportion of those went to the Pacific at the turn of the century or for some time thereafter. By the time these facts became clear, however, the glib rationalizations described above had already exerted their impact on United States government policies in the Pacific and East Asia.[54]

Julius Pratt went to the heart of the matter when he stated that "the need of

American business for colonial markets and fields for investment was discovered not by business men but by historians and other intellectuals, by journalists and politicians."[55] Such arguments, however, made it possible for successive administrations in Washington to take positions of commercial advocacy well in advance of the demonstrated desires, or needs, of the nation's business community. This was especially true with regard to China, and it led to a serious imbalance of American interests, commitments, and national power in the Pacific, ostensibly to protect a business stake vital to the nation's well-being. That imbalance, recognized too late by one of its architects, Theodore Roosevelt, would lead to repeated and increasingly serious foreign relations problems in the area in the twentieth century.

A "MISSION" FOR HUMANITY

An idealistic, humanitarian call to empire was a major force in winning over a sector of American public opinion that could not be moved to support aggressive actions by economic, political, or strategic appeals. The roots of this sentiment went deep into the American tradition. The appeals made to it at the turn of the century are reminiscent of those during the Manifest Destiny agitation of the 1840s that had fueled completion of the expansive drive across the North American continent. Any area and any people that fell under the sway of the United States, ran part of this argument, would be the better for it, politically in human freedom, economically in greater productivity and prosperity, and socially in sounder and more stable institutions.[56]

The reverend Josiah Strong put it well in 1885: "Every race which has deeply impressed itself on the human family has been the representative of some great idea—one or more—which has given direction to the nation's life and form to its civilization. The Anglo-Saxon is the representative of two great ideas, which are closely related. One of them is that of civil liberty. . . . The other . . . is that of a pure *spiritual* Christianity."[57] This combination of a civilizing mission, in terms of democratic institutions, with a religious one, usually in terms of American Protestant views, provided a powerful rationalization of expansion as a positive duty. Such arguments were repeated in press, pulpit, and the legislature over the following years, and they helped to reverse, for a time, old American prejudices against colonies and imperialism.[58]

When critics suggested that corruption and political jobbery in many parts of the contemporary American system hardly gave promise that the United States would bring unalloyed civic virtue to other peoples, their arguments, though supported with examples from city, state, or nation, were brushed aside. If there were blemishes on the American political and social scene, they were but minor imperfections in what was doubtless the best political system in the world, declared the expansionists. Besides, added Roosevelt, the sobering responsibility of governing and uplifting backward peoples would help purify both ideals and practice within the United States itself.[59]

INFLUENCES FROM ABROAD

International events and currents of thought also influenced policy making in the United States at the turn of the century. In the first place a "march of empire," the great outward thrust of European economic and military power associated with the "New Imperialism" of the late nineteenth century, served both as an example and as the source of an extensive literature of justification for conquests of "backward" areas, much of which was read by influential Americans.

The speeches of Henry Cabot Lodge, the writings of the Adams brothers, the letters of Theodore Roosevelt, all seemed to accept the idea that Europe's expansion, on balance, was evidence of a superior civilization inevitably expanding its influence. From there it was easy to conclude that similar American overseas adventures would be either desirable or inevitable. British writers and diplomats like Rudyard Kipling, Robert Louis Stevenson, and Sir Cecil Spring Rice were powerful influences in behalf of such thinking by those who might be termed an American policy elite.[60]

The threat that other powers, in their colonial or commercial expansion, might encroach on American interests abroad was also used as an argument for U.S. action. This sort of "preventive imperialism" was already familiar to Europeans with regard to Africa, Asia, and Oceania, and Great Britain was one of the oldest and favorite targets of such reasoning among Americans.

Mahan repeatedly cited the danger of British Caribbean bases to American military security and trade, and Theodore Roosevelt became exercised at the possibility that Germany might seek to establish footholds in the Americas, as well as in the Pacific. In time both Lodge and Roosevelt, already suspicious of Russian and French activities in East Asia, would include Japan as one of the nations that concerned Americans must face in defense of the "national interest."[61] Unless the Americans got there first, they argued, and thus joined in the very scramble for bases and concessions that many of them had so often denounced, there would soon be no free markets in which to sell nor pagans to convert without facing discriminatory barriers erected by rival powers.

OTHER INFLUENCES

During the peace negotiations between Spain and the United States, officers of both the army and navy were sent to Paris to inform and possibly advise the peace commissioners. It appears that those who testified supported acquisition of at least part of the Philippine archipelago. They may even have been selected for that purpose in view of the administration's increasingly expansionist policy. Yet, there seems to have been no strong navy push for acquisition of islands in the Marianas, outside of Guam, or in the Carolines or Marshalls despite an awareness evidenced of the strategic location of these islands between the United States and the Philippines. Navy views appear to have been divided even on

Guam and Wake. Naval stations, coaling bases, or cable connections were vaguely and variously cited, in and to Congress, as purpose for which those islands should be claimed.[62]

Cable considerations did emerge as one factor in discussions concerning the Pacific islands. Though Americans had developed an interest in telegraphic communication as early as the Civil War years, they were slower than the European nations in entering the field of ocean cable laying in the Pacific area. An early effort by an American group to construct a line from Alaska to Asia in the 1860s was abandoned when Danish-Russian interests opened overland telegraphic communications between Europe and East Asia. British firms, with government support, reached the Orient via their imperial holds to the south. The European firms then set out to prevent the introduction of further competition, except for local Japanese lines.

Thus, when Americans began to think of linking up with the Philippines and East Asia at the time of the Spanish-American War, they found cable access to the coasts of Asia in the hands of other nations whose governments supported private interests in essentially monopolistic arrangements. At one point representatives of a British firm even insisted that they had exclusive cable-landing rights in the Philippines by reason of prior arrangements with the Spanish.[63]

Under these circumstances, interested American telegraph firms, notably the Pacific Cable Company of New Jersey, the Pacific Cable Company of New York, and the Pacific Commercial Cable Company, began to seek active Washington support of their transpacific projects. They did not, however, except in certain rare instances, advocate government ownership or control of the industry. Bitter competition among the rival American firms made itself felt in Washington and delayed or impeded completion of an American cable even as far as Hawai'i until 1903.

Nevertheless, during the negotiations with Spain in 1898, cable interests advocated the acquisition of certain islands between Hawai'i and Asia as potential communications stations. Midway and Wake islands were mentioned in this connection. The former, of course, had been claimed for the United States in 1867 for use as a coaling station for transpacific steamships. In both cases, and even more in that of Guam, telegraph and navy interests were in 1898 at one in favor of acquisition.[64]

In other instances it was missionary and cable interests that seem to have been more closely linked, at least in the peace commissioners' minds. Kusaie, in particular, was portrayed to them as both a missionary center and a potential cable station. Impressed by the argument, the commissioners were at one point prepared to offer Spain a million dollars for the island, mentioning to Washington its potential as a naval base as well. The Spaniards, however, could not be moved from their agreement with Germany, and the offer was rebuffed. Similarly, although both the State Department and the American commissioners at Paris spoke briefly of possible acquisition of all the Carolines, nothing came of it.

There is, in fact, a feeling of unreality, founded on patent geographic igno-rance of the area, that pervades most of the discussion of Pacific islands in the whole peace settlement of 1898. In the end, the eagerness of both the Spanish and United States governments, for reasons of domestic politics, to wind up the whole peacemaking process had more to do with the final terms than did any sober calculation of Pacific interests. Both the Spanish and American negotia-tors, moreover, were anxious to get home for the holidays.

AFTERMATH

After the signing of the peace treaty with Spain, the debate in the United States over the question of American imperialism heated up considerably. In the Senate it centered first on the question of consenting to ratification of the treaty itself. The most crucial debates there, unfortunately for the historian, were con-ducted in executive session and did not become matters of public record. A good deal about the arguments presented, can be deduced, however, from state-ments made by senators in other places and other contexts.[65]

The debate in the House over the appropriations required by the treaty settle-ment involved many of the same arguments. Members of both houses of Con-gress expressed their views in speeches and articles, and both press and platform echoed them throughout the nation. Even after ratification of the treaty, the issue continued to be argued in the presidential campaign of 1900. From all this the voters at that time, and scholars since, have continued to argue the various motivations that succeeded in winning American acceptance of the responsibil-ities involved in acquiring an overseas empire.

The advocates of an expansive policy had the advantage of war-born excite-ment over a victorious cause and the wartime media identification of America's aims with all that was right and good. They had a dramatic program, the full nature and cost of which was yet shrouded in ignorance and uncertainty even for themselves. The issue of annexation was settled by treaty before the outbreak of the insurrection by Filipino nationalists revealed to many Americans the false-hood of much of what Lodge, McKinley, and others had told them about the eagerness of the island people for the blessings of American rule.

Lodge's errors in arguing that the Philippines would be a bastion of American military strength in East Asia, and that Manila would replace Hong Kong as the greatest commercial entrepôt there, would only be revealed by time and expe-rience. In the last analysis, probably the most important single argument in deciding the issue in 1899 was the fact that the United States was in the Phil-ippines and there seemed to be no politically satisfactory way to withdraw. Historians, in arguing the economic, strategic, or idealistic reasons for the an-nexation of 1898, seem to have underestimated the role played by simple pa-triotism and plain partisan politics.

While an Anti-Imperialist League was formed at the time to oppose ratifica-tion of the peace treaty, and though it included some most distinguished Americans, its cause never achieved the unity of purpose or the media popularity won by the expansionists. The policy of the anti-imperialists seemed essentially a negative one, especially with American armed forces actually in occupation of the Caribbean and Pacific islands at issue.

In retrospect, it seems unfortunate for the anti-imperialists' strategy in Congress that they put so much stress on the constitutional, legalistic side of the issue. Senator George G. Vest of Missouri stated their general theme, "under the Constitution of the United States no power is given to the Federal Government to acquire territory to be held and governed permanently as colonies." This provided endless opportunities for legalists like Senators Lodge of Massachusetts and Orville H. Platt of Connecticut to argue legal niceties until the issue was lost in the sea of words.

Another major handicap for the anti-imperialists lay in their lack of concrete knowledge of the Philippines and the Pacific with which to refute the glib, hazy generalities their opponents based on supposed strategic and economic advantages for the "national interest." When Theodore Roosevelt opined that the task of governing "backward peoples" would strengthen the moral fiber of Americans and call them to higher international responsibilities, no amount of factual research could be brought to bear against him. And when the editors of certain business journals and other "business" writers conjured up fantastic possibilities for profit in a "new Asia" yet to come, they did not fear documented disproof from their opponents.

Senator George Frisbie Hoar, Lodge's senior senate colleague from Massachusetts, struck quite another line of argument against annexation when he insisted that control of the Philippines would commit the United States to involvement in the tangled international politics of East Asia. More than that, he pointed out, it would involve the nation in a clear violation of the premises of the Monroe Doctrine. If the United States intervened in the affairs of other continents, he argued, how then could it deny others the right to meddle in the Americas?[66]

Anti-imperialists argued that the effort to maintain control over a distant population, different from that of the United States in race, culture, and tradition, would require the maintenance there of a military establishment and autocratic government completely out of keeping with the American democratic ideal. Aside from what this would mean for the people of the Philippines, opponents of annexation argued that it must end by corrupting free institutions in the United States.

"No nation," said the Democratic national platform of 1900, "can long endure half republic and half empire."[67] But partisan politics do strange things to arguments of high principle. William Jennings Bryan, the Democratic presidential candidate in 1900, helped bring about approval of the treaty with Spain by urging senators of his party to vote for its ratification. Although an anti-imperialist himself, Bryan apparently hoped to clear the campaign of the emotion-filled and divisive issue of expansionism. Victorious, the Democrats would then be able to free the islands later, if they so desired.

If that was indeed Bryan's motive, his tactics were fatally flawed. The imperialists had the stronger press by far, and "free silver" and the other domestic issues closer to Bryan's heart could not overcome their influence. No clear mandate on empire emerged from the election, unless one accepts the expansionists' claim that the victory of McKinley and Roosevelt represented in itself a vindication of their cause.[68]

There is an irony here. If the imperialists of 1898 had committed their nation to the assumption of Pacific island possessions, the anti-imperialists had at least as strong a voice in shaping American policies for the administration of those areas. If strategic and economic motivations loomed largest in the minds of Mahan, Lodge, Roosevelt, and others, it was largely on grounds of a national civilizing mission that this expansion was sold to the voting public. It was also on that basis, tempered by practical necessities, that two Philippine commissions, in 1899 and 1900, set up administrative policies aimed more at the welfare of the Filipinos, as the commissioners considered them, than at intensive economic exploitation of the islands by Americans.[69]

Only an exploitative policy similar to those created in Southeast Asia by France and the Netherlands, coupled with a powerful and continuing military establishment, and with free trade status for the port of Manila, could possibly have realized the expectations of Senator Lodge. To their credit, neither Lodge nor most of his expansionist colleagues actually advocated that kind of regime over the people and natural resources of the Philippines.

The result was an imbalance of national interests, commitments, and power in the western Pacific that launched the United States into the twentieth century with both feet planted firmly in midair so far as a realistic Pacific and Asian policy was concerned.

CONCLUSION

What interests, then, directed U.S. policies toward the Pacific Basin in the nation's first 115 years? The conclusion must be that they varied, both in time and space, with different groups rising and falling in importance as conditions at home and abroad dictated. Some, like whaling interests, disappeared altogether. The process was a gradual one, reflecting changes in American society, in technology, and in the state of international relations.

The first American interests in the Pacific were those of the American merchants and mariners who went there. The first American policies in the area were what the men in those groups developed and implemented to serve their interests. They asked little or nothing from government, in large part because their government then lacked the ability or the will to protect and promote their interests in far-distant lands.

For nearly a century, merchants in the United States, shippers and mariners on the high seas, and commission houses in China and Hawai'i formed the early "business interest." Their requests of government were apt to be specific, limited, and related to jobs and profits for Americans. At no time did they represent more than a minor fraction of total U.S. foreign trade.

The simple mercantile aims of the first Americans to ply the Pacific—merchants, fur traders, and whalers—were complicated by the introduction of missionaries and American settlers in the Pacific Basin. Their requests for protection brought diplomatic, consular, and naval officers into the field and thus created bureaucratic interests there. Politicians and publicists found fertile ground in the assertion of national interests in an area of which the general American public knew very little.

It is at least arguable that the inattention to the Pacific area that has characterized most of the American public throughout their national history permitted small groups, or even individuals, to exert disproportionate influence on the formation of national attitudes and policies there. Benton's expansionism, Reynolds's exploring expedition, and Seward's Alaska purchase might be cited as nineteenth-century examples. Both bureaucratic inertia and the rationalizing mythologies that supported the interests of such spokesmen gave rise to visions, even legends, of the Pacific and Asia quite at odds with the tangible interests of traders and investors there.

Politicians, publicists, bureaucrats, even missionaries when it seemed to serve their purpose, argued for the economic importance of the Pacific Basin to the United States. The responsible heads of business enterprises were much less active in seeking aggressive foreign policies there. This fairly obvious conclusion must be stressed because there has been so much simplistic identification of the "business community" as the moving force in Pacific and Asian policy. On the contrary, American businessmen either waited at home for someone to come for their goods or capital or they waged their own diplomacy in dealing with counterparts abroad.

As the nation's merchant marine expanded over its first half-century, maritime interests reached coast and islands throughout the Pacific world. Then, for reasons bound up in the economic and social history of the United States, that merchant marine declined. The whalers came no more, and the growing American trade with Asia began to travel increasingly in foreign ships. The interests of shipbuilders, shipowners, and mariners thus became less important to the framing of national policies in the Pacific.

Missionaries, slower than traders to enter the Pacific world, remained longer and were more obviously vocal in attempting to influence the views of Americans toward Pacific and Asian peoples. Though some of them became students of the islands' and Asian cultures, most simply reinforced attitudes of superiority and condescension toward the "heathen." Their attitudes were sometimes at variance with those of merchants, whalers, and consuls, and they seem to have had greater success in influencing popular opinion and public policies. Throughout the period of this study many of those who represented tangible interests in the Pacific were ready and able to conduct their own "diplomacy" with the people there. Government agents, from congressmen to consuls, might be either a help or a hindrance to their efforts. Frequently their principal value was in the relations with fellow Americans or with Europeans, rather than with Pacific peoples.

It is ironic that the political and strategic commitments of the United States in the Pacific Basin increased dramatically even as the commercial stake of the country's citizens seemed to be declining. As government replaced private interests in determining policies and relations, its diplomats and military officers paid no more attention than had their predecessors from the private sector to the impact of their policies on the interests of Pacific peoples, who were still viewed as objects to be manipulated rather than as people with whom common interests could be developed.

In 1898, over a century after the *Empress of China* became the first American ship to reach China, the United States government was still only slightly involved in the Pacific, and the interests of its citizens there formed only a minor part of American overseas enterprise. From there the gap between tangible interests and political commitments continued to grow. Seizure of the Philippines, as some predicted at the time, would involve Washington in the international politics of empire in the Pacific. From that point the United States government began to assume commitments out of all proportion to the real interests of its citizens and even more out of proportion to the military power that the nation possessed or was willing to use.

One major lesson that emerges from the record would appear to be that no simple definition of "national interest" will suffice, for any period. But unless the national interest is based on the tangible interests of the nation's citizens, the result is likely to be disappointing, possibly even disastrous.

7. John Franklin Jameson, *Privateering and Piracy in the Colonial Period: Illustrative Documents* (New York, 1923), preface and pp. 92–133, 149–50, 190–257; Gertrude Selwyn Kimball, "The East India Trade of Providence from 1787 to 1807," in *Papers from the Historical Seminary of Brown University* (Providence, 1896), VI, 3–4; Latourette, p. 11; William B. Weeden, *Economic and Social History of New England, 1629–1789* (Cambridge, MA, 1926), II, 559–65; Charles O. Paullin, *Diplomatic Negotiations of American Naval Officers, 1778–1883* (Baltimore, 1912), pp. 154–58.

8. Herbert L. Osgood, *The American Colonies in the Eighteenth Century* (New York, 1924), I, 528.

9. Ibid., pp. 530–31.

10. Weeden, I, 348–48.

11. Jameson, pp. 528–46; Osgood, pp. 542–47.

12. Paullin, pp. 154–58; Weeden, II, 539–40; Alice Morse Earle, *Customs and Fashions in Old New England* (New York, 1922), pp. 138, 180–82; Jonathan Goldstein, *Philadelphia and the China Trade, 1682–1846: Commercial, Cultural and Attitudinal Effects* (University Park, PA, 1978), pp. 1–3, 17–21.

13. "Higginson Letters," in Massachusetts Historical Society *Collections*, 3rd series, VII (Boston, 1838), 209.

14. James E. Gillespie, *The Influence of Overseas Expansion on England to 1700* (New York, 1920), pp. 58–59.

15. Alice Morse Earle, *Home and Child Life in Colonial Days* (New York, 1969), pp. 92–93.

16. Alice Morse Earle, *Customs and Fashions in Old New England* (New York, 1922), p. 180; Arthur M. Schlesinger, *The Colonial Merchants and the American Revolution, 1763–1776* (New York, 1918), pp. 108–109, 178–86, 265–77, 324, 363, 369.

17. Goldstein, pp. 1–3, 73–77; Taylor Biggs Lewis, *A Window on Williamsburg* (New York, 1966), contains photographs of the Chinese wallpaper in the governor's mansion.

18. John G.B. Hutchins, *The American Maritime Industries and Public Policy* (Cambridge, MA, 1941), pp. 130–59, 170–78; Timothy Pitkin, *A Statistical View of the Commerce of the United States of America* (New Haven, 1835), pp. 345–46; Latourette, p. 11.

19. Milburn, I, xxix–xxx, xlvi, liii; Morse, I, 14–15.

20. Dennett, pp. 5–6; Merrill Jensen, *The New Nation* (New York, 1950), pp. 179–218.

21. Dennett, pp. 5–6.

22. Pitkin, pp. 30–31; Weeden, II, 816–20; Albert A. Giesecke, *American Commercial Legislation before 1789* (New York, 1910), p. 127; Allan Nevins, *The American States During and After the Revolution, 1775–1789* (New York, 1924), pp. 563–64.

23. Nevins, p. 564; Anna C. Clauder, *American Commerce as Affected by the Wars of the French Revolution and Napoleon, 1793–1812* (Philadelphia, 1932), pp. 15, 26; Jensen, pp. 160–64.

24. Jensen, pp. 245–57.

25. Latourette, p. 13; Weeden, II, 280–81.

26. Jared Sparks, *The Life of John Ledyard* (Cambridge, MA, 1829), pp. 70, 121–70.

27. Ibid., p. 148.

28. Jefferson to Charles Thomson, Paris, September 20, 1787, in Julian P. Boyd, ed., *The Papers of Thomas Jefferson* (Princeton, 1950–), XII, 19.

29. Dennett, p. 138.

30. Ibid., p. 9; Hamilton A. Hill, "The Trade, Commerce, and Navigation of Boston, 1780–1880," in Justin Winsor, ed., *The Memorial History of Boston* (Boston, 1881), IV, 203–204; Foster Rhea Dulles, *The Old China Trade* (New York, 1930), p. 28.

31. Latourette, p. 13, cites Henry P. Johnston, ed., *The Correspondence and Public Papers of John Jay* (New York, 1891), III, 97; Goldstein, pp. 24–33, emphasizes Philadelphia's role in the *Empress*'s financing, preparation and publicity; see also Philip C.F. Smith, *The Empress of China* (Philadelphia, 1984), passim.

32. Samuel Shaw, *The Journals of Major Samuel Shaw* (Boston, 1847); U.S. Department of State, *The Diplomatic Correspondence of the United States of America* (Washington, DC, 1834), VIII, 430–72.

33. *Journals of the Continental Congress, 1774–1789* (Washington, DC, 1928), XXVI, 58–59, proceedings of January 29, 1784.

34. Smith, *Empress,* pp. 64–73.

35. *Journals of Continental Congress,* XXV, 816, proceedings of December 18, 1783, and XXVI, 1–2, proceedings of January 29, 1784.

36. Hill, p. 204; Goldstein, pp. 25, 34–35.

37. Shaw, pp. 151–65.

38. U.S. Department of State, *Letters of the Continental Congress,* I (December 1784 to December 1785), American letters, 281–89, 306, 312, 379–80, 429–31; Continental Congress, *Resolve Book,* no. 123, June 9, 1785.

39. Smith, *Empress,* pp. 19–30, 220–49; Goldstein, pp. 30–33, paints a more favorable view of the voyage's profitability, but Shaw's disappointment was clear. See also Clarence L. Ver Steeg, "Financing and Outfitting the First United States Ship to China," *Pacific Historical Review* (hereafter cited as *PHR*), XXII (1953), 1–12.

40. Dennett, P. 45, gives a table "rearranged from Melburn's [sic] *Oriental Commerce,* Vol. 2, p. 486." See also Dulles, pp. 210–11.

41. Dulles, p. 106; Hosea Ballou Morse and Harley F. MacNair, *Far Eastern International Relations* (Boston, 1931), p. 69.

42. Seward W. Livermore, "Early Commercial and Consular Relations with the East Indies," *PHR,* XV (1946), 31–33; Dennett, pp. 24, 27, 31.

43. Sydney Greenbie and Marjorie Greenbie, *Gold of Ophir or The Lure That Made America* (Garden City, NY, 1925), pp. xi–xvi.

44. Weeden, II, 819; Dennett, pp. 44–46; Latourette, pp. 27–28.

45. *American State Papers,* Commerce and Navigation, I, 599, and II, 63, offer data suggesting the part played by the East Indies trade in total U.S. commerce. See also Dulles, pp. 26–30.

46. Adams to Jay, London, November 11, 1785, in *Diplomatic Correspondence,* IV, 440–41; Charles Francis Adams, ed., *The Works of John Adams* (Boston, 1852–53), VIII, 343–44.

47. Nevins, pp. 556–63; Pitkin, pp. 31–32.

CHAPTER 2

1. John K. Fairbank, Edwin O. Reischauer, and Albert M. Craig, *East Asia: The Modern Transformation* (Boston, 1965), pp. 3–28; Samuel Wells Williams, *The Middle Kingdom* (New York, 1876), II, 381–467.

2. Latourette, pp. 10, 27, 29, 73; Shaw, pp. 229–36, 301, 351; William Speer, *The*

Oldest and Newest Empire: China and the United States (Pittsburgh, 1877), p. 410; Smith, *Empress*, pp. 31–42; Goldstein, pp. 21–22, 26–27, 30, 33–35, 47; Williams, *Middle Kingdom*, II, 412; John Macgregor, *Commercial Statistics of America* (London, 1845), pp. 822–24.

3. Kimball, "East India Trade," pp. 5–6; Samuel Eliot Morison, *The Maritime History of Massachusetts, 1783–1860*, (Cambridge, MA, 1961), pp. 122–23; Goldstein, pp. 24–30, 34–35, 46–48.

4. Kimball, "East India Trade," p. 30, quotes the *Providence Gazette*, September 14, 1793; Latourette, p. 28, cites the *United States Chronicle* of same date; Goldstein, pp. 47–48, notes a similar reaction in Philadelphia.

5. Pitkin, p. 303, table xvii; Dennett, pp. 18–21.

6. Greenbie, pp. xii–xiv.

7. Dulles, pp. 51–105.

8. Latourette, pp. 29–43, 73–76; Dulles, pp. 114–18; Dennett, pp. 24–34.

9. Dulles, p. 111; Dennett, pp. 24–34.

10. Robert E. Peabody, *Merchant Venturers of Old Salem* (Boston, 1912), pp. 58–64; Dennett, p. 24.

11. Dennett, p. 26.

12. Petition of Elias Hasket Derby "praying relief of duties on a case of tea" and a report on that petition, in *Annals of the Congress of the United States, 1789–1824*, 1st Congress, 2nd Session (hereafter cited as *Annals*) 1:2, pp. 1647, 1655. See also Peabody, pp. 95–96; Yenping Hao, "Chinese Teas to America—A Synopsis," in John K. Fairbank and Ernest R. May, eds., *America's China Trade in Historical Perspective* (Cambridge, MA, 1986), pp. 11–16. Latourette, pp. 78–79, gives a useful brief history of U.S. tariffs on imports from China to 1844.

13. Latourette, pp. 64–70; Goldstein, pp. 40–45, 61–66; Dennett, pp. 70–80.

14. Pitkin, pp. 245–306; Dulles, p. 210; *American State Papers*, Commerce and Navigation, I, 927–28.

15. Dulles, pp. 106–14.

16. Latourette, pp. 53–54, 63–84.

17. W. E. Cheong, "Trade and Finance in China, 1784–1834: A Reappraisal," *Business History*, VII (January 1965), 34–47; Latourette, pp. 53–54, 71–84; Dennett, pp. 69–80.

18. Dulles, p. 114; Peter Schram, "The Minor Significance of Commercial Relations between the United States and China, 1850–1931," in Fairbanks and May, pp. 237–38.

19. Latourette, pp. 60–70; Paullin, p. 162; Goldstein, pp. 40–45, 61, 66–67.

20. Dulles, p. 29; Latourette, pp. 64–65; Morison, pp. 213–24.

21. "Journal of the Brig 'Astrea,'" ms. Essex Institute, Salem, MA; Carl Seaburg and Stanley Paterson, *Merchant Prince of Boston: Colonel T. H. Perkins, 1764–1854* (Cambridge, MA, 1971), pp. 43–50.

22. Goldstein, pp. 43–45; Thomas Hart Benton, *Abridgment of the Debates of Congress from 1789 to 1856* (New York, 1857–1861), I, 32, 41–42.

23. John Bach McMaster, *The Life and Times of Stephen Girard, Mariner and Merchant* (Philadelphia, 1918), II, 171; Wildes, p. 157ff.; Kenneth W. Porter, *John Jacob Astor, Businessman* (Cambridge, MA, 1931), II, 650–52, 713–14; Goldstein, pp. 8–9.

24. Arthur M. Johnson and Barry E. Supples, *Boston Capitalists and Western Railroads: A Study in Nineteenth Century Investment Process* (Cambridge, MA, 1971), and

the Seaburg and Paterson biography of T. H. Perkins illustrate this point, as do Dennett, p. 8, and Goldstein, pp. 40–45.

25. Ibid.

26. Dennett, pp. 69–75.

27. Samuel Shaw to the President of the United States, December 7, 1790, enclosing a protest from Shaw to the Dutch governor general and council in Batavia, in *Diplomatic Correspondence*, VII, 473–78.

28. Seaburg and Paterson, pp. 48–50; Freeman Hunt, *Lives of American Merchants* (Reprint: New York, 1969), I, 38–48; Livermore, pp. 31–33; Dennett, pp. 31–32; Pitkin, p. 206.

29. Dennett, p. 26; Greenbie, pp. 98–99.

30. Livermore, pp. 40–44; Thomas R. McHale and Mary C. McHale, eds., *Early American-Philippine Trade: The Journal of Nathaniel Bowditch in Manila, 1796* (New Haven, 1962); Dennett, pp. 33–34; Latourette, pp. 58–59, 66, 72.

31. Shaw, pp. 162–63, 168, 237–48; Dennett, pp. 54, 80; Latourette, pp. 82–83, 91, 97–98; Greenbie, p. 160; Joseph Ingraham, "Journal of the Voyage of the Brigantine 'Hope' from Boston to the Northwest Coast of America, 1790 to 1792," Manuscript Division, Library of Congress, entries for December 1791–March 1792.

32. Ingraham, entry for December 1, 1791.

33. Shunzo Sakamaki, *Japan and the United States, 1790–1853* (Tokyo, 1939), pp. 4–11.

34. A major contribution to the history of this trade is James R. Gibson, *Otter Skins, Boston Ships, and China Goods: The Maritime Fur Trade of the Northwest Coast, 1785–1841* (Seattle, 1992), which builds on the early work of Frederick W. Howay and others. See also Morison, *Maritime History*, pp. 46–47, and Latourette, pp. 29–40.

35. James Morton Callahan, *American Relations in the Pacific and the Far East, 1784–1900* (Baltimore, 1901), p. 157.

36. Frederick W. Howay, ed., *Voyages of the Columbia to the North West Coast, 1787–1790*, in Massachusetts Historical Society *Collections*, vol. 79 (Boston, 1941); Dennett, p. 39.

37. "Solid Men of Boston in the Northwest," pp. 1–9. This manuscript, attributed to William Dane Phelps, may be found in the Bancroft Library, University of California, Berkeley. See also Dulles, pp. 54–55; Latourette, pp. 34–35; J. Wade Caruthers, *American Pacific Ocean Trade: Its Impact on Foreign Policy and Continental Expansion, 1784–1860* (New York, 1973), pp. 18–29.

38. Useful journals are those of Joseph Ingraham, and S. W. Jackman, ed., *The Journal of William Sturgis* (Victoria, BC, 1978); see also Frederick W. Howay, "Early Relations between the Hawaiian Islands and the Northwest Coast," in Albert P. Taylor and Ralph S. Kuykendall, eds., *The Hawaiian Islands* (Honolulu, 1930), pp. 11–38, and W. Patrick Strauss, *Americans in Polynesia, 1783–1842* (East Lansing, 1963), pp. 1–14.

39. Alexander Starbuck, *History of the American Whale Fishery from Its Earliest Inception to the Year 1876* (Waltham, MA, 1878), p. 90; see also Elmo Paul Hohman, *The American Whaleman* (New York, 1928), p. 37, and Edouard A. Stackpole, *The Sea-Hunters: New England Whalemen During Two Centuries, 1635–1835* (New York, 1953), pp. 145–53.

40. Callahan, p. 16; Shaw, pp. 118, 356–60; Dennett, pp. 31–32; Paullin, p. 165.

41. Joseph Barrell (Macao) to his principals in Boston, March 28, 1792, in Department

of State, Consular Despatches—Canton, vol. 1; Ingraham, II, chapter 4, entry for April 19–22; Foster Rhea Dulles, *America in the Pacific* (Boston, 1932), p. 36.

42. Adams to Jay, November 11, 1785, *Diplomatic Correspondence*, I, 440–41; Charles Francis Adams, pp. 343–44.

CHAPTER 3

1. Sparks, pp. xliv–xlix, 70, 200–201; Gibson, chapters 3 and 5; Harold W. Bradley, *The American Frontier in Hawai'i: The Pioneers, 1789–1843* (Stanford, 1942), pp. 12–23, 53–55, 73–79, 222–24.

2. Ingraham journal; Howay, *Voyages*, pp. 18–21; A. J. Krusenstern, *Voyage Round the World in the Years 1803, 1804, 1805, and 1806* (London, 1813), I, 83–95; Otto Von Kotzebue, *A New Voyage Round the World in the Years, 1823, 24, 25, and 26* (London, 1830), I, 64–66.

3. Hubert Howe Bancroft, *History of the Northwest Coast* (San Francisco, 1884), I, 185–209; Robert Greenhow, *The History of Oregon and California* (Boston, 1845), p. 181; Robert E. Johnson, *Thence Round Cape Horn* (Annapolis, 1962); John J. Johnson, "Early Relations of the United States with Chile," *PHR*, XIII (September 1944), 260–70.

4. "Correspondence Concerning Captain Kendrick and the Settlement of His Estate," manuscript in the Department of State Archives; W. R. Manning, "The Nootka Sound Controversy," American Historical Association *Annual Report,* 1904 (Washington, DC, 1905); Mark D. Kaplanoff, "Nootka Sound in 1789," *Pacific Northwest Quarterly,* LXV (1974), 157–63.

5. Ingraham journal, July 30, 1791; July 30, August 8–9, and September 10-October 9, 1792.

6. Manning, pp. 279–478; Greenhow, pp. 172–259.

7. "Solid Men of Boston," pp. 7–9, 14ff; Frederick W. Howay, Walter W. Sage, and Henry F. Angus, *British Columbia and the United States* (Toronto, 1942), pp. 3–4; Greenhow, pp. 164–83, 186–88.

8. Morison, *Maritime History,* pp. 60–61; "Solid Men of Boston," pp. 7–15; Ralph S. Kuykendall, *The Hawaiian Kingdom, 1778–1854* (Honolulu, 1938), p. 85, *The Hawaiian Kingdom, 1778–1854* (hereafter cited as Kuykendall, I) and the same author's *The Hawaiian Kingdom, 1854–1874* (hereafter cited as Kuykendall, II) (Honolulu, 1953), and the same author's *The Hawaiian Kingdom, 1874–1893* (hereafter cited as Kuykendall, III) (Honolulu, 1967).

9. *American State Papers:* Foreign Relations, Second Series, Class I (Washington, DC, 1858), V, 442, 445–46; Latourette, pp. 37–38, 55–56; Samuel Flagg Bemis, *John Quincy Adams and the Foundations of American Foreign Policy* (New York, 1956), I, 172–75, 182.

10. Bancroft, *Northwest Coast,* II, 342–48; Thomas Hart Benton, *A Thirty Years View* (New York, 1854–1856), I, 13–14, 50–54; Greenhow, pp. 331–32; *House Report No. 45,* 16:2; "Report on the Pacific Ocean Settlements," in *Annals,* 17:2, 398, 418, 423, 583–86; Latourette, pp. 56–57.

11. Howay, Sage, and Angus, p. 6; Gibson, pp. 299–314.

12. Dulles, *Old China Trade,* pp. 52–64; Jackman, pp. 113–22; Bancroft, *Northwest Coast,* I, 372–74; Dennett, pp. 39–41.

13. Dulles, *Old China Trade*, pp. 63–64; Bradley, pp. 220–24; Latourette, pp. 54–56.

14. William Sturgis, "The Northwest Fur Trade," in *Hunt's Merchants' Magazine and Commercial Review*, XIV (June 1846), 535–37; Robert G. Cleland, *History of California: The American Period* (New York, 1922), p. 9; Dulles, *Old China Trade*, pp. 55, 58.

15. Howay, Sage, and Angus, pp. 6–7.

16. Edmund Fanning, *Voyages to the South Seas, Indian and Pacific Oceans* (New York, 1838), pp. 137–50; Porter, I, 64–207; Washington Irving, *Astoria* (Norman, OK, 1964), pp. 108–14.

17. Dennett, p. 41; Oscar O. Winther, *The Great Northwest* (New York, 1947), p. 30; Howay, "An Outline Sketch of the Maritime Fur Trade," Canadian Historical Association, *Annual Report* (Ottawa, 1932), pp. 7–14; Caruthers, pp. 24–29.

18. Benton, I, 13, says that he and Floyd shared quarters in a Washington, DC, rooming house with two of Astor's employees and were influenced by their views.

19. Ingraham journal, April 19–22, 1791; Dulles, *America in the Pacific*, p. 16; Dennett, pp. 39–40; "Solid Men of Boston," pp. 40–50.

20. Kuykendall, I, 85, 434; Bradley, pp. 26–27.

21. R. A. Derrick, *History of Fiji* (Suva, 1946), p. 41; Dorothy Shineberg, *They Came for Sandalwood* (Melbourne, 1967), pp. 1–15.

22. "Solid Men of Boston," pp. 61–68, reproduces the contract in full, in addition to an account of the arrangement. See also Kuykendall, I, 86–87; Bradley, p. 30.

23. Charles S. Stewart, *A Visit to the South Seas in the U.S. Ship Vincennes during the Years 1829 and 1830* (New York, 1831), II, 211–19; Department of State, Consular Despatches—Honolulu, I, National Archives microfilm series #144 (hereafter cited as Consular Despatches—Honolulu), contains the reports of U.S. commercial agent John Coffin Jones.

24. W. P. Morrell, *Britain in the Pacific Islands* (Oxford, 1960), pp. 89–95.

25. Derrick, pp. 67–69; H. Stonehewer Cooper, *Coral Lands of the Pacific: Their Peoples and Their Products* (London, 1882), pp. 263–79; Ernest S. Dodge, *New England and the South Seas* (Cambridge, MA, 1965), pp. 86–111; Fanning, pp. 461–63.

26. Dodge, pp. 86, 90–95.

27. Theodore Morgan, *Hawai'i: A Century of Economic Change, 1778–1876* (Cambridge, MA, 1948), p. 174; Bradley, pp. 242, 244; Kuykendall, pp. 172–83; Strauss, pp. 23–32.

28. Sylvia Masterman, *The Origins of International Rivalry in Samoa, 1845–1884* (Stanford, 1934), pp. 57–60; Cooper, pp. 142–45.

29. C. Hartley Grattan, *The South West Pacific to 1900* (Ann Arbor, 1963), pp. 213–14, 485–86; Morrell, pp. 211–38, 297, 310.

30. Jean I. Brookes, *International Rivalry in the Pacific Islands, 1800–1875* (Berkeley, 1941), pp. 25, 61, 102–104, 307–309; Strauss, pp. 98–104; Grattan, p. 214.

31. The mission literature is voluminous. Basic documentary collections may be found in the Hawai'i Mission Children's Society Library, Honolulu, and in the Houghton Library at Harvard University. For a famous published example, see Hiram Bingham, *A Residence of Twenty-one Years in the Sandwich Islands* (Hartford, 1847).

32. Kuykendall, I, 100–69; Bradley, pp. 121–67; Strauss, pp. 61–63; Rufus Anderson, *History of the Sandwich Islands Mission* (Boston, 1870), pp. 38–74; Bradford Smith, *Yankees in Paradise* (Philadelphia, 1956), pp. 51–53; Sheldon Dibble, *History of the Sandwich Islands* (Honolulu, 1909), pp. 176–216.

33. Louis B. Wright and Mary Isabel Fry, *Puritans in the South Seas* (New York, 1936), pp. 270–86, 302–21; Department of State, Consular Despatches—Honolulu, I, 2.

34. Sylvester K. Stevens, *American Expansion in Hawai'i, 1842–1898* (Harrisburg, PA, 1945), p. 26; A. Gavan Daws, *Shoal of Time: A History of the Hawaiian Islands* (New York, 1968), pp. 75–81, 85–91; Wright and Fry, pp. 300–21.

35. Aarne A. Koskinen, *Missionary Influence as a Political Factor in the Pacific Islands* (Helsinki, 1953), p. 109; Smith, *Yankees*, p. 188; Strauss, pp. 63–7.

36. Jeremiah N. Reynolds, *Voyage of the United States Frigate Potomac in the years 1831, 1832, 1833, and 1834* (New York, 1835), pp. 418–19; Kuykendall, I, 144.

37. Strauss, pp. 68–71, 77–80, 87–95; Merze Tate, *The United States and the Hawaiian Kingdom: A Political History* (New Haven, 1965), pp. 1–13; Ralph S. Kuykendall, "American Interests and American Influence in Hawai'i in 1842," in Hawaiian Historical Society (hereafter cited as HHS), *39th Annual Report, 1930,* 1931, pp. 48–67.

38. *House Executive Documents No. 35,* 27:3, 1–2, "Message of President John Tyler, December 30, 1842, respecting the trade and commerce of the United States with the Sandwich Islands and of diplomatic intercourse with their government"; Stevens, *American Expansion,* pp. 3–12, 16–18, 24–31.

39. John Johnson, "Early Relations of the United States with Chile, *PHR,* XIII (1944), 260–65.

40. Henry Bernstein, *Origins of Inter-American Interest, 1700–1812* (Philadelphia, 1945), p. 81; Richard J. Cleveland, *A Narrative of Voyages and Commercial Enterprises* (Cambridge, MA, 1842), I, 168–86; Henry Clay Evans, Jr., *Chile and Its Relations with the United States* (Durham, 1927), p. 8; Roy F. Nichols, *Advance Agents of American Destiny* (Philadelphia, 1956), pp. 57–66; Johnson, "Early Relations," pp. 264–70; Charles Lyon Chandler, *Inter-American Acquaintances* (Sewanee, TN, 1917), pp. 46–75.

41. Morison, *Maritime History,* p. 62; Evans, pp. 12–16; Charles J. Stile, *Life and Service of Joel R. Poinsett* (Philadelphia, 1888), pp. 27–29; Starbuck, p. 94n; Johnson, "Early Relations," pp. 264–65.

42. Arthur P. Whitaker, *The United States and the Independence of Latin America, 1800–1830* (Baltimore, 1941), pp. 194–99; William R. Manning, *Diplomatic Correspondence of the United States Concerning the Independence of the Latin American Nations* (New York, 1925), passim.

43. Captain David Porter, *Journal of a Cruise Made to the Pacific Ocean . . . in the U.S. Frigate Essex, 1812–1814* (Philadelphia, 1815); Johnson, *Cape Horn,* pp. 3, 17; Raymond A. Rydell, *Cape Horn to the Pacific* (Berkeley, 1952), pp. 91–96.

44. Johnson, *Cape Horn,* pp. 3–15.

45. Henry M. Wriston, *Executive Agents in American Foreign Relations* (Baltimore, 1929), pp. 337–38; Strauss, p. 83–85. It may be that Porter and Fanning were in touch, since both made similar proposals at the same time.

46. Paullin, pp. 329–45; Johnson, *Cape Horn,* pp. 6–92; Rydell, pp. 91–110; William R. Stanton, *The Great United States Exploring Expedition of 1838–1842* (Berkeley, 1975), offers insight into navy thinking in the 1830s and 1840s and the political bickering and limited concepts that often hampered operations.

47. Oscar Lewis, *Sea Routes to the Gold Fields* (New York, 1949), passim; Rydell, pp. 25–75, 111–26.

48. Roland R. Duncan, "William Wheelwright: The Pioneer of Pacific Steam Navi-

gation, 1825–1882," unpublished doctoral dissertation, U. of California, Berkeley, 1960, passim.

49. Gordon Greenwood, *Early American-Australian Relations* (Melbourne, 1944), p. 117; Thomas Dunbabin, "Some American Actions and Reactions in Australian History," Australian Association for the Advancement of Science, *Report of the Nineteenth Meeting* (Hobart, 1928), p. 251; Werner Levi, *American-Australian Relations* (Minneapolis, 1947), pp. 1–3.

50. Greenwood, pp. 121–23; Levi, pp. 3–6; Lloyd G. Churchward, "Australia and America: A Sketch of the Origin and Early Growth of Social and Economic Relations between Australia and the United States of America, 1790–1876," unpublished M.A. thesis, U. of Melbourne, 1941, pp. 6–10, and the same author's "Australian-American Relations during the Gold Rush," *Historical Studies: Australia and New Zealand*, II (1942), 11–24.

51. Greenwood, pp. 138–41; Levi, pp. 5–9; Dunbabin, p. 251.

52. Greenwood, pp. 138–41; John M. Ward, *British Policy in the South Pacific, 1786–1893* (Sydney, 1948), pp. 14–30; Churchward, thesis, pp. 22–3, 45–7, and "Gold Rush," pp. 11–24.

53. Dunbabin, pp. 251–53; Greenwood, pp. 94–96; Ward, pp. 31–40.

54. Levi, p. 7.

55. Brookes, pp. 102–104; Grattan, pp. 154–55, 213–16; Strauss, pp. 101–104.

56. Strauss, pp. 101–104; Brookes, pp. 102–104; *Historical Records of New Zealand*, II, 608–21; Wilkes, *Narrative*, II, 375–80; James Davidson, "European Penetration of the South Pacific, 1779–1842," unpublished M. A. thesis, Cambridge University, 1942, pp. 201–207.

57. Churchward, thesis, pp. 49–56.

CHAPTER 4

1. The literature includes Herman Melville, *Moby Dick, or the Whale* (New York, 1851); Starbuck, *American Whale Fishery;* Charles M. Scammon, *The Marine Mammals of the Northwestern Coast of North America* (New York, 1874); Stackpole, *Sea-Hunters,* and *Whales and Destiny: The Rivalry Between America, France, and Britain for the Control of the Southern Whale Fishery* (Amherst, 1972). Foreign references include Robert Langdon, *Where the Whalers Went* (Canberra, 1984), and Honore Forster, *The South Sea Whaler* (Canberra, 1985).

2. Hohman, *American Whaleman,* gives an excellent account and analysis of the industry.

3. Gordon Jackson, *The British Whaling Trade* (Hamden, CT, 1978), pp. 91–142.

4. Ibid., pp. 104–11; Ward, *British Policy*, pp. 15–25; Starbuck, pp. 1–4, 23, 36, 90; Stackpole, *Whales and Destiny*, pp. 73–85, 123–31.

5. Starbuck, pp. 90, 186–89; Scammon, pp. 209–10; Stackpole, *Sea-Hunters*, pp. 152–54.

6. Starbuck, pp. 91–93; Stackpole, *Whales and Destiny*, pp. 25–235, 285–90.

7. Amasa Delano, *A Narrative of Voyages and Travels in the Northern and Southern Hemispheres* (Boston, 1817), pp. 257ff.; Morison, *Maritime History*, pp. 61–63; James Kirker, *Adventures to China: Americans in the Southern Oceans* (New York, 1970), pp. 3–49; Stackpole, *Sea-Hunters*, pp. 207–47.

8. Kirker, pp. 65–117; Delano, p. 306; Fanning, p. 21; Harry Morton, *The Whale's Wake* (Honolulu, 1982), pp. 105–24; Stackpole, *Sea-Hunters*, pp. 356–61.

9. Delano, p. 306; "Solid Men of Boston," pp. 14–26; Kirker, pp. 65–100; Dodge, pp. 65–73.

10. Scammon, pp. 141–63; Kirker, pp. 161–75; Dulles, *Old China Trade*, pp. 81–93, offers some variant figures and interesting accounts of individual voyages and sealing captains.

11. Fanning, pp. 330–499; Delano, pp. 304–53, 460–66; Morison, *Maritime History*, pp. 61–63; Dennett, p. 37; Strauss, pp. 14–16; Kirker, pp. 4, 79–95, 99–117.

12. Morison, *Maritime History*, pp. 54, 158; Stackpole, *Whales and Destiny*, pp. 341–46; Kirker, pp. 95–100; see Starbuck, 97n., for an oft-quoted example of such claims. J. M. Reynolds's 1828 report to Congress was another. Morison offers a more cautious and probably more accurate estimate of the whalers' island discoveries.

13. Levi, pp. 25–36; Greenwood, pp. 63–96.

14. Most of the dispatches that still exist have been published on microfilm by the National Archives under the title of the relevant port. Some, such as those of Jacques Moerenhout, at Papeete from 1835 to 1837, are remarkably full and informative. Others are extremely sketchy and infrequent. See also Hohman, pp. 48–93.

15. Starbuck, pp. 96–97.

16. Department of State, *Civil Affairs Handbook, Eastern Carolines* (Washington, 1944), p. 18, and same for *Mandated Marianas*, pp. 24–28; Hohman, pp. 39–40, 149–51; Tadao Yanaihara, *Pacific Islands Under Japanese Mandate* (Shanghai, 1939), pp. 12–13; Scammon, pp. 212–15.

17. Kuykendall, pp. 61–81. Bingham, pp. 81–245, and Anderson, pp. 16–50, offer missionary views of the whalers' impact on Hawai'i.

18. Starbuck, pp. 166–72; Kuykendall, I, 92–94; Bradley, pp. 79–82, 215–19.

19. Daws, pp. 166–72; *The Friend* (Honolulu), December 17, 1852.

20. Department of State, Consular Dispatches—Honolulu; Stewart, II, 213–19.

21. S. Rickard, *The Whaling Trade in Old New Zealand* (Auckland, 1965), pp. 7, 31–48, 60, 115; Greenwood, pp. 63–99; Dakin, pp. 12–21, 24–26, 58–71, 90–98, 113–20, 129–31, 161–69. Morton gives a valuable account for New Zealand, and Strauss, pp. 35–37, 104–14, is excellent on the American side.

22. Starbuck, pp. 100, 109–13; Hohman, pp. 84–88, 148–52, 297–99, 327–29; Scammon, p. 242.

23. Starbuck, pp. 99–113; Hohman, pp. 289–308.

24. Scammon, Starbuck, and Hohman offer numerous tables based on customs returns, local shipping records, and various private sources. Starbuck, pp. 11–14, notes the scarcity and unreliability of sources for at least the early years of whaling. The *Nantucket Inquirer*, *New Bedford Mercury*, and the *Whalemen's Shipping List* also published statistical material at various times. See also Hutchins, pp. 230, 269–70; Emory R. Johnson, ed., *History of Domestic and Foreign Commerce of the United States* (Washington, DC, 1915), II, 159; Hohman, pp. 3–8, 39–47, 292–96; Starbuck, pp. 98, 166, 660–702.

25. Hohman, pp. 4–6; John R. Spears, *The Story of the American Merchant Marine* (New York, 1910), p. 203.

26. Hohman, p. 4.

27. J. R. Williams, "The Whale Fishery," *North American Review*, XXXVIII (January 1834), 84–116.

28. Johnson, *Commerce*, I, 172.

29. "Annual Statistical Report for 1854," *Whalemen's Shipping List*, January 1855; Starbuck, p. 660.

30. Starbuck, pp. 58–92; Stackpole, *Sea-Hunters*, pp. 66–84, 97–115, 256–60, and *Whales and Destiny*, pp. 27–28, 43, 49, 350–51.

31. Fanning, pp. 259–67; Stanton, pp. 1–18; Strauss, pp. 107–109.

32. Starbuck, pp. 44, 94, seems to assume that Porter was instructed to enter the Pacific to protect American shipping, but this is not supported by navy records or by Porter's own account.

33. Stackpole, *Sea-Hunters*, pp. 457–58.

34. Stanton, pp. 68–69; Strauss, pp. 108–17; Aubrey Starke, "Poe's Friend Reynolds," *American Literature*, XI (March 1939–January 1940), 152–58; Robert F. Almy, "J. N. Reynolds: A Brief Biography with Particular Reference to Poe and Symmes," *The Colophon*, II, new series (1937), 227–45; Daniel M. Henderson, *The Hidden Coasts* (New York, 1953), pp. 29–35.

35. Starbuck, pp. 109–13.

36. Strauss, pp. 111–13.

37. Ibid., pp. 113–14.

38. Stanton, pp. 56, 61–62, 69; Strauss, pp. 114–16.

39. The most authoritative account of the expedition is that by its commander, Charles Wilkes. Stanton provides an excellent one-volume description, and Strauss covers the expedition, including its background and results, in pp. 107–45.

40. Strauss, p. 123.

41. Stanton, pp. 88–111; Strauss, pp. 124–25.

42. Strauss, pp. 124–27; Stanton, pp. 116–31.

43. Strauss, p. 127; Stanton, pp. 132–41.

44. Stanton, pp. 143–81; Strauss, pp. 127–28.

45. Stanton, pp. 186–89; Strauss, pp. 128–29.

46. Stanton, pp. 189–215; Strauss, pp. 131, 135–37.

47. Strauss, pp. 138–39.

48. Stanton, pp. 219–31; Strauss, p. 139.

49. Stanton, pp. 247–73; Strauss, p. 141.

50. Strauss, p. 142.

51. Stanton, pp. 316–77.

52. Strauss, pp. 142–43.

53. Strauss, pp. 143–45.

54. Strauss, p. 28.

55. Strauss, p. 38.

56. Cited in Strauss, p. 38.

57. Rhoda E.A. Hackler, "The Voice of Commerce," *Hawaiian Journal of History* (hereafter cited as *HJH*), III (1969), 42–47; and by the same author, "Our Men in the Pacific: A Chronicle of United States Consular Officers at Seven Ports in the Pacific Islands and Australias during the 19th Century," unpublished doctoral dissertation, University of Hawai'i at Manoa, 1978.

58. Kuykendall, I, 91–92, 122–23; Bradley, pp. 178–83; Bingham, pp. 284–303; Rose H. Gast, *Contentious Consul: A Biography of John Coffin Jones* (Los Angeles, 1976), pp. 64–68.

59. Hackler, "Commerce," pp. 42–45; Grattan, pp. 213–15.

CHAPTER 5

1. Hubert Howe Bancroft, *Northwest Coast,* and *History of California* (San Francisco, 1884–1890), comprise an extensive and still valuable treatment of this subject. See also Frederick Merk, *The Oregon Question* (Cambridge, MA, 1967), and Norman Graebner, *Empire on the Pacific* (New York, 1955).

2. Bancroft, *Northwest Coast,* II, 1–9, 126–236, 316–89; Greenhow, pp. 476–77; Merk, *Oregon,* pp. 1–29; Bemis, *Adams,* I, 280–85.

3. Bancroft, *Northwest Coast,* II, pp. 7, 18–21.

4. The controversy is described fully in Meares's own *Voyages,* and in Frederic A. Howay, ed., *The Dixon-Meares Controversy* (Toronto, 1929), as well as in Bancroft, *Northwest Coast,* I, 167–238, and Derek Pethick, *The Nootka Connection: Europe and the Northwest Coast, 1790–1795* (Vancouver, 1980), pp. 1–50.

5. W. R. Manning, "Nootka Sound Controversy," pp. 279–478.

6. Bancroft, *Northwest Coast,* I, 215, 251–53; Dorothy O. Johansen and Charles M. Gates, *Empire of the Columbia* (New York, 1967), pp. 38–43.

7. "Solid Men of Boston," pp. 28, 40–49; Bancroft, *Northwest Coast,* II, 130–35.

8. Jefferson to John Jacob Astor, November 9, 1813, in A. A. Lipscomb et al., eds., *The Writings of Thomas Jefferson* (Washington, DC, 1903), XIII, 432–34.

9. *House Document No. 112,* "Message from the President on claims set up by foreign governments to territories of the United States on the Pacific Ocean, April 17, 1822," 17:1, 13–17 and following documents. Note especially letter from R. B. Prevost (Monterey) to the secretary of state, November 11, 1818. See also Bancroft, *Northwest Coast,* I, 319–25, 525–28, and II, 330; Richard A. Pierce, *Russia's Hawaiian Adventure, 1815–1817* (Berkeley, 1965); Frank A. Golder, "Proposals for Russian Occupation of the Hawaiian Islands," in Albert P. Taylor and Ralph S. Kuykendall, eds., *The Hawaiian Islands* (Honolulu, 1930), pp. 34–49.

10. *American State Papers,* III, 731; Merk, *Oregon,* pp. 1–8; Bemis, *Adams,* I, 281–82; Bancroft, *Northwest Coast,* II, 331–33.

11. Frederick Merk, "The Genesis of the Oregon Question," *Mississippi Valley Historical Review,* XXXVI (March 1950), 593–94; Barry Gough, *The Royal Navy and the Northwest Coast of North America* (Vancouver, 1971), pp. 25–28; Merk, *Oregon,* pp. 17–45; *House Document No. 112,* 17:1, p. 7; Adams to Rush, May 20, 1818, in *American State Papers,* Foreign Relations, IV, 854.

12. Bemis, *Adams,* I, 280–86, 492–98, 512–16; Bradley, pp. 72–75.

13. Bemis, *Adams,* I, 278–86; Porter, I, 140–43; Johansen and Gates, 105–106.

14. *Annals,* 16:2 (December 19, 1820), p. 679.

15. Thomas Hart Benton, *Selections of Editorial Articles from the St. Louis "Enquirer" on the Subject of Oregon and Texas*...(St. Louis, 1844), pp. 4–6, 12–14, 18–23, 26–27; William N. Chambers, *Old Bullion Benton, Senator from the New West* (Boston, 1956), pp. 83–85; Elbert B. Smith, *Magnificent Missourian: The Life of Thomas Hart Benton* (New York, 1958), p. 880; Porter, II, 732n; Bemis, *Adams,* I, 329–40.

16. *Annals,* 16:2, 946–58; *House Report No. 45,* 16:2, January 25, 1821, "Report on the Pacific Ocean Settlements" (hereafter cited as *Floyd Report*), 1–45. This report was reprinted in the *Oregon Historical Quarterly,* XIII (March–December 1907), 51–75, 290–94.

17. *Floyd Report,* p. 12.

18. Ibid., pp. 13–14; Porter, II, 713–14, 732n.

19. Bancroft, *Northwest Coast*, I, 372–77, II, 316–54.

20. Merk, *Oregon*, pp. 107–53; Bradley, pp. 78–79.

21. Dexter Perkins, *Hands Off: A History of the Monroe Doctrine* (Boston, 1941), p. 30.

22. David Hunter Miller, ed., *Treaties and Other International Acts of the United States of America* (Washington, 1933), II, 151–55; Bemis, *Adams*, I, 516–36; Johansen and Gates, pp. 119–21.

23. Bemis, *Adams*, I, 510–36; Smith, pp. 82–91; Merk, *Oregon*, pp. 133–35.

24. Bemis, *Adams*, I, 510–36; Merk, *Oregon*, pp. 101–88.

25. Howay, Sage, and Angus, pp. 38–93; Arthur L. Throckmorton, *Oregon Argonauts* (Portland, 1981), pp. 3–13; Bancroft, *Northwest Coast*, II, 446–59, 542–621.

26. Washington Irving, *The Adventures of Captain Bonneville, U.S.A., in the Rocky Mountains and the Far West* (Reprint, Norman, OK, 1961).

27. Bancroft, *Oregon*, I, 54–56.

28. Earl Pomeroy, *The Pacific Slope* (Seattle, 1965), pp. 24–30; Johansen and Gates, pp. 159–77; Bancroft, *Oregon*, I, 78–138.

29. *House Report No. 101*, 25:3, March 16, 1838, p. 5.

30. Bancroft, *Oregon*, I, 231–34; Gough, pp. 11, 25, 30–32, 37–46.

31. Bancroft, *Oregon*, I, 292–314, 391–508; Johansen and Gates, pp. 127–30, 165, 173, 178–80, 187, 213.

32. Bancroft, *Northwest Coast*, II, 432–42, 519–20, 534–35, 592–96, 602–603, 687, 702–12; Howay, Sage, and Angus, pp. 66–119.

33. Jesse S. Reeves, *American Diplomacy Under Tyler and Polk* (Baltimore, 1907), pp. 249–54; Frederick Merk, "The Oregon Pioneers and the Boundary," *American Historical Review* (hereafter cited as *AHR*), XXIX (July 1924), 681–99; Howay, Sage, and Angus, pp. 120–30; Graebner, pp. 103–107, 123–49.

34. Reeves, pp. 258–64; Lester B. Shippee, *Canadian-American Relations, 1849–1874* (New Haven, 1939), passim; Johansen and Gates, pp. 209–10.

35. Graebner, pp. v–vii, 2–7, 217–28, carries his argument beyond what would appear a reasonable assessment of the true import of the Pacific trade as a shaping factor in either expansion to the Pacific coast or the delimitation of northern and southern boundaries there.

36. Bancroft, *California*, I, 539–40; Charles E. Chapman, *A History of California: The Spanish Period* (New York, 1930), pp. 216–31, 343–51; Robert Glass Cleland, *A History of California: The American Period* (New York, 1930), pp. 1–34; Andrew F. Holle, *California: A History* (New York, 1969), p. 101.

37. Bancroft, *Northwest Coast*, I, 306–309.

38. John W. Caughey, *California* (Englewood Cliffs, 1961), p. 174; Bancroft, *California*, II, 2; Rolle, pp. 101–104; Ralph J. Roske, *Everyman's Eden: A History of California* (New York, 1968), pp. 120–35.

39. Caughey, p. 174; Bancroft, *Northwest Coast*, I, 307–309.

40. "Solid Men of Boston," pp. 10–31, 40–59; Rolle, pp. 103–104.

41. Adele Ogden, "New England Traders in Spanish and Mexican California," in *Greater America: Essays in Honor of Herbert Eugene Bolton* (Berkeley, 1945), pp. 395–413; and by the same author, "Alfred Robinson: New England Merchant in Mexican California," *California Historical Society Quarterly*, XXIII (September 1944), 193–218; Nellie Van de Grift Sanches, *Spanish Arcadia* (Los Angeles, 1929), pp. 129–55.

42. Cleland, pp. 91–175; Caughey, pp. 262–68.

43. Caughey, pp. 266–68.

44. *Department of State, List of U.S. Consular Officers, 1789–1939*, Microcopy No. 587, roll 12 for Monterey and roll 17 for San Francisco; John A. Hawgood, ed., *First and Last Consul: Thomas Oliver Larkin and the Americanization of California* (Palo Alto, 1967).

45. Cleland, pp. 140–52, 176–89; Caughey, pp. 269–72; W. C. Binkley, *The Expansionist Movement in Texas* (Berkeley, 1925), pp. 28–29; Reeves, pp. 58–88; Graebner, pp. 65–82.

46. Caughey, pp. 269–72; Graebner, pp. 65–82; Cleland, pp. 176–89.

47. Reeves, pp. 100–102.

48. Ibid., pp. 98–113; Cleland, pp. 144–48; Caughey, pp. 232–33.

49. Quoted in Cleland, pp. 147–48.

50. Charles Sellers, *James K. Polk, Continentalist, 1843–1848* (Princeton, 1966), pp. 357–97; Richard R. Stenberg, "The Failure of Polk's Mexican War Intrigue of 1845," *PHR*, IV (March 1935), 39–86; Reeves, pp. 265–67; Graebner, pp. 103–22.

51. Cleland, p. 204.

52. Bancroft, *California*, V, 193–215.

53. Ibid., pp. 469–508, 524–57, 643; Caughey, pp. 265–68; Rolle, pp. 184, 189, 217. For a more doctrinaire view, see Lloyd C. Gardner, Walter F. LaFeber, and Thomas J. McCormick, *Creation of the American Empire* (Chicago, 1973), pp. 150–54, and Graebner, pp. 99–102, 154–228.

54. Miller, *Treaties*, V, 207–36.

CHAPTER 6

1. See Howay, *Voyages*, and "Early Relations," pp. 11–38; also Bernice Judd, *Voyages to Hawai'i Before 1860* (Honolulu, 1974), pp. 1–10.

2. Kuykendall, *Hawaiian Kingdom*, pp. 23–26.

3. Ibid., pp. 20–28, 82–88; Bradley, pp. 1–52; Morgan, pp. 57–73.

4. Kuykendall, I, 20–28, 82–8; Bradley, pp. 1–52; Morgan, pp. 57–73.

5. See, for example, Urey Lisiansky, *Voyage around the World in the Years 1803, 1804, 1805, and 1806 in the Ship Neva* (London, 1814), p. 115; Archibald Campbell, *A Voyage Round the World from 1806 to 1812* (Honolulu, 1967), pp. 118–19, 151–54.

6. William D. Westervelt, "Kamehameha's Cession of the Island of Hawai'i to Great Britain in 1784," HHS *22nd Annual Report* (1914), pp. 19–24; Kuykendall, I, 39–44; George Vancouver, *A Voyage of Discovery to the North Pacific Ocean in the Years 1790–1795* (London, 1801), V, 27–28, 47–53, 88–97; Kamehameha I to King George III, August 6, 1810, Archives of Hawai'i, Foreign Office and Executive File (hereafter cited as *FO&E*).

7. Campbell, *Voyage*, pp. 118–20.

8. Kuykendall, I, 82–89; Bradley, pp. 22–66; James Hunnewell, "Honolulu in 1817 and 1818," HHS *Papers*, No. 8 (1895); A. Gavan Daws, "Honolulu—The First Century: Influences in the Development of the Town to 1876," unpublished dissertation, U. of Hawai'i, 1966, pp. 2–6.

9. Peter Corney, *Voyages in the Northern Pacific, 1813–1818* (Honolulu, 1896), pp. 65–70; Louis Claude De Sauleses De Freycinet, *Voyage Around the World*, translated

into English by Ella L. Wiswell (Honolulu, 1978) p. 67; Jacques Arago, *Narrative of a Voyage Around the World . . . 1817, 1818, 1819, and 1820* (London, 1823), p. 122–23.

10. Kuykendall, I, 94; Bradley, pp. 58–65, 82–92.

11. Howay, "Early Relations," pp. 34–35; Klaus Mehnert, "The Russians in Hawai'i, 1804–1819," University of Hawai'i *Occasional Papers*, No. 38 (Honolulu, 1939), 1–21, 46–55, 61–68; Alexander Spoehr, "Fur Traders in Hawai'i: The Hudson's Bay Company in Honolulu, 1829–1861," *HJH*, XX (1986), 27–37; Alexander M'Konochle, "Considerations on the Propriety of Establishing a Colony on One of the Sandwich Islands," reprinted in HHS *14th Annual Report* (1907), pp. 29–43; Frank A. Golder, "Proposals for Russian Occupation of the Hawaiian Islands," in Taylor and Kuykendall, pp. 39–49.

12. Kuykendall, I, 85–92; Bradley, pp. 26–32, 53–71; Morgan, pp. 61–73; "Solid Men of Boston," pp. 61–68.

13. Andrew Bloxam, *Diary of Andrew Bloxam, Naturalist of the "Blonde," On Her Trip to the Hawaiian Islands from England, 1824–25* (Honolulu, 1925), pp. 41–42.

14. Gilbert Farquhar Mathison, *Narrative of a Visit to Brazil, Chile, Peru, and the Sandwich Islands During the Years, 1821 and 1822* (London, 1825), pp. 362–477.

15. Sir George Simpson, *An Overland Journey Round the World During the Years 1841 and 1842* (Philadelphia, 1847), I, 259–73.

16. Department of State, Consular Despatches—Honolulu, vol. 1; Gast, pp. 43–58, 77–96; Kuykendall, I, 89–92; Bradley, pp. 53–120.

17. "Acknowledgment of Indebtedness by Kings and Regents and Chiefs of the Sandwich Islands," November 2, 1828, *FO&E*, Folder 5; Stewart, *Visit*, II, 212.

18. Kuykendall, I, 70, 82, 93–95, 100–104; Bradley, pp. 79–82, 121–29.

19. Bingham, pp. 69–79; Samuel M. Kamakau, *Ruling Chiefs of Hawai'i* (Honolulu, 1961), pp. 219–28, 246–48; William D. Alexander, "The Overthrow of the Ancient Tabu System in the Hawaiian Islands," HHS *25th Annual Report* (1916), pp. 37–45; Stephanie Seto Levin, "A Reexamination of the Overthrow of the Kapu System in Hawai'i," (n.p., n.d.) in Hawaiian Collection, Hamilton Library, U. of Hawai'i at Manoa.

20. Bingham is filled with narrative fact and missionary interpretation, as are Dibble, *History,* and Anderson, *Mission.* For a contrary view see Wright and Fry, pp. 269–32.

21. Bradley, pp. 121–213; Kuykendall, I, 100–16; Daws, *Shoal of Time,* pp. 61–66, 75–81, 102–20.

22. Robert C. Lydecker, *Roster: Legislature of Hawai'i, 1841–1918* (Honolulu, 1918), pp. 3–5; W. D. Westervelt, "Hawaiian Printed Laws before the Constitution," HHS *16th Annual Report* (1908), pp. 54–57.

23. Interesting similarities can be found between the Puritan rule in seventeenth-century England and the missionary effort in nineteenth-century Hawai'i in, for example, Samuel Rawson Gardiner, *History of the Commonwealth and Protectorate, 1649–1656* (New York, 1965), III, 18, and IV, 27–40.

24. Reverend Henry T. Cheever, *Life in the Sandwich Islands* (New York, 1851), pp. 294–96.

25. From Bingham, pp. 215.

26. For a devastating indictment of the missionary influence on the Hawaiians by a contemporary observer, see H. Willis Baxley, M. D., *What I Saw on the West Coast of South and North America and at the Sandwich Islands* (New York, 1865), passim. Baxley was a "Special Commissioner of the United States" who visited the islands in 1860, 1861, and 1862.

27. Bingham, pp. 489–96; Anderson, pp. 121–26; Bradley, pp. 361–68; Kuykendall, I, 170–78, and "American Interests," pp. 54–57.

28. Bingham, pp. 529–30; Kuykendall, I, 153–59.

29. Kuykendall, I, 94; Morgan, pp. 59–73, 81–85.

30. Department of State, Consular Despatches—Honolulu, I; Stewart, II, 213–19.

31. Bingham, pp. 283–89; Gast, pp. 107–108, 112–16; Paullin, pp. 337–39; Hiram Paulding, *Journal of a Cruise of the United States Schooner Dolphin* (Honolulu, 1970), pp. 225–26.

32. Kuykendall, I, 79–81.

33. Department of State, Consular Despatches—Honolulu, vol. 1; Correspondence between the American Board of Commissioners for Foreign Missions and Members of the Sandwich Islands Mission, ms., Houghton Library, Harvard University; Miller, *Treaties,* III, 277–79; Stevens, p. 1; Kuykendall, I, 138, 207–208, 314–21.

34. Paullin, pp. 339–44; Stevens, pp. 1–12; Tate, pp. 1–19; Bradley, pp. 1–3, 89–97; Kuykendall, I, 138, 207–208, 314–21.

35. Jean Paul Faivre, *L'Expansion Francaise dans le Pacifique, 1800–1842* (Paris, 1953), pp. 217–93, 424–42; Brookes, pp. 69–92; Donald D. Johnson, "Powers in the Pacific: Tahiti and Hawai'i, 1825–1850," HHS *66th Annual Report* (1957), pp. 7–25.

36. Anderson, pp. 135–36; Bingham, pp. 529–30.

37. Walter F. Frear, *Anti-Missionary Criticism with Reference to Hawai'i* (Honolulu, 1935); Jarves, pp. 150–85, 189–98, 203–208; Kuykendall, I, 207, 234–36, 248–51; Bradley, pp. 399, 413–17; Daws, pp. 128–31.

38. Lydecker, pp. 4–5, 8–16; Kamakau, pp. 342–45, 336–78.

39. Bradley, pp. 402–408; Kuykendall, I, 189–94; the Archives of Hawai'i hold a small body of Farnham ms., and other pertinent documents may be found in *FO&E;* Brinsmade's activities may be followed in his consular dispatches, in *FO&E* files of the period, and in *Report of the Proceedings and Evidence in the Arbitration between the King and Government of the Hawaiian Islands and Messrs. Ladd & Co.* (Honolulu, 1846), all in Archives of Hawai'i.

40. Richard MacAllan, "Sir George Simpson and the Mission for Hawaiian Independence, 1840–1843," *HJH,* XX (1986), 67–82; Kuykendall, *Hawaiian Kingdom,* pp. 191–94.

41. William Richards's manuscript journals for this period may be found in the Archives of Hawai'i.

42. *Senate Executive Documents No. 77,* 52:2, VIII, 40–41; U.S. Department of State, *Papers Relating to the Foreign Relations of the United States* (hereafter cited as *Foreign Relations*), 1894, Appendix II, pp. 44–45; Stevens, pp. 1–11; Bradley, pp. 441–45; Kuykendall, I, 191–96.

43. *House Executive Documents No. 35,* 27:3, pp. 1–4; also in *Senate Executive Documents No. 77,* 52:2, pp. 35–36.

44. Kuykendall, I, 199–202; Stevens, pp. 16–20, 24–33, 44–45.

45. Ward, *British Policy,* pp. 127–37; Morrell, pp. 64–88; Brookes, pp. 124–38.

46. Great Britain, Foreign Office, File 58, 58/18, is an invaluable source, as are documents in Hawai'i *FO&E* for this period. See also Department of State, Instructions, Great Britain, Legare to Everett, June 13, 1843; George V. Blue, "The Policy of France toward the Hawaiian Islands from the Earliest Times to the Treaty of 1846," in Taylor and Kuykendall, pp. 51–93.

CHAPTER 7

1. Kuykendall, I, 236–39, 245–51, 368–82; Stevens, pp. 20–23.
2. *Senate Executive Documents No. 57*, 52:2, p. 13; *Foreign Relations*, 1894, pp. 60–61.
3. Kuykendall, I, 368–428; Daws, *Shoal of Time*, pp. 106–24, 128–36; Stevens, pp. 24–45.
4. Morgan, pp. 74–85, 96–194; Kuykendall, I, 170–84; Stevens, p. 12.
5. Spoehr, pp. 27–66; Kuykendall, I, 170–94; Morgan, pp. 96–194; Bradley, pp. 214–70; Jarves, pp. 189–203. Hawaiian government reports are of increasing value for the latter part of this period, especially after the establishment of formal ministries from 1845. These are found in the Archives of Hawai'i, Honolulu.
6. Stevens, pp. 46–50, 54–59, 61–140; Kuykendall, I, 331–33, 377–80, II, 37–47, 140–9, 198–200, 209–30, 247–57, III, 14–45; Morgan pp. 209–16; Tate, pp. 15, 20–21, 32–33.
7. Hawai'i, *Report of the Minister of Foreign Affairs*, 1850, appendix, pp. 41–87; Department of State, Diplomatic Despatches—Hawai'i, Ten Eyck to Secretary of State (Buchanan), 1848–1850; Department of State, Diplomatic Instructions—Hawai'i, II, Buchanan to Ten Eyck, No. 7, August 28, 1848; *Foreign Relations*, 1894, Appendix 2, pp. 79–95.
8. Kuykendall, I, 388–95; Brookes, pp. 189–96; Stevens, pp. 50–54.
9. *Congressional Globe*, 31:1, volume 24, part I, p. 16, message of President Millard Fillmore to Congress, December 2, 1851; Stevens, pp. 49–50.
10. Jacob Adler, ed., *The Journal of Prince Alexander Liholiho* (Honolulu, 1967); Laura Fish Judd, *Honolulu: Sketches of the Life, Social, Political, and Religious in the Hawaiian Islands from 1829 to 1861* (Honolulu, 1928), pp. 144–65; Gerrit P. Judd IV, *Dr. Judd: Hawai'i's Friend* (Honolulu, 1960), pp. 164–91.
11. Quoted in Kuykendall, I, 398.
12. Stevens, p. 56; Kuykendall, I, 410.
13. Kuykendall, I, 401–405.
14. Ibid., p. 402; Hawai'i, *Privy Council Records*, VI, 310–12, Archives of Hawai'i.
15. Laura Fish Judd, "A Suppressed Chapter of Hawaiian History," HHS *10th Annual Report* (1903), pp. 7–12; Kuykendall, I, 411–29; Stevens, pp. 57–76.
16. *Alta California* (San Francisco), April 22, 1851; *The Polynesian* (Honolulu), May 17, 1851; Kuykendall, I, 408–11.
17. Stevens, pp. 56–57; Kuykendall, I, 408–11.
18. William D. Alexander, "An Account of the Uncompleted Treaty of Annexation between the United States of America and the Hawaiian Kingdom Negotiated in 1854," HHS *Papers*, No. 9 (Honolulu, 1896); Pauline King Joerger, "A Political Biography of David Lawrence Gregg: American Diplomat and Hawaiian Official," unpublished Ph.D. diss., U. of Hawai'i, 1976; Kuykendall, I, 419–27.
19. *Congressional Globe*, 32:1, Part E, p. 2232, August 17, 1852.
20. Charles H. Hunter, ed., "The Turrill Collection," HHS *66th Annual Report* (1957), pp. 27–92 (see especially Charles R. Bishop to Joel Turrill, January 14, 1853, October 4, 1853, January 20, 1854, April 13, 1855, and William L. Lee to Turrill, June 1, 1851, January 15, 1853, and February 26, 1855); King, pp. 68–88; Kuykendall, I, 409–11, 413–28.

21. James D. Richardson, ed., *A Compilation of the Messages and Papers of the Presidents* (Washington, 1896–1899), V, 198–99.

22. Hawai'i, *FO&E* files contain much material on concern about filibustering and the general problem of maintaining order in Honolulu at this time. For general accounts see Kuykendall, I, 409–18; King, pp. 70–88; Daws, *Shoal of Time,* pp. 137–38, 148–49.

23. Quoted in Kuykendall, I, 418.

24. Department of State, Despatches—Hawai'i, Gregg to Marcy, No. 1, December 27, 1853.

25. King, p. 58.

26. Merze Tate, "Slavery and Racism as Deterrents in the Annexation of Hawai'i, 1854–1855," *Journal of Negro History,* XL (1962), 7–18; Kuykendall, I, 423–24; Stevens, pp. 72–76.

27. King, pp. 61–213; Kuykendall, I, 416–28.

28. Department of State, Despatches—Hawai'i, Gregg to Marcy, No. 76, March 12, 1855; Kuykendall, II, 39–42; King, pp. 104–109.

29. Kuykendall, I, 323–33, II, 140–49; Morgan, pp. 173–94, 209–15.

30. Hawai'i, *Report of the Minister of Foreign Relations,* 1856, pp. 13–14, Archives of Hawai'i; Department of State, Diplomatic Instructions—Hawai'i, March to Gregg, No. 25, October 2, 1856; Kuykendall, II, 44; Stevens, pp. 76–80.

31. Rhoda A. Hackler, "Elisha Hunt Allen, Son of New England—Man of Hawai'i," unpublished M.A. thesis, U. of Hawai'i, 1972; Kuykendall, II, 39–66; Stevens, pp. 60–84. The full text of the treaty is in *Senate Document No. 24,* 56:2.

32. Starbuck, p. 104; Kuykendall, II, 135–40; Morgan, pp. 140–53.

33. Kuykendall, II, 140–41.

34. Ibid., pp. 140–95; Jacob Adler, *Claus Spreckles: The Sugar King in Hawai'i* (Honolulu, 1966), pp. 3–15.

35. Kuykendall, II, 146–49, 228–30; Tate, pp. 27–40; Stevens, pp. 108–13.

36. Stevens, pp. 97–107; Kuykendall, II, 209–12, 216–30.

37. Department of State, Diplomatic Instructions—Hawai'i, Seward to McCook, February 1 and 7, 1867; Department of State, Despatches—Hawai'i, McCook to Seward, No. 1, May 29, 1867.

38. *Treaties, Conventions, International Acts, Protocols and Agreements between the United States of America and Other Powers, 1776–1904,* compiled by William M. Malloy (Washington, 1910–1938), I, 915–17.

39. The report was published in *Senate Executive Document No. 77,* 52:2, pp. 150–54, and in *AHR,* XXX (April 1925), 561–65. See also Stevens, p. 122; Kuykendall, II, 247–50; Thomas Walter Smails, "John McAllister Schofield: Military Diplomat," unpublished M.A. thesis, U. of Hawai'i at Manoa, 1966.

40. Donald W. Dozer, "The Opposition to Hawaiian Reciprocity, 1876–1888," *PHR,* XIV (June 1945), 157–84; Kuykendall, II, 248–57, and III, 17–45; Stevens, pp. 128–86.

41. Department of State, Diplomatic Instructions—Hawai'i, No. 113, p. 10, Blaine to James M. Comly, December 1, 1880; also printed in *Senate Executive Document No. 13,* 53:2, 7–12.

42. Alfred Thayer Mahan, "The United States Looking Outward," *Atlantic Monthly,* LXVI (December 1890), 816–24.

43. Andrew Lind, *An Island Community* (Chicago, 1938), pp. 47–52.

44. Lilikala Kame'eleihiwa, *Native Land and Foreign Desires* (Honolulu, 1992), passim.

45. Charles Pickering, M.D., *The Races of Man* (London, 1849), pp. 88–99; Pickering was a member of the Wilkes expedition.

46. Wilkes, I, 389–93.

47. See, for example, Francis Allyn Olmsted, *Incidents of a Whaling Expedition* (New York, 1841), p. 191.

48. See, for example, James L. Wisely, "Voyage to the Hawaiian Islands," clippings of his visit to Hawai'i in 1865 printed in a newspaper of that year, in Hawaiian Collection, Hamilton Library, U. of Hawai'i at Manoa.

49. Lawrence H. Fuchs, *Hawai'i Pono: A Social History* (New York, 1961), p. 21.

50. Ibid., pp. 24–25.

51. Charles Nordhoff, *Northern California, Oregon, and the Sandwich Islands* (Berkeley, 1974), pp. 70–71; Mabel Clare Craft, *Hawai'i Nei* (San Francisco, 1898), p. 59.

52. Kuykendall, II, 127–34; see also William R. Bliss, *Paradise in the Pacific* (New York, 1873), p. 50.

53. Kuykendall, II, 259–61.

54. John Wesley Bookwalter, *Canyon and Crater: Or, Scenes in California and the Sandwich Islands* (Springfield, OH, 1874), p. 184.

55. Kuykendall, III, 9–12.

56. Daws, *Shoal of Time*, pp. 207–50; Kuykendall, III, 186–473.

57. Fuchs, p. 29.

58. Daws, *Shoal of Time*, p. 246.

59. Ibid.; Tate, pp. 86–95; Stevens, pp. 151–53; Kuykendall, III, 356–72.

60. Tate, pp. 95–100; Daws, *Shoal of Time*, pp. 255–58; Kuykendall, III, 423–30.

CHAPTER 8

1. Johnson, *Commerce*, II, 84–85; *Statistical Abstract of the United States,* 1895 (Washington, 1896), p. 387, table 133; Hutchins, pp. 304–24, 397–440.

2. Johnson, *Commerce*, II, 301–3; Hutchins, pp. 316–24; Elisha P. Douglass, *The Coming of Age of American Business* (Chapel Hill, 1971), pp. 96–100.

3. Hutchins, pp. 397–400; Dennett, pp. 578, 586.

4. Brookes, pp. 317–25; Masterman, pp. 111–30; Barry Rigby, "Private Interests and the Origins of American Involvement in Samoa, 1872–1877," *Journal of Pacific History,* VIII (1973), 75–87; K. Jack Bauer, "The Golden Age," pp. 57–60, and Lawrence C. Allin, "The Civil War and the Period of Decline, 1861–1913," pp. 65–78, both in Robert A. Kilmarx, ed., *America's Maritime Legacy* (Boulder, 1979).

5. Quoted in Count Otto zu Stolberg-Wernigerode, *Germany and the United States of America during the Era of Bismarck* (Reading, PA, 1937), p. 201.

6. Brookes, p. 317, cites Truxton to George M. Robeson (secretary of the navy), May 27 and July 3, 1870, in Department of the Navy, Official Memoranda, 1869–1870. See also Peirce to Fish, August 18, 1870, in Department of State, Despatches—Hawai'i, vol. 13.

7. Johnson, *Commerce*, I, 172.

8. Brookes, pp. 316–21. Highly colored accounts of Hayes's career may be found in Frank Clune, *Captain Bully Hayes: Blackbirder and Bigamist* (London, 1970), and A. T. Saunders, *Bully Hayes* (Perth, 1932); Department of State, List of United States Consular Officers, Microcopy No. 587.

9. Hutchins, pp. 287–324, 448–51.

10. *House Committee Report No. 595,* 30:1, May 4, 1848, "Steam Communication with China and the Sandwich Islands"; *Congressional Globe,* 30:1, May 4, 1848, p. 724.

11. Samuel E. Morison, *"Old Bruin": Commodore Matthew C. Perry, 1794–1858* (Boston, 1967), pp. 127–32, 256–60; Allin, pp. 80–85.

12. Kwang-ching Liu, *Anglo-American Steamship Rivalry in China, 1862–1874* (Cambridge, MA, 1962), pp. 9–11; Robert Bennet Forbes, *Personal Reminiscences, with Recollections of China* (Boston, 1892).

13. Forbes, pp. 9–63; Dennett, pp. 585–86; George F. Seward to Secretary of State Hamilton Fish, January 30, 1877, in *Foreign Relations,* 1877, pp. 88–91.

14. George H. Preble, *A Chronological History of the Origin and Development of Steam Navigation* (Philadelphia, 1895), pp. 218–19; Will Lawson, *Pacific Steamers* (Glasgow, 1927), pp. 29–37.

15. "An Act to Authorize the Establishment of Ocean Mail Steamship Service between the United States and China," February 17, 1865, in *Statutes at Large and Treaties of the United States of America* (Boston, 1865), p. 430; John H. Kemble, "A Hundred Years of the Pacific Mail," *American Neptune,* X (April 1950), 123–43.

16. *Senate Report No. 194,* 40:3, January 28, 1869, p. 1; Dennett, pp. 584–85; Callahan, p. 70.

17. George H. Ryden, *The Foreign Policy of the United States in Relation to Samoa* (New Haven, 1933), pp. 43–49; Brookes, pp. 318–25.

18. See chapter 9.

19. John H. Kemble, *The Panama Route, 1848–1869* (Berkeley, 1943); Lewis, *Sea Routes;* Rydell, *Cape Horn.* All give useful accounts of this phase of American activity in the eastern Pacific. See also Hutchins, pp. 359–61, 367.

20. Preble, p. 211; Lawson, pp. 17–18; Kemble, *Panama Route,* pp. 22–35; Lewis, pp. 166–69, 195–200, 225–29; T. M. Van Metre, "Coastwise Trade of the Pacific Coast and the Intercoastal Trade," in Johnson, *Commerce,* I, 360–61.

21. Willis Fletcher Johnson, *Four Centuries of the Panama Canal* (New York, 1907), pp. 44–77; Gerstle Mack, *The Land Divided: A History of the Panama Canal and Other Isthmian Canal Projects* (New York, 1944), pp. 120–35, 171–206.

22. Ryden, pp. 42–46, 354, 438, 466; Masterman, pp. 81–85, 109–22; H. Stonehewer Cooper, *The Coral Lands of the Pacific: Their Peoples and Their Products* (London, 1882), preface, p. 336.

23. Mary Wilhelmine Williams, *Anglo-American Isthmian Diplomacy, 1815–1915* (Washington, DC, 1916), pp. 26–138; Mack, pp. 181–87, 191–94, 204–206; Edwin C. Hoyt, *National Policy and International Law: Case Studies from American Canal Policy* (Denver, 1966), pp. 5–25.

24. Mack, pp. 207–23, 226–78, 306–10; Williams, pp. 270–99; Johnson, *Commerce,* II, 78–98.

25. Richardson, *Messages and Papers,* VII, 585–86; *Senate Document No. 237,* 56:1, "Correspondence in Relation to an Interoceanic Canal," pp. 469–70.

26. Mack, pp. 317–76; Johnson, *Commerce,* II, 78–107.

27. Norman Harper, *Australia and the United States* (Melbourne, 1971), pp. 2–8; Levi, pp. 37–48.

28. Lloyd C. Churchward, "Australian-American Trade Relations, 1791–1939," *Economic Record,* XXVI (June 1950), 71–77; Dunbabin, p. 255; L. E. Fredman, *The United*

States Enters the Pacific (Sydney. 1969), pp. 44–45; Churchward, "Gold Rush," 11–24; Grattan, pp. 275–76; J. A. Alexander, *The Life of George Chaffey* (Melbourne, 1928), pp. 30–96.

29. Hutchins. pp. 265–69, 304–307, 371–77; Johnson, *Commerce,* II, 72–85; Churchward, "Trade Relations," pp. 73–74.

30. *New South Wales Statistical Register for 1906 and Previous Years* (Sydney, 1908), p. 115, tables 17, 18, and note.

31. Commonwealth Bureau of Census and Statistics, *Bulletin* No. 1, "Monthly Summary of Australian Statistics," January 1912.

32. Lloyd C. Churchward, "The American Influence on the Australian Labour Movement," *Historical Studies: Australia and New Zealand,* V (November 1952), 258–77.

33. Department of State, List of Consular Officers, Microfilm Series: Apia, roll one; Lauthala, roll ten; Papeete, roll 14; Suva, roll 19.

34. Levi. pp. 75–80; Stolberg-Wernigerode, pp. 201–204.

35. Brookes, pp. 223–24; Levi, pp. 75–80.

36. Boutwell to Commodore William Mervine, December 21, 1855, enclosed in Boutwell to Secretary of State Fish, September 20, 1869, in Department of State, Despatches—Lauthala, Microfilm No. 561, roll 4; Brookes, p. 173, 232–38; Derrick, I, 132–37; Peter France, *The Charter of the Land: Custom and Colonization in Fiji* (Melbourne, 1969), pp. 56–58.

37. Derrick, pp. 132–51; France, pp. 71–83, 92–101; Brookes, pp. 304–91.

38. Levi, pp. 30–33; Dunbabin, pp. 256–77.

39. Owen W. Parnaby, *Britain and the Labor Trade in the Southwest Pacific* (Durham, NC, 1964), passim; Deryck Scarr, "Recruits and Recruiters: A Portrait of the Labour Trade," in Deryck Scarr and J. W. Davidson, eds., *Pacific Islands Portraits* (Canberra, 1970), pp. 225–51; Ward, *British Policy,* pp. 218–36; 261–66; Morrell, pp. 171–86; Brookes, pp. 294–302, 368–85.

40. Ryden, pp. 62–63; Saunders, pp. 300–304; Alfred R. Lubbock, *Bully Hayes: South Sea Pirate* (Boston, 1931), pp. 201–10; Meade to Robeson, February 29, 1872, in Department of the Navy, Commanders' Letters, January–April 1872, p. 111.

41. Brookes, p. 385; Ward, *British Policy,* pp. 229–30, 261–62.

42. Owen W. Parnaby, "The Labour Trade," in R. Gerard Ward, ed., *Man in the Pacific Islands* (Oxford, 1972), pp. 124–44; Douglas Oliver, *The Pacific Islands* (Cambridge, MA, 1962), pp. 125–40; Morrell, pp. 148–68, 171, 186, 205–38; Ward, *British Policy,* pp. 218–87, 303–10.

43. Roy F. Nichols, *Advance Agents of American Destiny* (Philadelphia, 1956), pp. 157–201; Edwin H. Bryan, Jr., *American Polynesia and the Hawaiian China* (Honolulu, 1942), pp. 28–32.

44. "An Act to Authorize Protection to be Given to Citizens of the United States who may Discover Deposite [sic] of Guano," August 18, 1856, in *Statutes at Large,* VI, 119–20.

45. John Bassett Moore, *Digest of International Law* (Washington, DC, 1906), I, 556–80; Bryan, pp. 28–58; Nichols, p. 205.

46. David N. Leff, *Uncle Sam's Pacific Islets* (Stanford, 1940), pp. 2–3, 7–10; Bryan, pp. 32–34.

47. Nancy J. Morris, "Hawaiian Missionaries Abroad, 1852–1909," unpublished dissertation, U. of Hawai'i at Manoa, 1987; Henry P. Judd, "The Hawaiian Mission to Marquesa and Micronesia," in *The Centennial Book: One Hundred Years of Christian*

35; Albertine Loomis, "The Longest Legislature," HHS *71st Annual Report* (1962), pp. 7–14.

33. Russ, pp. 28–68; Kuykendall, III, 470–581; Tate, 111–54. For partisan accounts by major participants in the overthrow, see Lorrin A. Thurston, *Memoirs of the Hawaiian Revolution* (Honolulu, 1936), and Liliuokalani, *Hawai'i's Story by Hawai'i's Queen* (Rutland, VT, 1964).

34. *House Executive Document No. 47*, 53:2, "Report of Commissioner to the Hawaiian Islands" (Blount Report), p. 120.

35. Stevens, pp. 222–40; 245–50; Russ, pp. 113–64; Julius W. Pratt, *Expansionists of 1898: The Acquisition of Hawai'i and the Spanish Islands* (Baltimore, 1936), pp. 110–87; Tate, pp. 228–34.

36. Tate, pp. 228–29, 234–37; Russ, pp. 167–71; Thurston, pp. 230–33; Kuykendall, III, 534–35, 622–23; Pratt, pp. 124–31.

37. Kuykendall, III, 631–47; Pratt, pp. 140–46; Tate, pp. 235–51; Russ, pp. 221–93; Stevens, pp. 247–50.

38. William A. Russ, *The Hawaiian Republic, 1894–1898, and Its Struggle to Win Annexation* (Selinsgrove, PA, 1961); Thomas J. Osborne, *"Empire Can Wait": American Opposition to Hawaiian Annexation, 1893–1899* (Kent, OH, 1981), pp. 68–108; Tate, pp. 251–73; Stevens, pp. 261–84.

39. Osborne, pp. viii–xv, 17–27, 68–137; Pratt, pp. 146–87; Russ, *Republic*, pp. 130f. For an economic determinist view, see Walter F. LaFeber, *The New Empire: An Interpretation of American Expansion 1860–1898* (Ithaca, 1963), pp. 140–96.

40. Thomas A. Bailey, "Japan's Protest against the Annexation of Hawai'i," *Journal of Modern History*, III (1931), 46–61; Tate, pp. 266, 282–84, 299–300; Russ, *Republic*, pp. 23–25, 130–77; *Japan Times*, August 5, 1897, quoted in *Literary Digest*, May 22, 1898; Stevens, pp. 281–84.

41. Russ, *Republic*, pp. 178–94; Pratt, p. 219; *Senate Report No. 681*, 55:2.

42. Bailey, "Protest," pp. 54–60; Pratt, pp. 220–21; Russ, *Republic*, pp. 145–49, 173–74.

43. Howard K. Beale, *Theodore Roosevelt and the Rise of America to World Power* (Baltimore, 1956), pp. 39–44, 53, 57, 65–67, 233; Russ, *Republic*, pp. 141–43; Pratt, p. 218.

44. Robert L. Beisner, *Twelve Against Empire: The Anti-Imperialists, 1898–1900* (New York, 1968), pp. iii–x, 18–35, 139–64, 215–39.

45. Thomas A. Bailey, "The United States and Hawai'i during the Spanish-American War," *AHR*, XXXVI (April 1931), 550–60; Tate, pp. 296–99; Pratt, pp. 319–28; Thurston, pp. 569–70; Osborne, pp. 122–27.

46. *Journal of the Executive Proceedings of the Senate*, 55:1, p. 230.

CHAPTER 10

1. Thomas A. Bailey, "America's Emergence as a World Power: The Myth and the Verity," *PHR*, XXX (February 1961), 1–16; Pratt, pp. 1–33; David Healy, *U.S. Expansionism: The Imperialist Urge in the 1890s* (Madison, 1970), pp. 3–47; William Appleman Williams, *The Roots of the Modern American Empire* (New York, 1969), pp. 4–46, are just a few of the attempts by historians to explain the causes of American expansionism. See also, Weinberg; Merk; and Marilyn B. Young, "The Quest for Empire,"

in Ernest R. May and James C. Thomson, Jr., eds., *American-East Asian Relations: A Survey* (Cambridge, MA, 1972).

2. Healy, pp. 52–54; Christopher Lasch, "The Anti-Imperialists, the Philippines, and the Inequality of Man," *Journal of Southern History*, XXIV (April 1958), 319–31.

3. A.V.B. Hartendorp, *History of Industry and Trade of the Philippines* (Manila, 1958), pp. 7–11.

4. Bowditch, passim; Johnson, *Commerce*, II, 107–108.

5. Johnson, *Commerce*, II, 108–109.

6. Hartendorp, pp. 10–11.

7. Roosevelt to Lodge, September 21, 1897, in Henry Cabot Lodge, ed., *Selections from the Correspondence of Theodore Roosevelt and Henry Cabot Lodge, 1884–1918* (New York, 1925), I, 278–79; Healy, pp. 110–13; Elting E. Morison, ed., *The Letters of Theodore Roosevelt* (Cambridge, MA, 1951–1954), I, 746, II, 842; Beale, p. 70.

8. Henry F. Pringle, *Theodore Roosevelt: A Biography* (New York, 1931), p. 178; Joseph B. Bishop, *Theodore Roosevelt and His Time* (New York, 1925), I, 278–79; Beale, p. 62.

9. Braisted, pp. 21–22; George Dewey, *Autobiography of George Dewey, Admiral of the Navy* (New York, 1931), pp. 167–79; Walter Millis, *The Martial Spirit: A Study of Our War with Spain* (New York, 1931), pp. 111–12; Philip Y. Nicholson, "George Dewey and the Transformation of American Foreign Policy," unpublished dissertation, U. of Michigan, 1913, pp. 80–82; John A.A. Grenville and George B. Young, *Politics, Strategy, and American Diplomacy: Studies in Foreign Policy, 1873–1917* (New Haven, 1966), pp. 269–76.

10. Rhoda E.A. Hackler, "Discoverer of Aguinaldo?" *Foreign Service Journal*, January 1970, pp. 32–34, 44.

11. Ibid.; Dean C. Worcester, *The Philippines Past and Present* (New York, 1921), pp. 18–66; Emilio Aguinaldo and V.A. Pacis, *A Second Look at America* (New York, 1957), pp. 32–39; *Senate Document No. 52*, 55:3, I, 336–42 and 355–58, reprints some of the reports of Consuls Pratt and Wildman. See also Alice W. McDiarmid, "Consuls Out of Contact," *Foreign Service Journal*, March 1988, pp. 34–36.

12. Aguinaldo and Pacis, pp. 32–39; Garel A. Grunder and William E. Livezey, *The Philippines and the United States* (Norman, OK, 1951), pp. 21–25.

13. H. H. Kohlsaat, *From McKinley to Harding: Personal Recollections of Our Presidents* (New York, 1923), p. 68.

14. French E. Chadwick, *The Relations of the United States and Spain* (New York, 1911), II, 369.

15. Ibid., II, 363.

16. Ibid., II, 364.

17. Ibid., II, 372.

18. Ibid., II, 396–98, quotes McKinley's order of May 19 to the secretary of war concerning military occupation policy, and pp. 459–60 quotes the peace commissioners' views based on this. See also John A. Garraty, *Henry Cabot Lodge* (New York, 1953), pp. 196–200, and, for a different view, Charles S. Campbell, *The Transformation of American Foreign Relations, 1865–1900* (Chicago, 1966), pp. 60–65.

19. Carl Schurz, "Thoughts on American Imperialism," *Century Illustrated Monthly Magazine*, XXXIV (1898), 781–88; John R. Proctor, "Isolation or Imperialism?" *The Forum*, XXVI (1898), 14–26; *Congressional Record*, 55:1, 2, and 3, and House and Senate documents of the period offer a mountain of documentation on these points.

20. Lodge to Day, August 11, 1898, quoted in Garraty, pp. 197–98.

21. Lodge to Roosevelt, June 24, 1898, in Lodge, *Selections,* I, 312–14; Garraty, pp. 198–202; Pratt, pp. 326–33.

22. *Senate Document No. 148,* 56:2, "Papers Relating to the Treaty with Spain," p. 35; Pratt, p. 338.

23. "Treaty for Cession of Outlying Islands of the Philippines, November 7, 1900," in Malloy, II, 1696–97.

24. Lodge, *War with Spain,* pp. 191–93; Robert G. Neale, *Great Britain and United States Expansion* (East Lansing, 1966), pp. 1–93; Bertha Ann Reuter, *Anglo-American Relations during the Spanish-American War* (New York, 1924), pp. 61–149.

25. Thomas A. Bailey, "Dewey and the Germans at Manila Bay," *AHR,* XLV (October 1939), 59–81; Lester B. Shippee, "Germany and the Spanish-American War," *AHR,* XXX (July 1925), 754–77; Neale, pp. 15–22, 32–36, 85–91; G.J.A. O'Toole, *The Spanish War: An American Epic—1898* (New York, 1984), pp. 99–100, 104–108, 191–92, 250–51, 364–65.

26. Pratt, p. 342; Shippee, pp. 769–70; White to Day, July 12 and 30, 1898, in *Foreign Relations,* 1898.

27. Neale and Reuter offer valuable accounts of this phase of the Spanish-American conflict.

28. Bailey, "Dewey and the Germans," pp. 59–81.

29. P.E. Quinn, "The Diplomatic Struggle for the Carolines, 1898," *PHR,* XIV (September 1945), 290–302; H. Wayne Morgan, ed., *Making Peace with Spain: The Diary of Whitelaw Reid, September–December, 1898* (Austin, 1965), pp. 143–76; Pratt, pp. 342–44; Shippee, pp. 770–77; Germany, *Die Grosse Politik der Europaischen Kabinette, 1871–1914* (Berlin, 1935), XV, 211–30.

30. Roosevelt to Frederic R. Coudert, July 3, 1901, in Morison, *Letters,* III, 105; Healy, p. 114. "Papers Relating to the Treaty with Spain," in *Senate Document No. 148,* 56:2, and Whitelaw Reid's diary for the period give indispensable information on the attitudes and rationalizations of the American peace commissioners.

31. Bryan, pp. 208–10; Leff, pp. 21–22; Julius W. Pratt, *America's Colonial Experiment* (New York, 1950), pp. 76–77; *House Document No. 3,* 56:2, "Report of the Secretary of the Navy, 1900," p. 415.

32. Paul Carano and Pedro C. Sanchez, *A Complete History of Guam,* (Rutland, VT, and Tokyo, 1964), pp. 170–77; Braistead, pp. 28–29.

33. Carroll Miner Dwight, *The Fight for the Panama Route* (New York, 1940), pp. 17–116; Philippe Bunau Varilla, *Panama: The Creation, Destruction, and Resurrection* (London, 1913), pp. 159–67; Pratt, *Colonial Experiment,* pp. 83–94; *Senate Document No. 474,* 63:2, "Diplomatic History of the Panama Canal."

34. Gray, *Amerika Samoa,* pp. 92–102.

35. Ibid., pp. 105–52; Ryden, pp. 558–81; Roger H. Herwig, *Politics of Frustration: The United States in German Naval Planning, 1889–1941* (Boston, 1976), pp. 13–39; Paul M. Kennedy, *The Samoan Tangle: A Study in Anglo-German-American Relations, 1898–1900* (New York, 1974), pp. 136–37.

36. Thomas F. Darden, *Historical Sketch of the Administration of the Government of American Samoa* (Washington, DC, 1952), passim.

37. Much of the earlier literature was designed to justify expansion; the bulk of more recent writings has been critical of "imperialism," and has ascribed it largely to economic motives. See, for example, Thomas C. Paterson, *American Imperialism and Anti-*

Imperialism (New York, 1973); Henry Cabot Lodge, *The War with Spain;* Chadwick; Marilyn Blatt Young, *The Rhetoric of Empire: American China Policy, 1895–1901* (Cambridge, MA, 1968); LaFeber; and Beisner, for the various arguments advanced in the discussion in addition to other works cited earlier.

38. For example, Henry Cabot Lodge, "Our Blundering Foreign Policy," *The Forum,* XIX (March 1895), p. 16; *Congressional Record,* 53:2, March 2, 1895, p. 3082. The *Record* carries many of Lodge's statements on foreign affairs from 1887 to 1893 in the House, and from the latter year into the 1920s in the Senate.

39. Healy, pp. 60–61; William E. Livezey, *Mahan on Sea Power* (Norman, OK, 1947), pp. 182–83; LaFeber, p. 92; William D. Puleston, *Mahan: The Life and Work of Captain Alfred Thayer Mahan, U.S.N.* (New Haven, 1939), pp. 186–87, 193–94.

40. Walter F. LaFeber, "A Note on the 'Mercantilistic Imperialism' of Alfred Thayer Mahan," *Mississippi Valley Historical Review,* XLVIII (March 1962), 677; Livezey, pp. 241–42; Karsten, pp. 336–39.

41. Grenville and Young, pp. 201–38.

42. Beale, pp. 58–59, quotes this as from the *New York Sun,* February 13, 1898, but Tate, p. 247n, records his inability to find such a quote in that issue of the *Sun.*

43. Stevens, pp. 281–88; Russ, *Hawaiian Republic,* pp. 130–77.

44. *PRPFE,* especially George Blakeslee's paper, "The Islands of the Pacific," pp. 1045–1154. See also Ernest Dodge's introduction to Ward, *American Activities.*

45. William W. Kimball, Lt., USN., "War with Spain, 1896. General Considerations of the War, the Results Desired, and the Consequent Kind of Operations to Be Undertaken," Records Group No. 313, Naval Operating Forces, North Atlantic Station, Entry 43, Box 11, U.S. Navy Department Archives; O'Toole, pp. 97–99.

46. John A.S. Grenville, "American Naval Preparations for War with Spain, 1896–1898," *Journal of American Studies,* VII (April 1968), 33–48. See also Grenville and Young, pp. 269–79.

47. Alfred W. Griswold, *Far Eastern Policy of the United States* (New York, 1938), pp. 9–15; Karsten, pp. 328–47.

48. See, for example, Charles S. Campbell, *Special Business Interests and the Open Door Policy* (Hamden, CT, 1968); Charles Vevier, *The United States and China, 1906–1913* (New Brunswick, NJ, 1955); Thomas J. McCormick, *China Market: America's Quest for Informal Empire, 1893–1901* (Chicago, 1967); Young, *Rhetoric of Empire;* William Appleman Williams, *The Tragedy of American Diplomacy* (Cleveland, 1959); Pratt, *Expansionists;* Charles F. Remer, *American Investments in China* (Honolulu, 1929), and by the same author, *Foreign Investments in China* (New York, 1933). See also Paul A. Varg, *The Making of a Myth: The United States and China, 1897–1912* (East Lansing, 1968).

49. Mahan, "Looking Outward," pp. 816–24; Josiah Strong, *Our Country, Its Possible Future and Its Present Crisis* (New York, 1885).

50. See, for example, Brooks Adams, *America's Economic Supremacy* (Reprint: New York, 1947), pp. 72, 89, 98, 104–105.

51. Brooks Adams, "Reciprocity or the Alternative," *Atlantic Monthly,* 88 (August 1901), 145–55; Healy, pp. 101–102; Theodore Roosevelt to Brooks Adams, September 27, 1901, in Morison, *Letters,* III, 152–53.

52. *House Document No. 483,* 55:23, "Commercial Relations of the United States with Foreign Countries during the Years 1896 and 1897," pp. 19, 21; see also Uriah H. Crocker, *The Depression of Trade and the Wages of Labor* (Boston, 1886); Edward

SELECTED BIBLIOGRAPHY

GOVERNMENT DOCUMENTS

Germany

Die Grosse Politik der Europaischen Kabinette, 1871–1914. 40 vols. Berlin, 1924–1927.

Great Britain

Foreign Office, File 58.

Kingdom of Hawai'i

Foreign Office and Executive File.
Privy Council Records.
Report of the Minister of Foreign Relations.

New Zealand

New Zealand Official Yearbook. Wellington, 1896– .

United States

Congress

Annals of the Congress of the United States, 1789–1824. 42 vols. Washington, DC, 1834–1856.
Congressional Globe, 1833–1873. 46 vols. Washington, DC, 1834–1873.
Journals of the Continental Congress, 1774–1781. 31 vols. Washington, DC, 1904–1934.
Register of Debates in Congress, 1824–1837. 14 vols. Washington, DC, 1825–1838.

Statutes at Large of the United States of America. Boston, 1845–1873; Washington, DC, 1875–1934.

House of Representatives

House Committee Report No. 595, 30:1, May 4, 1848. "Steam Communication with China and the Sandwich Islands."

House Document No. 3, 56:2. "Report of the Secretary of the Navy, 1900."

House Document No. 112, 17:1, April 17, 1822. "Message from the President on claims set up by foreign governments to territories of the United States on the Pacific Ocean."

House Executive Document No. 177, 40:2. "Memorial of the Legislature of Washington Territory to the President."

House Executive Document No. 35, 27:3. "Message of President John Tyler, December 30, 1842, respecting the trade and commerce of the United States with the Sandwich Islands and of diplomatic intercourse with their Government."

House Executive Document No. 47, 53:2. "Report of Commissioner to the Hawaiian Islands." [The Blount Report.]

House Document No. 483, 55:2. "Commercial Relations of the United States with Foreign Countries during the Years 1896 and 1897."

House Executive Document No. 105, 22:2. "A Report of J.N. Reynolds in relation to islands, reefs, and shoals in the Pacific Ocean."

House Report No. 45, 16:2, January 25, 1821. "Report on the Pacific Ocean Settlements."

Senate

Journal of the Executive Proceedings of the Senate, 55:1.

Senate Document No. 62, 55:3. Part 1. "Our Administration in Guam."

Senate Document No. 148, 56:2. "Papers Relating to the Treaty with Spain."

Senate Document No. 174, 56:1.

Senate Document No. 237, 56:1. "Correspondence in Relation to Interoceanic Canal."

Senate Document No. 474, 63:2. "Diplomatic History of the Panama Canal."

Senate Document No. 871, 54:1. May 6, 1896. "Pacific Cables."

Senate Executive Document No. 13.

Senate Executive Document No. 57.

Senate Executive Document No. 77, 52:2.

Department of the Navy

Commanders Letters.

Official Memoranda, 1869–1870.

Department of State

American State Papers: Class I, Foreign Relations. 6 vols. Washington, DC, 1832–1859; Class IV, Commerce and Navigation, 2 vols. Washington, DC, 1832–1834.

Civil Affairs Handbook, Eastern Carolines. Also, *Mandated Marianas.* 1944. Consular Despatches—Honolulu. National Archives. Microfilm series #144.

Consular Instructions, Honolulu. Microcopy No. 78.

"Correspondence Concerning Captain Kendrick and the Settlement of His Estate." MS, Department Archives.

The Diplomatic Correspondence of the United States of America. 3 vols. Washington, DC, 1833–1834.

Diplomatic Despatches—Hawai'i.

Instructions, Great Britain, Legare to Everett, June 13, 1843.

Letters of the Continental Congress.

List of U.S. Consular Officers, 1789–1939. Microcopy No. 587.

Treaties, Conventions, International Acts, Protocols and Agreements between the United States of America and Other Powers, 1776–1904. 4 vols. Compiled by William M. Malloy. Washington, DC, 1910–1938.

Papers Relating to the Foreign Relations of the United States. Washington, DC, 1862–.

Papers Relating to the Treaty with Spain. Washington, DC, 1901.

Papers Relating to Pacific and Far Eastern Affairs Prepared for American Delegates to the Conference on Limitation of Armaments. Washington, DC, 1922.

MANUSCRIPT COLLECTIONS

Correspondence between the American Board of Commissioners for Foreign Missions and Members of the Sandwich Islands Mission. Houghton Library, Harvard University.

William Heath Davis Papers. California State Library, Sacramento.

Ingraham, Joseph. "Journal of the Voyage of the Brigantine 'Hope' from Boston to the Northwest Coast of America, 1790 to 1792." Manuscript Division, Library of Congress.

"Journal of the Brig 'Astrea.' " Essex Institute, Salem, MA.

Report of the Proceedings and Evidence in the Arbitration between the King and Government of the Hawaiian Islands and Messrs. Ladd and Co. Honolulu, 1846. Archives of Hawai'i.

"Solid Men of Boston in the Northwest." Bancroft Library, University of California, Berkeley.

OTHER UNPUBLISHED MATERIALS

Churchward, Lloyd G. "Australia and America: A Sketch of the Origin and Early Growth of Social and Economic Relations between Australia and the United States of America, 1790–1876." M.A. thesis. U. of Melbourne, 1941.

Davidson, James. "European Penetration of the South Pacific, 1779–1842." M.A. thesis. Cambridge University, 1942.

Daws, A. Gavan. "Honolulu—The First Century: Influences in the Development of the Town to 1878." Ph.D. dissertation. U. of Hawai'i, 1966.

Duncan, Roland R. "William Wheelwright: The Pioneer of Pacific Steam Navigation, 1825–1882." M.A. thesis. U. of California, Berkeley, 1960.

Hackler, Rhoda E.A. "Elisha Hunt Allen: Son of New England—Man of Hawai'i." M.A. thesis. U. of Hawai'i, 1972.

———. "Our Men in the Pacific." Ph.D. dissertation. U. of Hawai'i, 1978.

Kimball, William W., Lt., USN. "War with Spain, 1896. General Considerations of the War, the Results Desired, and the Consequent Kind of Operations to Be Undertaken." Records Group No. 313, Naval Operations Forces, North Atlantic Station. Entry 43, Box 11. Navy Department Archives, Washington, DC.

King, Pauline N. "A Political Biography of David Lawrence Gregg, American Diplomat and Hawaiian Official." Ph.D. dissertation. U. of Hawai'i, 1976.

Levin, Stephanie Seto. "A Reexamination of the Overthrow of the Kapu System in Hawai'i." (n.p., n.d.). Hawaiian Collection, Hamilton Library, U. of Hawai'i at Manoa.

Morris, Nancy J. "Hawaiian Missionaries Abroad, 1852–1909." Ph.D. dissertation. U. of Hawai'i, 1987.

Nicholson, Philip Y. "George Dewey and the Transformation of American Foreign Policy." Ph.D. dissertation. U. of Michigan, 1971.

Rigby, Barry. "The Grant Administration and the Pacific Islands." M.A. thesis. U. of Hawai'i, 1972.

Smails, Thomas W. "John McAllister Schofield: Military Diplomat." M. A. thesis. U. of Hawai'i at Manoa. 1966.

Taylor, William H. "The Hawaiian Sugar Industry." Ph.D. dissertation. U. of California, Berkeley, 1935.

Wisely, James L. "Voyage to the Hawaiian Islands," clippings of his visit to Hawai'i in 1865 printed in a newspaper of that year. Hawaiian Collection, Hamilton Library, U. of Hawai'i at Manoa.

PUBLISHED ARTICLES

Adams, Brooks. "Reciprocity or the Alternative." *Atlantic Monthly,* 88 (August 1901), 145–55.

Alexander, William D. "An Account of the Uncompleted Treaty of Annexation between the United States of America and the Hawaiian Kingdom Negotiated in 1854." Hawaiian Historical Society *Papers,* No. 9. Honolulu, 1896.

———. "The Overthrow of the Ancient Tabu System in the Hawaiian Islands. Hawaiian Historical Society *25th Annual Report* (1916), pp. 37–45.

Allin, Lawrence C. "The Civil War and the Period of Decline, 1861–1913." In Robert A. Kilmarx, ed., *America's Maritime Legacy* (Boulder, 1979), pp. 65–78.

Almy, Robert F. "J.N. Reynolds: A Brief Biography with Particular Reference to Poe and Symmes." *The Colophon,* II, New Series (1937), 227–45.

"Annual Statistical Report for 1854." *Whalemen's Shipping List.* (January 1885).

Austin, Oscar P. "Problems of the Pacific—the Commerce of the Great Ocean." *National Geographic Magazine,* August 1902.

Bailey, Thomas A. "America's Emergence as a World Power: The Myth and the Verity." *Pacific Historical Review,* XXX (1961), 1–16.

———. "Dewey and the Germans at Manila Bay." *American Historical Review,* XLV (October 1939), 59–81.

———. "Japan's Protest against the Annexation of Hawai'i," *Journal of Modern History,* III (1931), 46–61.

———. "Why the United States Purchased Alaska." *Pacific Historical Review,* III (1934), 39–50.

————. "The United States and Hawai'i During the Spanish-American War." *American Historical Review*, XXXVI (April 1931), 550–60.

Bauer, K. Jack. "The Golden Age." In Robert A. Kilmarx, ed., *America's Maritime Legacy*, Boulder, 1979, pp. 27–63.

Blue, George V. "The Policy of France toward the Hawaiian Islands from the Earliest Times to the Treaty of 1846." In Albert P. Taylor and Ralph S. Kuykendall, eds., *The Hawaiian Islands* (Honolulu, 1930), pp. 51–93.

————. "The Report of Captain LaPlace on his Voyage to the Northwest Coast and California in 1839." *California Historical Society Quarterly*, XVIII (1930), 315–28.

Cheong, W.E. "Trade and Finance in China, 1784–1834: A Reappraisal." *Business History*, VII (January 1965), 34–56.

Churchward, Lloyd G. "The American Influence on the Australian Labour Movement." *Historical Studies: Australia and New Zealand*, V (November 1952).

————. "Australian-American Relations during the Gold Rush." *Historical Studies: Australia and New Zealand*, II (1942).

————. "Australian-American Trade Relations, 1791–1939." *Economic Record*, XXVI (1950), 71–77.

Dennett, Tyler. "Seward's Far Eastern Policy." *American Historical Review*, XXVIII (1922), 45–62.

Downs, Jacques M. "American Merchants and the Chinese Opium Trade, 1800–1840," *Business History Review*, XLII (1968), 418–21.

Dozer, Donald W. "The Opposition to Hawaiian Reciprocity, 1878–1888." *Pacific Historical Review*, XIV (1945), 117–84.

Dunbabin, Thomas. "Some American Actions and Reactions in Australian History." Australian Association for the Advancement of Science, *Report of the Nineteenth Meeting* (Hobart, 1928), pp. 250–57.

Ettinger, A.A. "The Proposed Anglo-French-American Treaty, 1852, to Guarantee Cuba to Spain." Royal Historical Society *Transactions*, 4th Series, XLIII (1930), 149–85.

Golder, Frank A. "Proposals for Russian Occupation of the Hawaiian Islands." In Albert P. Taylor and Ralph S. Kuykendall, eds., *The Hawaiian Islands* (Honolulu, 1930), pp. 39–49.

————. "The Purchase of Alaska." *American Historical Review*, XXV (1920), 411–15.

Grenville, John A.S. "American Naval Preparations for War with Spain, 1896–1898." *Journal of American Studies*, VII (April 1968), 33–48.

Hackler, Rhoda E.A. "Discoverer of Aguinaldo?" *Foreign Service Journal*, January 1970, pp. 32–34, 44.

————. "The Voice of Commerce." *Hawaiian Journal of History*, III (1969), 42–47.

Hao, Yenping. "Chinese Teas to America—A Synopsis." In John K. Fairbank and Ernest R. May, eds., *America's China Trade in Historical Perspective* (Cambridge, MA, 1986), pp. 11–16.

Harrington, Fred H. "The Anti-Imperialist Movement in the United States, 1898–1900." *Mississippi Valley Historical Review*, XXII (1935), 211–30.

"Higginson Letters." Massachusetts Historical Society *Collections*. 3rd Series. Volume 7. Boston, 1838.

Hill, Hamilton A. "The Trade, Commerce, and Navigation of Boston, 1780–1880." In

Justin Winsor, ed., *The Memorial History of Boston* (Boston, 1881), IV, 203–204.

Hinckley, Ted C. "Sheldon Jackson and Benjamin Harrison." *Pacific Historical Review,* LIV (1963), 66–74.

Howay, Frederick W. "Early Relations between the Hawaiian Islands and the Northwest Coast." In Albert P. Taylor and Ralph S. Kuykendall, eds., *The Hawaiian Islands* (Honolulu, 1930), pp. 11–38.

———. "An Outline Sketch of the Maritime Fur Trade." Canadian Historical Association *Annual Report* (Ottawa, 1932), pp. 7–14.

Hunnewell, James. "Honolulu in 1817 and 1818." Hawaiian Historical Society *Papers,* No. 8 (1895).

Hunter, Charles H., ed. "The Turrill Collection." Hawaiian Historical Society *66th Annual Report* (1957), pp. 27–92.

Johnson, Donald D. "Powers in the Pacific: Tahiti and Hawai'i, 1825–1850." Hawaiian Historical Society *66th Annual Report* (1957), pp. 7–25.

Johnson, John J. "Early Relations of the United States with Chile." *Pacific Historical Review,* XIII (September 1944), 260–70.

Judd, Henry P. "The Hawaiian Mission to Marquesa and Micronesia." In *The Centennial Book: One Hundred Years of Christian Civilization in Hawai'i, 1820–1920* (Honolulu, 1920), pp. 44–46.

Judd, Laura F. "A Suppressed Chapter of Hawaiian History." Hawaiian Historical Society *10th Annual Report* (1903), pp. 7–12.

Kaplanoff, Mark D. "Nootka Sound in 1789." *Pacific Northwest Quarterly,* LXV (1974), 157–63.

Kemble, John H. "A Hundred Years of the Pacific Mail." *American Neptune,* X (1950), 123–43.

Kimball, Gertrude Selwyn. "The East India Trade of Providence from 1787 to 1807." *Papers from the Historical Seminary of Brown University.* Volume 6. (Providence, 1896).

Kuykendall, Ralph S. "American Interests and American Influence in Hawai'i in 1842." Hawaiian Historical Society *39th Annual Report* (1931), pp. 48–67.

LaFeber, Walter F. "A Note on the 'Mercantilistic Imperialism' of Alfred Thayer Mahan." *Mississippi Valley Historical Review,* XLVIII (March 1962), 677.

Lasch, Christopher. "The Anti-Imperialists, the Philippines, and the Inequality of Man." *Journal of Southern History,* XXIV (April 1958), 319–31.

Livermore, Seward W. "Early Commercial and Consular Relations with the East Indies." *Pacific Historical Review,* XV (1946), 31–58.

Lodge, Henry Cabot, "Our Blundering Foreign Policy." *The Forum,* XIX (March 1895).

Loomis, Albertine. "The Longest Legislature." Hawaiian Historical Society *71st Annual Report* (1962), pp. 7–14.

MacAllan, Richard. "Sir George Simpson and the Mission for Hawaiian Independence, 1840–1843." *Hawaiian Journal of History,* XX (1986), 67–82.

McDiarmid, Alice M. "Consuls Out of Contact." *Foreign Service Journal,* March 1988, pp. 34–36.

M'Konochle, Alexander. "Considerations on the Propriety of Establishing a Colony on One of the Sandwich Islands." Reprinted in Hawaiian Historical Society *14th Annual Report* (1907), pp. 29–43.

McPherson, Hallie M. "The Interest of William McKendree Gwin in the Purchase of Alaska, 1856–1861." *Pacific Historical Review,* III (1934), 357–86.

Mahan, Alfred Thayer. "Hawai'i and Our Future Sea Power." *The Forum,* XV (1893), 1–11.

———. "Possibilities of an Anglo-American Reunion." *North American Review,* CLIX (1894), 551–73.

———. "The United States Looking Outward." *Atlantic Monthly,* LXVI (1890), 816–24.

Manning, W.R. "The Nootka Sound Controversy" American Historical Association *Annual Report,* 1904. Washington, DC, 1905.

Martin, Toradash. "Steinberger of Samoa: Some Biographical Notes." *Pacific Northwest Quarterly,* LXVIII (April 1977), 49–59.

Maury, Matthew F. "Communication with the Pacific." *National Intelligencer,* November 4, 1849.

Mazour, Anatole G. "The Prelude to Russia's Departure from America." *Pacific Historical Review,* X (September 1941), 311–19.

Mehnert, Klaus. "The Russians in Hawai'i, 1804–1819." University of Hawai'i *Occasional Papers,* No. 38 (Honolulu, 1939).

Melville, George W. "Our Future in the Pacific—What We Have There to Hold and Win." *North American Review,* XXXVI (1898), 181–96.

Merk, Frederick. "The Genesis of the Oregon Question." *Mississippi Valley Historical Review,* XXXVI (March 1950), 583–612.

———. "The Oregon Pioneers and the Boundary." *American Historical Review,* XXIX (1924), 681–99.

Miller, Stuart C. "The American Trader's Image of China, 1785–1840." *Pacific Historical Review,* XXXVI (1967), 375–95.

Morison, Samuel Eliot. "Historical Notes on the Gilbert and Marshall Islands." *American Neptune,* IV (1944), 25–27.

Muller, Dorothea R. "Josiah Strong and American Nationalism: A Reevaluation." *Journal of American History,* LIII (1966), 487–503.

Ogden, Adele. "Alfred Robinson, New England Merchant in Mexican California." *California Historical Society Quarterly,* XXIII (September 1944), 193–218.

———. "New England Traders in Spanish and Mexican California." In *Greater America: Essays in Honor of Herbert Eugene Bolton* (Berkeley, 1945), pp. 395–413.

Parnaby, Owen W. "The Labour Trade." In R. Gerard Ward, ed., *Man in the Pacific Islands* (Oxford, 1972), pp. 124–44.

Proctor, John R. "Isolation or Imperialism?" *The Forum,* XXVI (1898), 14–26.

Quinn, P.E. "The Diplomatic Struggle for the Carolines, 1898." *Pacific Historical Review,* XIV (September 1945), 290–302.

Rigby, Barry. "Private Interests and the Origins of American Involvement in Samoa, 1872–1877." *Journal of Pacific History,* VIII (1973), 75–87.

Robinson, Edward Van Dyke. "The Caroline Islands and the Terms of Peace." *The Independent,* L (October 13, 1898), 1046.

Roske, Ralph J. "The World Impact of the California Gold Rush, 1849–1857." *Arizona and the West,* V (1963), 187–232.

Scarr, Deryck. "Recruits and Recruiters: A Portrait of the Labour Trade." In Deryck Scarr and J.W. Davidson, eds., *Pacific Islands Portraits* (Canberra, 1970), pp. 225–51.

Schram, Peter. "The Minor Significance of Commercial Relations between the United States and China, 1850–1931." In John K. Fairbank and Ernest R. May, eds., *America's China Trade in Historical Perspective* (Cambridge, MA, 1986), pp. 237–38.

Schurz, Carl. "Thoughts on American Imperialism." *Century Illustrated Monthly Magazine,* XXXIV (1898), 781–88.

Shelmidine, Lyle S. "The Early History of Midway Islands." *American Neptune,* VIII (1948), 179–95.

Shippee, Lester B. "Germany and the Spanish-American War." *American Historical Review,* XXX (1925), 754–77.

Spoehr, Alexander. "Fur Traders in Hawai'i: The Hudson's Bay Company in Honolulu, 1829–1861." *Hawaiian Journal of History,* XX (1986), 27–37.

Squier, George O., Capt. "The Influence of Submarine Cables upon Military and Naval Supremacy." *National Geographic Magazine,* XII (January 1901).

Starke, Aubrey. "Poe's Friend Reynolds." *American Literature,* XI (1939–1940), 152–58.

Stathis, Stephen M. "Albert B. Steinberger: Grant's Man in Samoa." *Hawaiian Journal of History,* XVI (1982), 86–111.

Stelle, Charles C. "American Trade in Opium to China Prior to 1820." *Pacific Historical Review,* IX (1940), 425–27.

Stenberg, Richard R. "The Failure of Polk's Mexican War Intrigue of 1845." *Pacific Historical Review,* IV (March 1935), 39–86.

Stephan, John J. "Russian-American Economic Relations in the Pacific: A Historical Perspective." In John J. Stephan and W.P. Chichkanov, eds., *Soviet-American Horizons on the Pacific* (Honolulu, 1986), pp. 61–83.

Stockton, Charles H., Capt., USN. "The American Interoceanic Canal: A Study of the Commercial, Naval, and Political Conditions." *United States Naval Institute Proceedings,* XXVI (1889), 752–97.

Strauss, W. Patrick. "Preparing the Wilkes Expedition: A Study in Disorganization." *Pacific Historical Review,* XXVIII (1959), 221–32.

Strong, E.W. "Spain and the Caroline Islands." *American Monthly Review of Reviews,* XVII (June 1898), 706–708.

Sturgis, William. "The Northwest Fur Trade." *Hunt's Merchants' Magazine and Commercial Review,* XIV (June 1846), 535–37.

Tate, Merze. "Slavery and Racism as Deterrents in the Annexation of Hawai'i, 1854–1855." *Journal of Negro History,* XL (1962), 7–18.

Torodash, Martin. "Steinberger of Samoa: Some Biographical Notes." *Pacific Northwest Quarterly,* LXVII (1977), 48–59.

Van Metre, T.M. "Coastwise Trade of the Pacific Coast and the Intercoastal Trade." In Emory Johnson, *History of Foreign and Domestic Commerce of the United States* (Washington, DC, 1915), I, 360–61.

Ver Steeg, Clarence L. "Financing and Outfitting the First United States Ship to China." *Pacific Historical Review,* XXII (1953), 1–12.

Westervelt, William D. "Hawaiian Printed Laws before the Constitution," Hawaiian Historical Society *16th Annual Report* (1908), pp. 54–57.

———. "Kamehameha's Cession of the Island of Hawai'i to Great Britain in 1784." Hawaiian Historical Society *22nd Annual Report* (1914), pp. 19–24.

Williams, J.R. "The Whale Fishery." *North American Review*, XXXVIII (January 1834), 84–116.
Young, Marilyn B. "The Quest for Empire." In Ernest R. May and James C. Thomson, Jr., eds., *American-East Asian Relations: A Survey* (Cambridge, MA, 1972).

BOOKS

Adams, Brooks. *America's Economic Supremacy.* Reprint, New York, 1947.
Adams, Charles Francis, ed. *The Works of John Adams.* 10 volumes. Boston, 1850–1856.
Adler, Jacob. *Claus Spreckles: The Sugar King in Hawai'i.* Honolulu, 1966.
———. *The Journal of Prince Alexander Liholiho.* Honolulu, 1967.
Aguinaldo, Emilio, and V.A. Pacis. *A Second Look at America.* New York, 1957.
Alexander, J.A. *The Life of George Chaffey.* Melbourne, 1928.
Anderson, Rufus. *History of the Sandwich Islands Mission.* Boston, 1870.
Arago, Jacques. *Narrative of a Voyage around the World . . . 1817, 1818, 1819, and 1820.* London, 1823.
Baker, John N.L. *A History of Geographical Discovery and Exploration.* Boston, 1931.
Bancroft, Hubert Howe. *History of Alaska, 1730–1885.* San Francisco, 1886.
———. *History of California.* 2 vols. San Francisco, 1884–1890.
———. *History of the Northwest Coast.* 3 vols. San Francisco, 1884–1886.
———. *History of Oregon.* 2 vols. San Francisco, 1886. Barnes, William, and John H. Morgan. *The Foreign Service of the United States: Origins, Development, and Functions.* Washington, DC, 1961.
Baxley, H. Willis, M.D. *What I Saw on the West Coast of South and North America and at the Sandwich Islands.* New York, 1865.
Beaglehole, John C. *The Exploration of the Pacific.* 2nd ed. London, 1947.
Beale, Howard K. *Theodore Roosevelt and the Rise of America to World Power.* Baltimore, 1956.
Beardsley, Charles. *Guam: Past and Present.* Rutland, VT, and Tokyo, 1964.
Beers, Henry P. *American Naval Occupation and Government of Guam, 1899–1902.* Washington, DC, 1944.
Beisner, Robert L. *Twelve Against Empire: The Anti-Imperialists, 1898–1900.* New York, 1968.
Bemis, Samuel Flagg. *John Quincy Adams and the Foundations of American Foreign Policy.* New York, 1956.
Benton, Thomas Hart. *Abridgement of the Debates of Congress from 1789 to 1856.* 16 vols. New York, 1857–1861.
———. *Selections of Editorial Articles from the St. Louis "Enquirer" on the Subject of Oregon and Texas as Originally Published in that Paper in the Years 1818–1819.* St. Louis, 1844.
———. *A Thirty Years View.* 2 vols. New York, 1854–1856.
Bernstein, Harry. *Origins of Inter-American Interest, 1700–1812.* Philadelphia, 1945.
Bingham, Hiram. *A Residence of Twenty-one Years in the Sandwich Islands.* Hartford, CT, 1847.
Binkley, W.C. *The Expansionist Movement in Texas.* Berkeley, 1925.
Bishop, Joseph B. *Theodore Roosevelt and His Time.* 2 vols. New York, 1925.
Bletz, Donald F. *The Role of the Military Professional in U.S. Foreign Policy.* New York, 1972.

Bliss, William R. *Paradise in the Pacific*. New York, 1873.

Bloxam, Andrew. *Diary of Andrew Bloxam, Naturalist of the "Blonde," On Her Trip to the Hawaiian Islands from England, 1824–25*. Honolulu, 1925.

Bookwalter, John Wesley. *Canyon and Crater: Or, Scenes in California and the Sandwich Islands*. Springfield, OH, 1874.

Boyd, Julian B., ed. *The Papers of Thomas Jefferson*. 21 vols. Princeton, 1950–.

Bradford, William. *History of Plymouth Plantation, 1620–1647*. 2 vols. Boston, 1912.

Bradley, Harold W. *The American Frontier in Hawai'i: The Pioneers, 1789–1843*. Stanford, 1942.

Braisted, William R. *The United States Navy in the Pacific, 1897–1909*. Austin, 1958.

Brookes, Jean I. *International Rivalry in the Pacific Islands, 1800–1875*. Berkeley, 1941.

Bryan, Edwin H., Jr. *American Polynesia and the Hawaiian Chain*. Honolulu, 1942.

Bunau Varilla, Philippe. *Panama: The Creation, Destruction, and Resurrection*. London, 1913.

Byron, Lord George Anson. *Voyage of HMS Blonde to the Sandwich Islands in the Years 1824–1825*. London, 1826.

Callahan, James Morton. *American Relations in the Pacific and the Far East, 1784–1900*. Baltimore, 1901.

Campbell, A.E. *Expansion and Imperialism*. New York, 1970.

Campbell, Archibald. *A Voyage Round the World from 1806 to 1812*. Reprint, Honolulu, 1967.

Campbell, Charles S. *Anglo-American Understanding, 1884–1918*. Baltimore, 1957.

———. *Special Business Interests and the Open Door Policy*. Hamden, CT, 1968.

———. *The Transformation of American Foreign Relations, 1865–1900*. Chicago, 1966.

Carano, Paul, and Pedro C. Sanchez. *A Complete History of Guam*. Rutland, VT, and Tokyo, 1964.

Caruthers, J. Wade. *American Pacific Ocean Trade: Its Impact on Foreign Policy and Continental Expansion, 1784–1860*. New York, 1973.

Caughey, John W. *California*. 2nd edition. Englewood Cliffs, NJ, 1961.

———. *History of the Pacific Coast of North America*. New York, 1938.

Chadwick, French E. *The Relations of the United States and Spain*. New York, 1911.

Challener, Richard D. *Admirals, Generals, and American Foreign Policy, 1898–1914*. Princeton, 1973.

Chambers, William N. *Old Bullion Benton, Senator from the New West*. Boston, 1956.

Chandler, Charles Lyon. *Inter-American Acquaintances*. 2nd edition. Sewanee, TN, 1917.

Chapman, Charles E. *A History of California: The Spanish Period*. New York, 1930.

Cheever, Henry T. Rev. *Life in the Sandwich Islands*. New York, 1851.

Clauder, Anna C. *American Commerce as Affected by the Wars of the French Revolution and Napoleon, 1793–1812*. Philadelphia, 1932.

Cleland, Robert Glass. *A History of California: The American Period*. New York, 1930.

Cleveland, Richard J. *A Narrative of Voyages and Commercial Enterprises*. Cambridge, MA, 1842.

Clune, Frank. *Captain Bully Hayes: Blackbirder and Bigamist*. London, 1970.

Conniff, Michael L. *Panama and the United States: The Forced Alliance*. Athens, GA, 1992.

Cooper, H. Stonehewer. *The Coral Lands of the Pacific: Their Peoples and Their Products*. London, 1882.

Corney, Peter. *Voyages in the Northern Pacific, 1813–1818*. Honolulu, 1896.

Corpuz, O.D. *The Philippines.* Englewood Cliffs, NJ, 1965.

Craft, Mabel C. *Hawai'i Nei.* San Francisco, 1898.

Crawford, David, and Leona Crawford. *Missionary Adventures in the South Pacific.* Tokyo, 1967.

Crocker, Uriah H. *The Depression of Trade and the Wages of Labor.* Boston, 1886.

Dakin, John. *Whalemen Adventurers.* Sydney, 1934.

Dana, Richard Henry. *Two Years Before the Mast.* New York, 1840.

Darden, Thomas F., Capt., USMC. *Historical Sketch of the Administration of the Government of American Samoa.* Washington, DC, 1952.

Daws, A. Gavan. *Shoal of Time: A History of the Hawaiian Islands.* New York, 1968.

Delano, Amasa. *A Narrative of Voyages and Travels in the Northern and Southern Hemispheres.* Boston, 1817.

Dennett, Tyler. *Americans in Eastern Asia.* New York, 1922.

Derrick, R.A. *A History of Fiji.* Suva, 1946.

Dewey, George. *Autobiography of George Dewey, Admiral of the Navy.* New York, 1913.

Dibble, Sheldon. *A History of the Sandwich Islands.* Honolulu, 1909.

Dodge, Ernest S. *New England and the South Seas.* Cambridge, MA, 1965.

Douglass, Elisha P. *The Coming of Age of American Business.* Chapel Hill, 1971.

Dudden, Arthur P. *The American Pacific.* New York, 1992.

Dulles, Foster Rhea. *America in the Pacific.* Boston, 1932.

————. *The Old China Trade.* New York, 1930.

Dwight, Carroll Miner. *The Fight for the Panama Route.* New York, 1940.

Earle, Alice Morse. *Customs and Fashions in Old New England.* New York, 1922.

————. *Home and Child Life in Colonial Days.* New York, 1969.

Ellison, Joseph W. *Opening and Penetration of Foreign Influence in Samoa to 1880.* Corvallis, 1938.

Evans, Henry Clay, Jr. *Chile and Its Relations with the United States.* Durham, 1927.

Fairbank, John K., Edwin O. Reischauer, and Albert M. Craig. *East Asia: The Modern Transformation.* Boston, 1965.

Faivre, Jean Paul. *L'Expansion Francaise dans le Pacifique, 1800–1842.* Paris, 1953.

Fanning, Edmund. *Voyages Round the World.* New York, 1833.

————. *Voyages to the South Seas, Indian and Pacific Oceans.* 5th edition. New York, 1838.

Forbes, Robert Bennet. *The Isthmus Ship Railway and Canal as Commercial Routes.* N.p., [c1886].

————. *Personal Reminiscences, with Recollections of China.* 3rd edition. Boston, 1892.

————. *Remarks on China and the China Trade.* Boston, 1844.

Forbes, William Cameron. *The Philippine Islands.* Boston, 1928.

Forster, Honore. *The South Sea Whaler.* Canberra, 1985.

Foster, John W. *American Diplomacy in the Orient.* Boston, 1903.

France, Peter. *The Charter of the Land: Custom and Colonization in Fiji.* Melbourne, 1989.

Frear, Walter J. *Anti-Missionary Criticism with Reference to Hawaii.* Honolulu, 1935.

Fredman, L.E. *The United States Enters the Pacific.* Sydney, 1969.

Freeman, Otis W., ed. *Geography of the Pacific.* New York, 1951.

Freycinet, Louis Claude De Sauleses De. *Voyage Around the World.* Translated into English by Ella L. Wiswell. Honolulu, 1978.

Friend, Theodore. *Between Two Empires.* New Haven, 1965.

Friis, Herman R., ed. *The Pacific Basin: A History of its Geographical Discovery and Exploration.* New York, 1967.

Fuchs, Lawrence H. *Hawai'i Pono: A Social History.* New York, 1961.

Gardiner, Samuel Rawson. *History of the Commonwealth and Protectorate, 1649–1656.* New York, 1965.

Gardner, Lloyd C., Walter F. LaFeber, and Thomas J. McCormick. *Creation of the American Empire.* Chicago, 1973.

Garraty, John A. *Henry Cabot Lodge.* New York, 1953.

Gast, Ross H. *Contentious Consul: A Biography of John Coffin Jones.* Los Angeles, 1976.

Gibson, James R. *Otter Skins, Boston Ships, and China Goods: The Maritime Fur Trade of the Northwest Coast, 1785–1841.* Seattle, 1992.

Giesecke, Albert A. *American Commercial Legislation Before 1789.* New York, 1910.

Gillespie, James E. *The Influence of Overseas Expansion on England to 1700.* New York, 1920.

Gilson, Richard P. *Samoa, 1830–1900: The Politics of a Multi-Cultural Community.* Melbourne, 1970.

Gleeck, Lewis E., Jr. *The Manila Americans.* Manila, 1977.

Goldstein, Jonathan. *Philadelphia and the China Trade, 1682–1846: Commercial, Cultural, and Attitudinal Effects.* University Park, PA, 1978.

Golovnin, V.M. *Round the World in the Kamchatka, 1817–1819.* Reprint, Honolulu, 1979.

Gough, Barry. *The Royal Navy and the Northwest Coast of North America.* Vancouver, 1971.

Graebner, Norman. *Empire on the Pacific.* New York, 1955.

Grattan, C. Hartley. *The Southwest Pacific to 1900.* Ann Arbor, 1963.

Gray, John A.C., Capt., USN. *Amerika Samoa: A History of American Samoa and Its United States Naval Administration.* Annapolis, 1960.

Greenbie, Sydney and Marjorie Greenbie. *Gold of Ophir, or the Lure That Made America.* Garden City, NY, 1925.

Greenhow, Robert. *The History of Oregon and California.* Boston, 1845.

Greenwood, Gordon. *Early American-Australian Relations.* Melbourne, 1944.

Grenville, John A.A., and George B. Young. *Politics, Strategy, and American Diplomacy: Studies in Foreign Policy, 1873–1917.* New Haven, 1966.

Griswold, Alfred W. *Far Eastern Policy of the United States.* New York, 1938.

Gruening, Ernest. *The State of Alaska.* New York, 1954.

Grunder, Garel A., and William E. Livezey. *The Philippines and the United States.* Norman, OK, 1951.

Hammond, George P., ed. *The Larkin Papers.* 10 vols. Berkeley, CA, 1951–1964.

Harper, Norman. *Australia and the United States.* Melbourne, 1971.

Harris, Harold L. *Australia's National Interests and National Policies.* Melbourne, 1938.

Hartendorp, A.V.B. *History of Industry and Trade of the Philippines.* Manila, 1958.

Hawgood, John A., ed. *First and Last Consul: Thomas Oliver Larkin and the Americanization of California.* Palo Alto, 1967.

Hayden, Joseph R. *The Philippines: A Story of National Development.* New York, 1945.

Healy, David. *U.S. Expansionism: The Imperialist Urge in the 1890s.* Madison, WI, 1970.

Henderson, Daniel M. *The Hidden Coasts.* New York, 1953.

Henderson, John B., Jr. *American Diplomatic Questions.* New York, 1901.

Herwig, Roger H. *Politics of Frustration: The United States in German Naval Planning, 1889–1941.* Boston, 1976.

Hogan, J. Michael. *The Panama Canal in American Politics.* Carbondale, IL, 1986.

Hohman, Elmo Paul *The American Whaleman.* New York, 1928.

Holle, Andrew F. *California: A History.* New York, 1969.

Howay, Frederic W., ed. *The Dixon-Meares Controversy.* Toronto, 1929.

———, ed. *Voyages of the Columbia to the North West Coast, 1787–1790.* Massachusetts Historical Society *Collections.* vol. 79. Boston, 1941.

———, Walter W. Sage, and Henry F. Angus. *British Columbia and the United States.* Toronto, 1942.

Hoyt, Edwin C. *National Policy and International Law: Case Studies from American Canal Policy.* Denver, 1966.

Hunt, Freeman. *Lives of American Merchants.* 2 vols. 1856. Reprint, New York, 1969.

Hunt, Michael R. *The Making of a Special Relationship: The United States and China to 1914.* New York, 1983.

Hunter, William C. *Bits of Old China.* London, 1885.

Hutchins, John G.B. *The American Maritime Industries and Public Policy.* Cambridge, MA, 1941.

Irving, Washington. *The Adventures of Captain Bonneville, U.S.A., in the Rocky Mountains and the Far West.* Reprint, Norman, OK, 1961.

———. *Astoria.* Reprint, Norman, OK, 1964.

Jackman, S.W., ed. *The Journal of William Sturgis.* Victoria, BC, 1978.

Jackson, Gordon. *The British Whaling Trade.* Hamden, CT, 1978.

Jackson, S.W., ed. *The Journal of William Sturgis.* Victoria, B.C., 1978.

Jameson, John Franklin. *Privateering and Piracy in the Colonial Period: Illustrative Documents.* New York, 1923.

Jarves, James Jackson. *History of the Hawaiian Islands.* 3rd edition. Honolulu, 1847.

Jenkins, James T. *A History of the Whale Fisheries.* London, 1921.

Jensen, Merrill. *The New Nation.* New York, 1950.

Johansen, Dorothy, and Charles M. Gates. *Empire of the Columbia.* 2nd edition. New York, 1967.

Johnson, Arthur M., and Barry Supples. *Boston Capitalists and Western Railroads: A Study in Nineteenth Century Investment Process.* Cambridge, MA, 1971.

Johnson, Donald D. *The City and County of Honolulu: A Governmental Chronicle.* Honolulu, 1991.

———, and Michael F. Miller. *Hawai'i's Own: A History of the Hawai'i Government Employees Association.* Honolulu, 1986.

Johnson, Emory R., ed. *History of Domestic and Foreign Commerce of the United States.* 2 vols. Washington, DC, 1915.

Johnson, Robert E. *Thence Round Cape Horn.* Annapolis, 1962.

Johnson, Willis Fletcher. *Four Centuries of the Panama Canal.* New York, 1907.

Johnson, Henry P., ed. *The Correspondence and Public Papers of John Jay.* New York, 1891.

Judd, Bernice. *Voyages to Hawai'i Before 1860.* Honolulu, 1974.

Judd, Gerrit P., IV. *Dr. Judd: Hawaii's Friend.* Honolulu, 1960.

Judd, Laura Fish. *Honolulu: Sketches of the Life, Social, Political, and Religious in the Hawaiian Islands from 1829 to 1861.* Honolulu, 1928.

Kamakau, S.M. *Ruling Chiefs of Hawai'i.* Honolulu, 1961.

Kame'eleihiwa, Lilikala. *Native Land and Foreign Desires.* Honolulu, 1992.

Kaplanoff, Mark D., ed. *Joseph Ingraham's Journal of the Brigantine Hope on a Voyage to the Northwest Coast of North America, 1790–92.* Barre, MA, 1971.

Karsten, Peter. *The Naval Aristocracy: The Golden Age of Annapolis and the Emergence of Modern American Navalism.* New York, 1972.

Kelley, Hall J. *A General Circular to All Persons of Good Character Who Wish to Emigrate to the Oregon Territory.* Charleston, MA, 1831.

———. *A Geographical Sketch of That Part of North America Called Oregon.* Boston, 1830.

Kemble, John H. *The Panama Route, 1848–1869.* Berkeley, 1943.

Kennedy, Paul M. *The Samoan Tangle: A Study in Anglo-German-American Relations, 1898–1900.* New York, 1974.

Kilmarax, Robert A., ed. *America's Maritime Legacy.* Boulder, 1979.

King, Pauline N., ed. *The Diaries of David Lawrence Gregg, an American Diplomat in Hawaii, 1853–1858.* Honolulu, 1982.

Kirk, Grayson. *Philippine Independence: Motives, Problems, and Prospects.* New York, 1936.

Kirker, James. *Adventures to China: Americans in the Southern Oceans.* New York, 1970.

Kohlsaat, H.H. *From McKinley to Harding: Personal Recollections of Our Presidents.* New York, 1923.

Koskinen, Aarne A. *Missionary Influences as a Political Factor in the Pacific Islands.* Helsinki, 1953.

Kotzebue, Otto Von. *A New Voyage Round the World in the Years 1823, 24, 25, and 26.* London, 1830.

Krusenstern, A.J. *Voyage Round the World in the Years, 1803, 1804, 1805, and 1806.* London, 1813.

Kuykendall, Ralph S. *The Hawaiian Kingdom.* 3 volumes. Honolulu, 1938–1967.

LaFeber, Walter. *The New Empire: An Interpretation of American Expansion.* Ithaca, NY, 1963.

Langdon, Robert. *Where the Whalers Went.* Canberra, 1984.

Latourette, Kenneth Scott. *The History of Early Relations Between the United States and China, 1784–1844.* New Haven, 1917.

Lawson, Will. *Pacific Steamers.* Glasgow, 1927.

Leech, Margaret. *In the Days of McKinley.* New York, 1959.

Leff, David N. *Uncle Sam's Pacific Islets.* Stanford, 1940.

Levi, Werner. *American-Australian Relations.* Minneapolis, 1947.

Lewis, Oscar. *Sea Routes to the Gold Fields.* New York, 1949.

Lewis, Taylor Biggs. *A Window on Williamsburg.* New York, 1966.

Liliuokalani. *Hawaii's Story by Hawaii's Queen.* Reprint, Rutland, VT, and Tokyo, 1964.

Lind, Andrew W. *An Island Community: Ecological Succession in Hawaii.* Chicago, 1938.

Lipscomb, A.A., et al., eds. *The Writings of Thomas Jefferson.* 20 vols. Washington, DC, 1903–1906.

Lisiansky, Urey. *Voyage around the World in the Years 1803, 1804, 1805, and 1806 in the Ship Neva.* London, 1814.

Liss, Sheldon B. *The Canal: Aspects of United States-Panamanian Relations.* Notre Dame, IN, 1967.

Liu, Kwang-ching. *Anglo-American Steamship Rivalry in China, 1862–1874.* Cambridge, MA, 1962.

Livezey, William E. *Mahan on Sea Power.* Norman, OK, 1947.

Lockwood, Stephen C. *Augustine Heard and Company, 1858–1862: American Merchants in China.* Cambridge, MA, 1971.

Lodge, Henry Cabot, ed. *Selections from the Correspondence of Theodore Roosevelt and Henry Cabot Lodge, 1884–1918.* 2 vols. New York, 1925.

———. *The War with Spain.* New York, 1899.

Loomis, Albertine. *To All People: History of the Hawai'i Conference of the United Church of Christ.* Honolulu, 1970.

Lubbock, Alfred B. *Bully Hayes, South Sea Pirate.* Boston, 1931.

Lydecker, Robert C. *Roster: Legislature of Hawaii, 1841–1918.* Honolulu, 1918.

McCormick, Thomas J. *China Market: America's Quest for Informal Empire, 1893–1901.* Chicago, 1967.

MacGregor, John. *Commercial Statistics of America.* London, 1845.

McHale, Thomas R., and Mary C. McHale, eds. *Early American-Philippine Trade: The Journal of Nathaniel Bowditch in Manila, 1796.* New Haven, CT, 1962.

Mack, Gerstle. *The Land Divided: A History of the Panama Canal and Other Isthmiam Canal Projects.* New York, 1944.

McMaster, John Bach. *The Life and Times of Stephen Girard, Mariner and Merchant.* Philadelphia, 1918.

MacNair, Harley F., and Hosea Ballou Morse. *Far Eastern International Relations.* Boston, 1931.

Mahan, Alfred Thayer. *The Interest of America in Sea Power, Present and Future.* Boston, 1898.

Manchester, Curtis A., Jr. *The Exploration and Mapping of the Pacific.* New York, 1951.

Manning, William R. *Diplomatic Correspondence of the United States Concerning the Independence of the Latin American Nations.* New York, 1925.

Masterman, Sylvia. *The Origins of International Rivalry in Samoa, 1845–1884.* Stanford, 1934.

Mathison, Gilbert Farquhar. *Narrative of a Visit to Brazil, Chile, Peru, and the Sandwich Islands During the Years 1821 and 1822.* London, 1825.

May, Ernest R. *American Imperialism: A Speculative Essay.* New York, 1968.

Meares, John. *Voyages Made in the Years 1788 and 1789 from China to the North West Coast of America.* London, 1790.

Melville, Herman. *Moby Dick, or, The Whale.* New York, 1851.

———. *Narrative of a Four Months' Residence among the Natives of a Valley of the Marquesas Islands.* London, 1846.

Merk, Frederick. *Manifest Destiny and Mission in American History.* New York, 1963.

———. *The Oregon Question.* Cambridge, MA, 1967.

Milburn, William. *Oriental Commerce.* 2 vols. London, 1823.

Miller, David Hunter, ed. *Treaties and Other International Acts of the United States of America.* 8 vols. Washington, DC, 1931–1948.

Millis, Walter. *The Martial Spirit: A Study of Our War with Spain.* New York, 1931.

Monaghan, Jay. *Australians and the Gold Rush: California and Down Under, 1849–1854.* Berkeley, 1973.

———. *Chile, Peru, and the California Gold Rush of 1849.* Berkeley, 1973.

Moore, John Bassett. *Digest of International Law.* 8 vols. Washington, DC, 1906.

Morgan, H. Wayne, ed. *Making Peace with Spain: The Diary of Whitelaw Reid, September–December, 1898.* Austin, TX, 1965.

Morgan, Theodore. *Hawaii: A Century of Economic Change, 1778–1876.* Cambridge, MA, 1948.

Morison, Elting E., ed. *The Letters of Theodore Roosevelt.* 8 vols. Cambridge, MA, 1951–1954.

Morison, Samuel Eliot. *The Maritime History of Massachusetts, 1783–1860.* Cambridge, MA, 1961.

———. *"Old Bruin": Commodore Matthew C. Perry, 1794–1858.* Boston, 1967.

Morrell, W.P. *Britain in the Pacific Islands.* Oxford, 1960.

Morse, Hosea Ballou. *The Chronicles of the East India Company Trading to China, 1635–1834.* 5 vols. Oxford, 1926–1929.

———. *The International Relations of the Chinese Empire.* London, 1910.

———, and Harley F. MacNair. *Far Eastern International Relations.* Boston, 1931.

Morton, Harry. *The Whale's Wake.* Honolulu, 1982.

Munford, James E., ed. *John Ledyard's Journal of Captain Cook's Last Voyage to the Pacific Ocean.* Corvallis, 1963.

Neale, Robert G. *Great Britain and United States Expansion.* East Lansing, 1966.

Nevins, Allan. *The American States During and After the Revolution, 1775–1789.* New York, 1924.

———. *Hamilton Fish and the Inner History of the Grant Administration.* New York, 1936.

Nichols, Jeannette Paddock. *Alaska: A History of the Administration, Exploitation, and Industrial Development During the First Half Century Under the Rule of the United States.* Cleveland, 1924.

Nichols, Roy F. *Advance Agents of American Destiny.* Philadelphia, 1956.

Nordhoff, Charles. *Northern California, Oregon, and the Sandwich Islands.* Berkeley, 1974.

O'Connor, Richard. *Pacific Destiny.* Boston, 1969.

Oliver, Douglas. *The Pacific Islands.* Revised edition. Cambridge, MA, 1962.

Olmsted, Francis Allyn. *Incidents of a Whaling Expedition.* New York, 1841.

Osborne, Thomas J. *"Empire Can Wait": American Opposition to Hawaiian Annexation, 1893–1899.* Kent, OH, 1981.

Osgood, Herbert L. *The American Colonies in the Eighteenth Century.* New York, 1924.

O'Toole, G.J.A. *The Spanish War: An American Epic—1898.* New York, 1984.

Parnaby, Owen W. *Britain and the Labor Trade in the Southwest Pacific.* Durham, NC, 1964.

Paterson, Thomas C. *American Imperialism and Anti-Imperialism.* New York, 1973.

Paulding, Hiram, Lt., USN. *Journal of a Cruise in the United States Schooner Dolphin.* Reprint, Honolulu, 1970.

Paullin, Charles O. *Diplomatic Negotiations of American Naval Officers, 1778–1883.* Baltimore, 1912.

Peabody, Robert E. *Merchant Venturers of Old Salem.* Boston, 1912.

Perkins, Dexter. *Hands Off: A History of the Monroe Doctrine.* Boston, 1941.

———. *The Monroe Doctrine.* Cambridge, MA, 1927.

Perkins, Whitney T. *Denial of Empire: The United States and Its Dependencies.* Leyden, 1952.

Pethick, Derek. *First Approaches to the Northwest Coast.* Vancouver, 1976.

————. *The Nootka Connection: Europe and the Northwest Coast, 1790–1795.* Vancouver, 1980.

Pickering, Charles, M.D. *The Races of Man.* London, 1849.

Pierce, Richard A. *Russia's Hawaiian Adventure, 1815–1817.* Berkeley, 1965.

Pitkin, Timothy. *A Statistical View of the Commerce of the United States of America.* New Haven, 1835.

Pomeroy, Earl. *The Pacific Slope.* Seattle, 1965.

Pomeroy, Earl S. *Pacific Outpost: American Strategy in Guam and Micronesia.* Stanford, 1951.

Porter, David, Capt., USN. *Journal of a Cruise Made to the Pacific Ocean by Captain David Porter in the U.S. Frigate Essex, 1812–1814.* Philadelphia, 1815.

Porter, Kenneth W. *John Jacob Astor, Businessman.* 2 vols. Cambridge, MA, 1931.

Porter, Kirk H., and Donald Bruce Johnson, comps. *National Party Platforms, 1840–1964.* 2 vols. Urbana, 1973.

Potter, E.B., ed. *Sea Power: A Naval History.* Englewood Cliffs, NJ, 1960.

Pratt, Julius W. *America's Colonial Experiment.* New York, 1950.

————. *Expansionists of 1898: The Acquisition of Hawai'i and the Spanish Islands.* Baltimore, 1936.

Preble, George H. *A Chronological History of the Origin and Development of Steam Navigation.* Philadelphia, 1895.

Pringle, Henry F. *Theodore Roosevelt: A Biography.* New York, 1931.

Puleston, William D. *Mahan: The Life and Work of Captain Alfred Thayer Mahan, U.S.N.* New Haven, 1939.

Quincy, Josiah, ed. *The Journals of Major Samuel Shaw.* Boston, 1847.

Reeves, Jesse S. *American Diplomacy Under Tyler and Polk.* Baltimore, 1907.

Remer, Charles F. *American Investments in China.* Honolulu, 1929.

————. *Foreign Investments in China.* New York, 1933.

Reuter, Bertha Ann. *Anglo-American Relations during the Spanish-American War.* New York, 1924.

Reynolds, Jeremiah N. *Voyage of the United States Frigate Potomac in the Years 1831, 1832, 1833, and 1834.* New York, 1835.

Reynolds, Stephen. *The Voyage of the "New Hazard" to the Northwest Coast, Hawaii, and China, 1810–1813.* Salem, MA, 1938.

Richardson, James D. *A Compilation of the Messages and Papers of the Presidents.* 10 vols. Washington, DC, 1896–1899.

Rickard, S. *The Whaling Trade in Old New Zealand.* Auckland, 1965.

Rolle, Andrew F. *California: A History.* New York, 1969.

Roske, Ralph J. *Everyman's Eden: A History of California.* New York, 1968.

Russ, William A. *The Hawaiian Republic, 1894–1898, and Its Struggle to Win Annexation.* Selinsgrove, PA, 1961.

————. *The Hawaiian Revolution, 1893–94.* Selinsgrove, PA, 1959.

Russel, Robert R. *Improvement of Communication with the Pacific Coast as an Issue in American Politics, 1783–1864.* Cedar Rapids, IA, 1948.

Ryan, Paul B. *The Panama Canal Controversy: U.S. Diplomacy and Defense Interests.* Stanford, 1977.

Rydell, Raymond A. *Cape Horn to the Pacific.* Berkeley, 1952.

Ryden, George H. *The Foreign Policy of the United States in Relation to Samoa.* New Haven, 1933.

Sakamaki, Shunzo. *Japan and the United States, 1790–1853*. Tokyo, 1939.

Sanches, Nellie Van de Grift. *Spanish Arcadia*. Los Angeles, 1929.

Saunders, A.T. *Bully Hayes*. Perth, 1932.

Savelle, Max. *The Foundations of American Civilization: A History of Colonial America*. New York, 1942.

Scammon, Charles M. *The Maritime Mammals of the Northwestern Coast of North America*. New York, 1874.

Scarr, Deryck. *Fragments of Empire: A History of the Western Pacific High Commission, 1877–1914*. Canberra and Honolulu, 1968.

———, and James W. Davidson, eds. *Pacific Islands Portraits*. Canberra, 1970.

Schlesinger, Arthur M. *The Colonial Merchants and the American Revolution, 1763–1776*. New York, 1918.

Seaburg, Carl, and Stanley Paterson. *Merchant Prince of Boston: Colonel T.H. Perkins, 1754–1854*. Cambridge, MA, 1971.

Sellers, Charles. *James K. Polk, Continentalist, 1843–1848*. Princeton, 1966.

Seybert, Adam. *Statistical Annals of the United States*. Philadelphia, 1818.

Shaler, William. *Journal of a Voyage between China and the Northwestern Coast of America Made in 1804*. Claremont, CA, 1935.

Shaw, Samuel. *The Journals of Major Samuel Shaw*. Boston, 1847.

Shineberg, Dorothy. *They Came for Sandalwood*. Melbourne, 1967.

Shippee, Lester B. *Canadian-American Relations, 1849–1874*. New Haven, 1939.

Simpson, George, Sir. *An Overland Journey Round the World During the Years 1841 and 1842*. 2 vols. Philadelphia, 1847.

Smith, Bradford. *Yankees in Paradise*. Philadelphia, 1956.

Smith, Elbert B. *Magnificent Missourian: The Life of Thomas Hart Benton*. New York, 1958.

Smith, Philip C.F. *The Empress of China*. Philadelphia, 1984.

Sparks, Jared. *The Life of John Ledyard*. Cambridge, MA, 1829.

Spears, John R. *The Story of the American Merchant Marine*. New York, 1910.

Speer, William. *The Oldest and Newest Empire: China and the United States*. Pittsburgh, 1877.

Stackpole, Edouard A. *The Sea-Hunters: New England Whalemen During Two Centuries, 1635–1835*. New York, 1953.

———. *Whales and Destiny: The Rivalry Between America, France, and Britain for Control of the Southern Whale Fishery*. Amherst, 1972.

Stanton, William. *The Great United States Exploring Expedition of 1838–1842*. Berkely, 1975.

Starbuck, Alexander. *History of the American Whale Fishery from Its Earliest Inception to the Year 1876*. Waltham, MA, 1878.

Stevens, Sylvester K. *American Expansion in Hawaii, 1842–1898*. Harrisburg, PA, 1945.

Stevenson, Robert Louis. *A Footnote to History: Eight Years of Trouble in Samoa*. London, 1892.

———. *In the South Seas*. London, 1900.

Stewart, Charles S. *A Visit to the South Seas in the U.S. Ship Vincennes during the Years 1829 and 1830*. 2 vols. New York, 1831.

Stile, Charles J. *Life and Service of Joel R. Poinsett*. Philadelphia, 1888.

Stolberg-Wernigerode, Otto zu. *Germany and the United States of America During the Era of Bismarck*. Reading, PA, 1937.

Strauss, W. Patrick. *Americans in Polynesia, 1783–1842.* East Lansing, 1963.

Strong, Josiah. *Our Country: Its Possible Future and Its Present Crisis.* New York, 1885.

Taft, William Howard. *Four Aspects of Civic Duty.* New York, 1907.

Tate, Merze. *The United States and the Hawaiian Kingdom: A Political History.* New Haven, 1965.

Taylor, Eva G.R. *Late Tudor and Early Stuart Geography, 1583–1650.* London, 1934.

Throckmorton, Arthur L. *Oregon Argonauts.* Portland, 1981.

Thurn, Everard, and Leonard C. Wharton, eds. *The Journal of William Lockerby, Sandalwood Trader in the Fijian Islands, 1808–1809.* London, 1925.

Thurston, Lorrin A. *Memoirs of the Hawaiian Revolution.* Honolulu, 1936.

Tompkins, E. Berkeley. *Anti-Imperialism in the United States: The Great Debate, 1890–1920.* Philadelphia, 1970.

Trask, David F. *The War with Spain in 1898.* New York, 1981.

Vancouver, George. *A Voyage of Discovery to the North Pacific Ocean in the Years 1790–1795.* 2nd edition. London, 1801.

Varg, Paul A. *The Making of a Myth: The United States and China, 1897–1912.* East Lansing, 1968.

Varilla, Philippe Bunau. *Panama: The Creation, Destruction, and Resurrection.* London, 1913.

Vevier, Charles. *The United States and China, 1906–1913.* New Brunswick, NJ, 1955.

Wakeman, Edgar. *Report on the Islands of the Samoan Group.* New York, 1872.

Ward, John M. *British Policy in the South Pacific, 1786–1893.* Sydney, 1948.

Ward, R. Gerard, ed. *American Activities in the Central Pacific, 1790–1870.* 8 vols. Ridgewood, NJ, 1966–1967.

Waters, Thomas F. *Augustine Heard and His Friends.* Salem, MA, 1916.

Watson, Robert M. *A History of Samoa.* Wellington, NZ, 1918.

Wayland, John W. *The Pathfinder of the Sea: The Life of Matthew Fontaine Maury, Scientist of the Sea.* New Brunswick, NJ, 1963.

Weeden, William B. *Early Oriental Commerce in Providence.* Cambridge, MA, 1908.

———. *Economic and Social History of New England, 1629–1789.* Cambridge, MA, 1926.

Weinberg, Albert K. *Manifest Destiny.* Baltimore, 1935.

Westcott, Allan F., ed. *American Sea Power Since 1775.* Chicago, 1947.

Whitaker, Arthur P. *The United States and the Independence of Latin America, 1800–1830.* Baltimore, 1941.

Wildes, Harry Emerson. *Lonely Midas: The Story of Stephen Girard.* New York, 1943.

Wilkes, Charles, Lt., USN. *Narrative of the United States Exploring Expedition during the Years 1838, 1839, 1840, 1841, 1842.* Philadelphia, 1845.

Williams, Frederick W. *Life and Letters of Samuel Wells Williams.* New York, 1889.

Williams, Mary Wilhelmine. *Anglo-American Isthmian Diplomacy, 1815–1915.* Washington, DC, 1916.

Williams, Samuel Wells. *The Middle Kingdom.* 2 vols. New York, 1876.

Williams, William Appleman. *American-Russian Relations, 1781–1947.* New York, 1952.

———. *The Roots of the Modern American Empire.* New York, 1969.

———. *The Tragedy of American Diplomacy.* Cleveland, 1959.

Willoughby, William F. *Territories and Dependencies of the United States.* New York, 1905.

Winther, Oscar O. *The Great Northwest.* New York, 1967.

Worcester, Dean C. *The Philippines: Past and Present.* New York, 1921.

Wright, Louis B., and Mary Isabel Fry. *Puritans in the South Seas.* New York, 1936.

Wriston, Henry M. *Executive Agents in American Foreign Relations.* Baltimore, 1929.

Yanaihara, Tadao. *Pacific Islands Under Japanese Mandate.* Shanghai, 1939.

Young, Marilyn Blatt. *The Rhetoric of Empire: American China Policy, 1895–1901.* Cambridge, MA, 1968.

Younger, Edward. *John A. Kasson: Politics and Diplomacy from Lincoln to McKinley.* Iowa City, 1955.

Yzendoorn, Reginald. *History of the Catholic Mission in the Hawaiian Islands.* Honolulu, 1927.

INDEX